Theory and Policy of International Competitiveness

Theory and Policy of International Competitiveness

Fidelis Ezeala-Harrison

PRAEGER

Westport, Connecticut
London

Library of Congress Cataloging-in-Publication Data

Ezeala-Harrison, Fidelis.
    Theory and policy of international competitiveness / Fidelis
Ezeala-Harrison.
        p.   cm.
    Includes bibliographical references and index.
    ISBN 0–275–96414–0 (alk. paper)
    1. Competition, International.   I. Title.
HF1414.E98   1999
382′.104—dc21   98–37153

British Library Cataloguing in Publication Data is available.

Library of Congress Catalog Card Number: 98–37153
ISBN: 0–275–96414–0

First published in 1999

Praeger Publishers, 88 Post Road West, Westport, CT 06881
An imprint of Greenwood Publishing Group, Inc.
www.praeger.com

Printed in the United States of America

The paper used in this book complies with the
Permanent Paper Standard issued by the National
Information Standards Organization (Z39.48–1984).

10 9 8 7 6 5 4 3 2 1

To my wife, *Chichi Ezeala*, for all our endeavors together.

Contents

PART III: STRATEGIES OF GLOBAL COMPETITION AND COMPETITIVENESS

Tables and Figures

TABLES

FIGURES

Preface

This book is about the international competitiveness of nations. It is about how competitiveness could make the difference in what international trade proves to be, or not to be, to a nation's economic prosperity. This book explores the details of what competitiveness is and what it is not. It examines the international competitiveness concept both at the micro (firm/industry) level and the macro (national) level, and analyzes their sources, effects, and potentials for a country's economic progress. The expositions offer pertinent guidelines and policy prescriptions of how a nation could achieve and maintain international competitiveness in order to sustain the long-term prosperity of its firms and businesses in particular, and overall economic growth in general.

Today's world is one in which national and international division of labor and specialization have resulted in massive production of goods and services across all regions of the world. Often, the major constraint that most societies face is the availability of the market for the profitable disposal of their products. This tends to set limits on the extent of the growth of national and regional economies. For this reason, the extent and pace of economic growth in every country have come to be dictated by the extent and pace of the country's ability to maintain relative competitiveness in all facets of its economic transactions with the rest of the world.

Could the nature of a country's international competitiveness be the crucial factor determining the country's ability to benefit from freer flow of trade in the global economy? A proper understanding of the meaning of international competitiveness and the implications it holds for an economy is crucial in today's short- and long-term economic policy formulation of nations. This volume offers a complete outline of how international competitiveness may be pursued, with a view to its proper role toward a country's overriding pursuit of steady economic progress.

The book is constituted of eleven chapters of original research, arranged in three parts. *Part I* contains the four chapters on the theme of *Theory of International Competitiveness*. These analyze: the concept of international trade and the place of international competitiveness in it; the various conceptions and misconceptions of international competitiveness; the theories of competitive advantage and comparative advantage, and what they mean for international competitiveness; and the expounding of the impact of international competitiveness for short- and long-term progress.

Part II of the book is on the *Policy Issues of International Competitiveness*. This contains the four chapters dealing with: the policy analysis of structural reforms for promoting a country's international competitiveness; the impact of globalization and the role of Communication and Information Technology (CIT), strategic trade policies, and environmental issues. *Part III* contains the three chapters on the theme of *Strategies of Global Competition and Competitiveness*. These give the background analysis of the strategic interaction that govern competition in today's global market environment, for which international competitiveness has become the necessary attribute for any firm to survive.

The present volume is intended for students and teachers in economics and business in universities and colleges; researchers, policy makers, business practitioners, and trade policy formulators involved within governmental and international agencies. It is meant for trade policy strategists and regional development planners in development agencies.

This book is written in nontechnical language and is designed to be accessible to all readers regardless of their previous knowledge of economics and business. However, a background in economics would be very helpful for a much deeper appreciation of the principles and issues addressed in the book. It is intended that all readers could avail themselves of the book's step-by-step approach in studying the subject of international competitiveness from its first principles through to advanced levels.

Saint John, N.B.   *F.E-H.*
CANADA

Acknowledgments

This book project benefited from the help of many colleagues, friends, and family members. Gratitude is due to my wife, Chichi, and our children, for their understanding and support during those times that this work took me away from our family life.

My thanks are due to my faculty colleagues at the University of New Brunswick, Saint John, especially Dr. Mohammed Kabir for his warm friendship and encouragement, and Dr. Ken Coates for reading chapter 6 and providing helpful comments. Many thanks also go to Dr. Amir Mahmood of the University of Newcastle, Australia, for collaborative research support and for organizing the Departmental seminar given in Australia in furtherance of the research for this book. I appreciate the insightful comments and criticisms offered by the participants at the seminar in Australia, which gave much impetus toward the scope and focus of the research.

Dr. Dennis McConnell of the University of Maine at Orono, whom I met in Indonesia, provided very thoughtful comments and insights. I extend thanks to two anonymous reviewers who carefully evaluated the various chapters and gave appreciated comments. My sincere thanks also go to my research assistant. Finally, I thank the staff at Greenwood Publishing Group, especially my Production Editor, Betty Pessagno, for much cooperation and patience.

PART I

THEORY OF INTERNATIONAL COMPETITIVENESS

1

International Trade and International Competitiveness

International trade has come to occupy the center stage in the economic activity, growth, and development processes of most modern societies. The present-day world economic (dis)order has simply rendered almost every modern economy to be heavily dependent on its foreign trade sector. This situation goes against the traditional belief that foreign trade dependence is a mark of economic underdevelopment. It is a reflection of how trends have changed, and with it, the dramatic shifts of national and international economic pursuits. And in no aspect is this trend more remarkable than the aspect of international competitiveness and the immense importance it now holds for the prospects of survival or failure of nations in their ability to obtain the maximum economic potentials from international trade. Precisely, then, it can be stated that where international trade may be an "engine" that drives economic growth of nations, international competitiveness represents the "fuel" that empowers that engine.

Most present-day developed, as well as developing, countries depend on foreign markets for sale of significant portions of their domestic production of goods and services. They also depend on foreign sectors for the sources of major resource inputs in the form of direct investment, aid, grants, loans, and the like. For this reason, competence in international trade, together with its attendant need to achieve and maintain strong international competitiveness, has become a necessary prerequisite for ensuring steady economic growth and progress of any modern economy. In this regard, many countries have adopted various measures aimed at promoting their international trade sectors: some have entered into multilateral trade agreements, and others have concluded strong regional integration of their economies with neighboring partners.

International trade has been posited to be a most important, if not the most important, single factor that shaped the development achievements and the underdevelopment situations of countries during the twentieth century. Over this period, primary product exports have traditionally accounted for the bulk of the gross domestic product (GDP) of almost all the less developed countries (LDCs) of Africa, Asia, the Middle East, and Latin America and the Caribbean. Many researchers believe that this trend has remained unchanged today.[1]

International trade permeates every facet of a country's economic life in ways over and beyond ordinary imports and exports of goods and services. It involves international transactions as well as administrative rules of conduct in short- and long-term international payments, banking services, currency exchanges, capital movements, technological transfers, and even sociopolitical transactions such as sports and cultural exchanges.

This chapter presents an expositional discourse on the various aspects of trade, with a view to stressing its place in a nation's ability to achieve growth and development. It is against this background that the main focus of this book, international competitiveness, will be viewed.

ROLE OF TRADE IN ECONOMIC GROWTH OF NATIONS

The importance of international trade in economic growth and development may have been recognized as early as the mercantilist era of economic thought. Mercantilism is the economic doctrine that appeared between the Middle Ages and the period of the universal dominance of *laissez-faire*. It emphasizes the importance of international trade, and pioneered the accounting notion of the balance of payments between a nation and the rest of the world.[2]   However, the mercantilist notion of international trade was based on the idea that a country might have *absolute advantage* (in terms of lower production costs) over another in production of an item, so that this country would export its more competitive products and take advantage of the markets of its trading partner. The Ricardian *comparative advantage* paradigm, on the other hand, advocates that this country should rather specialize in production of the output in which it has greatest comparative advantage, while its partner specializes in the other.

Later in this chapter we discuss a range of issues concerning the subject of international trade and economic growth, covering the basic ideas of the so-called New Trade Theory, as well as other trade matters such as formation of trading blocs and international financial movements.

The Classical Notion of Trade and Development

The classical theory of international trade and its role in economic development is based on the principle of comparative advantage. The comparative advantage paradigm states that a country performs better by concentrating on the production of those goods and services for which it possesses a comparative advantage over others, and then trade those goods for those of other countries.

By so doing, each country, with its comparative cost advantage, can produce its products more cheaply than others, so that through trade all countries would benefit immensely by way of obtaining goods more cheaply than they would have if they produced all goods themselves.[3]

In determining the degree of comparative advantage, the costs of production are measured in terms of opportunity costs—the real costs of individual items in terms of the foregone alternatives that must be sacrificed in order to obtain them. For example, the real cost of 1,000 tons of wheat produced in Canada is the (supposedly) 400 heads of cattle that cannot be produced because five hectares of land must be transferred from livestock rearing to the production of the 1,000 tons of wheat. To illustrate, let us assume that country A has a comparative advantage relative to country B in the production of manufactured goods, because A can produce manufactured goods at lower costs in terms of agricultural products foregone, as against B. Following this situation, A should specialize in the production of manufactured goods and trade it for agricultural produce with B, who also specializes in the production of agricultural produce in which it has comparative advantage. In this way, not only do the total of goods exchanged increase massively, but also the costs of acquiring these goods are much lower through trade, for both countries A and B.

The leading figure in classical economic thought, Adam Smith, in his *Inquiry into the Causes of the Wealth of Nations*, stressed the idea that trade would enable a country to reap full benefits from the advantages of economies of scale. Putting this in modern microeconomic terms, we state that trade enables the country to utilize its productive resources more efficiently, and thus move onto a point on its production possibility frontier.

The comparative advantage phenomenon has provided a major impetus for global free-trade policies. Through such free trade and exchange, over time international income redistributions take place as free product and factor mobilities equalize prices and incomes across countries. This implies a more equitable distribution of the benefits of international progress, and therefore a more even spread of economic development across the world. International trade is thus an engine of growth and development. This has been the conclusion of at least classical and neoclassical economics, for whom trade is a *vent for surplus*, for it is trade that enables a country to overcome the limits set by the extent of the market against specialization and the division of labor.[4]

Trade as an Engine of Growth

Adam Smith had argued that only the size of the market could limit the level of economic growth that a society could achieve. In this tradition, classical and neoclassical economics vigorously supports free and unrestricted trade among nations in asserting that trade opens up opportunities for people in all countries to improve their welfare.

The "trade as engine of growth" paradigm is espoused by classical economic thinkers. A brief review of its key tenets may be useful here as a prelude to highlighting the potentials of genuine trade in fostering growth. Historical evidence indicates that, indeed, international trade was a powerful engine of economic growth and development for most present-day developed countries. This is because, as nations are inherently self-insufficient, (free) trade offers the following immense advantages to a country.

Market for Mass Exports

Mass export of primary agricultural produce, as well as industrial manufactured products, creates foreign exchange for the purchase of vital capital resources for industrialization and infrastructural development. International trade simply removes the constraints that limited market demand might place on a country's pace of development.

Capital Acquisition through Trade

International trade opens up opportunities for a country to acquire much needed capital equipment to apply to its industrial and infrastructural needs. This enables an economy to be able to apply diversified machinery, tools, equipment, and semifinished products in its everyday economic activities without being restricted to equipment that it alone could produce domestically. This gives the country greater opportunity to obtain capital resources for growth.

Capital Acquisition through Borrowing

A country is able to receive loans, grants, trade credits, aid, and the like from its richer international trading partners. Such resources are crucial to a country's development as it could apply them toward importation of capital or other development needs. Moreover, a country could access borrowing and aid facilities available in international financial institutions such as the International Bank for Reconstruction and Development (IBRD) or the World Bank, the International Monetary Fund (IMF), and the United Nations Development Program (UNDP).

Technological Transfer

A country could easily apply foreign technologies that it encounters through international trade, in order to enhance its own production systems and methods. Such ready-made technology that is available through the constant interaction that only international trade allows would otherwise be unavailable or very slow and expensive to develop and apply.

In echoing the standard classical arguments in favor of free trade, some recent studies have emphasized the technological aspects of the gains from trade. In a recent study on the importance of technological diffusion as a source of comparative advantage of nations, Dollar (1993) noted some important short- and long-run global benefits of an open global (international) trading regime. These benefits are summarized as follows:

1. In the short run, global free trade would enhance income redistribution among factors of production within each trading country. This is because of the equal access that domestic firms would have to export markets as long as there are no internal restrictions (such as preferential subsidies or selective licences). This is a short-run effect that allows each sector to expand production as far as is technologically feasible without facing the constraint of limited market demand.

2. In the long run, global free trade would accelerate overall technological advances in the world to the benefit of all trading nations, in general, and innovating countries, in particular.

3. In the long run, free trade would accelerate the diffusion of technology from the innovating countries to the developing countries.

Thus, we observe that international trade does act as an added stimulant to innovation, and it lies behind the rapid technological breakthroughs and the accompanying high economic growth rates achieved by the outward-looking, trade-oriented, Newly Industrializing Countries (NICs) of East Asia.[5]

International Friendship and Sociocultural Exchanges

Through the constant and frequent interaction between countries in the course of international trade, international goodwill and friendly relations develop. They learn each other's consumption patterns, other institutional and organizational arrangements, values, ideas, and lifestyles. International cultural exchanges through sports and the arts flourish. This promotes world peace and harmony, enabling growth and development.

TERMS AND PATTERNS OF INTERNATIONAL TRADE

The world's international trade patterns are governed by the various policies, attitudes, and strategies adopted by the various countries, regions, and trading blocs that have been formed over the decades in which global trade has occurred. The pattern of world trade is instrumental in determining the outcome of any trading arrangement between the various countries of the world. This is so because countries engage in trade with the express objectives of deriving economic benefits from it. However, despite the propositions of the comparative advantage principle, trade transactions do not always result in win-win outcomes for trading partners. Many trade transactions are clear zero-sum games. That is, the outcome of the trade transaction is such that the gains accruing to one partner amount to the losses sustained by the other partner. And several factors may be responsible for such a situation. Before we consider these issues, we must understand the following terms and definitions.

The Terms of Trade

The terms of trade (TOT) facing a country is the relationship between the average price of the country's exports and the average price of its imports. If the average price of exports is higher than the average price of imports, the country is said to have a favorable terms of trade; if otherwise, it has an unfavorable (or adverse) terms of trade. This depiction of the TOT is used to formulate an explicit formula for the TOT, termed the *net barter terms of trade* and defined simply as the ratio of the average price of a country's exports to the average price of its imports.

Let the average price of exports and imports, respectively, be: P_X and P_M; then the TOT is given by:

$$TOT = P_X/P_M \qquad\qquad (1.1)$$

From this expression it is clear that as P_X rises relative to P_M, the country's TOT improves, and as P_M rises relative to P_X, the country's TOT deteriorates.

Much of the evidence based on many recent empirical studies (such as Cuddington and Urzua, 1989) as well as evidence from World Bank data (1991) indicate that the TOT of manufactured goods have been much more favorable relative to that of primary products, thereby lending support to the structuralist position. The question is whether or not a country could influence its TOT level, and to what degree. The current thought being advanced in this book is that through the achievement and maintenance of relative international competitiveness, a country could influence its TOT level, and therefore be capable of influencing the level of revenue realized from its exports and the expenditure incurred on its imports. In this way, its economy would be more effectively protected against the unpredictability of world market fluctuations.

A country cannot easily influence the level of its terms of trade. It is not very easy to fix commodity prices in international markets which are apt to be highly competitive. Moreover, a typical country would be only one of many trading partners in the world market for any given commodity, so that commodity prices would be subject to world (international) market supply and demand conditions.

However, through achieving and maintaining international competitiveness, a country can influence its TOT level. The ability to influence the world market commodity prices of a country's products (the key determinant of the TOT level) depends on how internationally competitive the products of that country are in the international marketplace. A country that achieves relative competitiveness for its products by, say, producing and marketing its products at minimum unit costs (micro level competitiveness) and that enables its firms and exporters to market products more efficiently through maintenance of stable foreign exchange rate of its currency (macro level competitiveness) could ensure a desired level for the prices of its exports. While international competitiveness would yield a premium price for a country's exports, it would also mean that its imports would be at relative disadvantage (subject to retaining standard or superior quality composition) in terms of their unit cost-price combinations. These issues will be analyzed further in the chapters that follow.

The Balance of Trade

Trade balance relates to volumes. The balance of trade facing a country is the relationship between the volume of the country's exports (X), and the volume of its imports (M), over a given time period. If the volume of exports is greater than the volume of imports over the given time period, the country is said to have a favourable trade balance; otherwise, it has an adverse trade balance.

Letting

V_X = Volume of exports (measured in terms of a denominated currency unit)

V_M = Volume of imports (measured in terms of a denominated currency unit)

the balance of trade (BOT) may be depicted as

$$\text{BOT} = V_X/V_M \qquad (1.2)$$

This expression indicates that as V_X rises relative to V_M, the country's BOT improves, and as V_M rises relative to V_X, the country's BOT deteriorates.

A country could influence its BOT level by simply raising the volume of its exports or by reducing the volume of its imports through various measures ranging from devaluation of its currency to adoption of trade restrictionist actions. However, these measures tend to involve some undesirable results: devaluation may lead to undervaluation of the national currency and to inflation; trade restrictions may lead to retaliation from trading partners. Therefore, it is important that a country be able to influence its BOT though without such undesirable results. Achievement and maintenance of international competitiveness seems to be a very effective means of being able to influence the BOT.

As will be analyzed in chapter 2, firms in a country achieve *micro level* international competitiveness through production and marketing of products at minimum unit costs. *Macro level* competitiveness is achieved through maintenance of an *economic liberalization* regime in the economy. These *necessary and sufficiency conditions* together enable the country's exporting and import-competing firms to market products in foreign and domestic markets, respectively, more efficiently relative to trading partners. This yields greater sales volumes and enables the country to influence its BOT level.

Import Penetration

As a country opens its borders to other countries with whom it transacts business, there is a degree to which its economy opens up. This would indicate how far, and with what level of ease, its trading partners could effectively reach its markets. This is the measure of the country's *import penetration*.

Import penetration (IP) may be defined as the ratio of the volume of imports to the total volume of goods and services transacted within the economy during a given time period (say, one year). Using the gross domestic product (GDP) as a proxy for the total volume of transacted goods and services over one year, a country's IP may be depicted as

$$IP = V_M/Y \tag{1.3}$$

where
$$Y = GDP$$

Equation (1.3) indicates that a country's import penetration would rise or fall with the relative size of imports in the GDP. Thus, it is not with the absolute volume of imports, *per se*, that a country should be concerned. Rather, it is the size of imports relative to the GDP (over a certain time span) that should be watched in deciding whether or not a country has a high or low import penetration. In the context of the free market environment in which the world operates, a high IP level would be undesirable for a country. A high IP level would mean that the country's import-competing firms are relatively uncompetitive and the economy would suffer unemployment and balance-of-payments adversity.

However, a country's state of international competitiveness would affect both of the two parameters that determine its IP level, namely, its volume of imports and GDP level. Achievement of micro level competitiveness would raise the GDP, and with all other things remaining unchanged, thereby reduce its IP. Achievement of macro level competitiveness would reduce the volume of imports and, again, reduce its IP, under all other things remaining unchanged.

Export Intensity

Export intensity (EI) is a term that may be used to qualify the degree of export orientation of an economy. In effect, the EI would indicate how much an economy depends on foreign markets. It would show how sensitive the economy would be to changes in the international market place.

An economy's EI may be defined as the ratio of the volume of exports to the total volume of goods and services transacted within the economy (GDP) during a given time period (say, one year):

$$EI = V_X/Y \qquad\qquad (1.4)$$

A country's export performance can easily be verified by using equation (1.4). Again, the state of a country's international competitiveness is crucial in determining its export intensity. In fact, the EI represents a popular competitiveness parameter that have been adopted by many in the past, often referred to as *trade performance*.

Again, an economy's state of international competitiveness would affect both of the two parameters that determine its EI level. All other things remaining constant, achievement of micro level competitiveness would raise the volume of exports and thereby raise the level of EI, indicating the close connection between a country's export intensity and its international competitiveness (at the micro level). Micro level competitiveness would also raise the GDP, indicating that EI would be reduced, all other things remaining constant. This could presumably be interpreted as a situation where the achievement of competitiveness enables an economy eventually to become less dependent on its export sector for growth. Macro level competitiveness does not appear to be very crucial in affecting EI.

The Balance of Payments

A country's balance-of-payments (BOP) account at some point in time (say, at the end of one yearly period) is the relationship between the total receipts (inflows) that it procures and the total payments (outflows) that it incurs in the course of its international trading transactions with the rest of the world over that period. The BOP, as a typical statement of account, is made up of two sides: the credit side (of all receipts entries) and the debit side (of all payments entries). Furthermore, each of these two sides is composed of three sections: the current account section, the capital account section, and the net reserves section.

Current account covers entries of all visible and invisible items of trade. Visible items of trade are merchandise exports (in the credit section) and merchandise imports (in the debit section). The invisible items include services in both sections (such as banking, shipping, insurance, tourism, etc.). The *capital account* includes all money lent or invested from abroad. It also includes all monetary and financial transfers involving such things as profit, interest payments, and dividends repatriated across borders. A prominent example is the cash remittances that foreign workers send to their home countries.

By definition, the BOP must balance annually. A country with, say, a $2 billion deficit on its current account (due to a huge deficit balance of trade) may get $2 billion in the form of a short-term (or long-term) grant or loan from another country or external financial institution to finance this deficit and thus balance its BOP. This means that the country balances its BOP by running a surplus on its capital account in the amount of $2 billion. Alternatively, most countries have official reserves of foreign currency and gold that they can draw from and use to cover any current account deficits that might arise.[6]

Ultimately, however, whether or not a country's official reserve changes depends on its exchange rate policy. Therefore, we need to fully understand how the exchange rates of currencies are determined and maintained.

Exchange Rates and Exchange Rate Policies

The exchange rate of a country's currency is the rate at which that currency exchanges for the currencies of other countries. Its value at any time depends on the exchange rate policy that is being pursued by the country concerned. A country may pursue a *fixed* exchange rate policy (in which case the exchange rate is pegged at some level), a *flexible* exchange rate policy (in which case its level is determined by the currency's supply and demand in the free international money market), or a *quasi-fixed* exchange rate policy (in which case the currency is allowed to float, but the rate is not allowed to rise above or fall below certain levels).

A country's currency exchange rate is a major factor in the country's state of international competitiveness, at the macro level. This is because in order for the country's products to be sold in the world market, the foreign buyers must obtain the country's currency in order to pay for the country's products. However, in order to obtain (purchase) the country's currency, its price, that is, the exchange rate, must be considered. The higher its price (the higher its exchange rate), the lower would be the amount of it that is purchased, and hence the lower would be the amount of the country's exports that would be bought/sold (demanded) in the world market. Therefore, a country would be considered to have lost international competitiveness (at the macro level) when its currency exchange rate increases, and to have gained competitiveness when its currency exchange rate decreases.

The country's currency exchange rate (x) is the rate at which the currency is bought and sold in the international currency market. It is the rate at which the currency exchanges with those of other countries that it trades with. The value of a country's currency exchange rate is simply given by the ratio of one unit of the country's currency to one unit of the (rest of world's) representative foreign currency. This is determined as follows.

Consider two countries, A and B, that engage in trade with each other and whose currency denominations are $\$^A$ and $\$^B$, respectively. Then, for country A, the exchange rate, x^A, is

$$x^A = \$^A1/\$^B1 \tag{1.5}$$

This expression indicates that x^A, the currency exchange rate of country A, would rise as the value of $\$^A$ rises or the value of $\$^B$ falls, and would fall as the value of $\$^A$ falls or the value of $\$^B$ rises. Consequently, these factors affect the country's competitiveness, as follows:

1. If x^A rises, country A's currency is said to have appreciated, and country A has lost some degree of international competitiveness.
2. If x^A falls, country A's currency is said to have depreciated, and country A has improved its international competitiveness.

Three major factors determine the rise and fall of a country's currency exchange rate. These are:

1. The size of the country's exports: As the country's exports rise, there would be greater demand for the country's currency in the international market (to pay for the exports). This would result in a higher price of the currency, which is, higher exchange rate. The reverse is the case for a decrease in exports.
2. *The size of the country's imports*: As the country's imports rise, there would be greater supply of the country's currency in the international market (to pay for the imports). This would result in a lower price of the currency, which is, lower exchange rate. The reverse is the case for a decrease in imports.
3. *The level of domestic interest rate*: As the country's domestic interest rate level rises, there would be greater demand for the country's currency in the international market from foreign investors wishing to invest in the country (being attracted by the relatively higher interest rate earnings). This would result in a higher price of the currency, which is, higher exchange rate. The reverse is the case for a decrease in domestic interest rate.

Maintaining competitiveness, again, at the macro level regarding currency exchange rate, would imply avoiding the anti-export bias that are signaled by adopting a policy such as fixed exchange rate regime. This would be achieved by maintaining a flexible exchange rate regime and pursuing policies for stable (moderate) exchange rate of the country's currency.

Devaluation

Devaluation is a special type of fixed exchange rate policy whereby the rate is fixed and maintained below its current level, or below the level that the free market (supply and demand) would yield. A country's currency may also be *overvalued*, if the exchange rate is fixed and maintained above its market value.

Devaluation of a country's currency effectively raises the domestic prices of imports in the country and lowers the prices of the country's exports in foreign markets. Apparently, the purpose of devaluation is to encourage higher export sales and discourage imports, probably in an effort to correct a balance of trade deficit. This may succeed, however, only if the country's exports have elastic demand in foreign markets, while its imports also have elastic demand in the domestic market.[7]

Under the Bretton Woods system of fixed exchange rates, the central banks of various countries frequently intervene in the international currency market to "regulate" the value of their currencies.[8] For example, if their exchange rate goes under pressure to depreciate, they sell foreign exchange from their reserves to buy (and thereby effectively raise the demand for) their own currency. This action provides support for the currency and stabilizes its exchange rate around the current level.

If, on the other hand, a country's exchange rate gets too high, its central bank may buy foreign exchange to increase its reserve, thereby increasing the supply of its currency and reducing its price, the exchange rate, in the international money market. A country might occasionally allow its currency to depreciate because it might be lacking sufficient reserves of foreign exchange to support it.

As a country's exchange rate is assumed to be the price at which it bought imports and sold exports, changes in its exchange rate policies amount to adjusting this price and altering the volume of export and import transactions. Capital flows are also affected by exchange rate policies because the amount of foreign capital inflow and outflow depends on the relative strength or weakness of the domestic currency. Thus, the exchange rate is a central parameter in the degree of international trade, and therefore in the degree to which development is transmitted through trade.

Purchasing Power Parity

In a free-trade world with floating exchange rates, a state of relative parity would be established among the currencies of all the trading partners. This situation has been explained by a theory known as the *Purchasing Power Parity* (PPP) theorem. It states that exchange rates tend toward equality in international purchasing power with each other. This is because free adjustments in their exchange rates allow each currency to achieve relative parity in line with the relative strengths of their economies. To illustrate the PPP concept, let us consider one major economic factor that easily affects a country's exchange rate, namely, inflation.

Inflation erodes a currency's purchasing power. The difference between inflation rates in different countries determines the relative strengths of their respective currencies, and the extent to which one country's currency erodes in terms of the others. For example, if, say, a country's inflation rate grows faster than its trading partner's inflation rate, the country's currency depreciates (or devalues, presumably by the amount of the difference between the inflation rates); and if its inflation grows slower, it revalues its currency. In this way, that country brings its costs back into line with the international norm and thus would not be trading at an unfair disadvantage (under higher inflation) or advantage (under lower inflation). This indicates that "real exchange rates are constant," the real exchange rate being the exchange rate adjusted for differential inflation rate.

A practical example that is very close to the experiences of many countries will illuminate the PPP explanation. Suppose two countries, A and B, have equal purchasing power (their exchange rates are at par) at a point in time, year 1, with zero inflation rate in either country. Assuming that by the end of year 2, an inflation rate of 5 percent arises in country A. According to the PPP model, country A's exchange rate would, over time, depreciate by 5 percent in order for country A to maintain stability in the volume of trade that it transacts with country B.

The PPP may be depicted simply as

$$P_d = xP_f \tag{1.6}$$

where

P_d = average domestic price level
P_f = average foreign price level
x = exchange rate of the given country

This implies that traded goods and services are purchased at virtually similar prices across all trading nations. From this PPP relationship, the exchange rate is found as

$$x = P_d/P_f \tag{1.7}$$

This gives the exchange rate in terms of price levels as compared to the definition given earlier in terms of currency units.

GLOBAL TRADE EXPERIENCES, COMPETITIVENESS AND GROWTH

International trade has grown leaps and bounds globally since the end of World War II. However, close study of global trade statistics reveals that world trade follows well-defined and well-established characteristic patterns across the various regions, and among the various countries, according to their associations and levels of development. For instance, World Bank data indicate that, since the post-World War II period, whereas the rate of growth of exports of the developing countries taken together has been less than one-half of that of the OECD countries taken together, the developing countries' rate of growth of imports far exceeds that of the OECD countries.[9]

Associated with this pattern of trade is the fact that the developing countries tend to have unfavorable TOTs and deficit BOTs, although the BOT deficits tend to be offset by net capital flows from the OECD countries to the developing countries. The data, however, further reveal that this pattern is fast changing if not already changed. Over the decade of the 1980s, the rate of growth of exports of the developing countries rose sharply and exceeded that of the developed countries, as the pattern of imports was also reversed. At the same time, capital flows from the developed to the developing countries declined significantly. This recent trade and capital flows pattern reflects the problems of instability, especially introduced in the international economic order by the debt crises that erupted during this time.

The debt crises of the 1980s spelled a major shift in the patterns of trade of the developing world. Prior to this period, imports expanded far more rapidly than exports, and trade deficits were offset by capital inflows. The reverse became the case after the 1980s, a shift that was especially very prominent in Latin America and the Caribbean, the Middle East, and North Africa; the major debtor nations of the world. Sub-Saharan Africa, whose trade is dominated by primary produce, experienced very high rates of export growth which exceeded import growth during the pre-1980s period. During the 1980s, however, they had absolute declines in both export and import growth. This region has been particularly hurt by international trade imbalances: persistent adverse TOT has perhaps retarded economic growth and development far more in Sub-Saharan Africa than anywhere else in the world.

Asia's trade performance has been the most impressive among the developing regions of the world. Except for the two big economies of China and India, both of which pursued major trade-restrictionist policies during the post-World War II era, it could be safely inferred for this region that international trade has played the "engine of growth" role that it did for the nineteenth-century developing countries. The most rapid expansion of trade occurred in the so-called Newly Industrializing Countries (NICs) of East Asia, notably Singapore, South Korea, Taiwan, Thailand, and, to a lesser extent, Malaysia, Indonesia, China, India, and the Latin American countries of Brazil and Mexico (see Table 1.1). In these countries, export expansion far exceeded import expansion, yielding consistent balance of trade surpluses throughout much of the post-World War II period. This trend has basically continued to date, despite the rather unexpected economic reversals that were experienced in these economies as a result of the instabilities which have developed in their capital markets since mid-1997.[10] Through all these, the two South Asian "sleeping giants," China and India, witnessed a rapid opening up of their economies to international trade in the 1980s and 1990s. For after it launched its economic (liberalization) reforms in the late 1970s, China turned from a third-world closed economy to a dynamic growth-oriented and competitive economy going into the new millennium.

The relative successes of the Asian NICs are attributable to their abilities to diversify their structure of trade, quickly adapt to changing realities, and adopt necessary reforms needed to promote competitiveness.[11] Unlike the other LDCs, the Asian NICs were able to reduce the primary-product composition of their exports. World Bank data indicate that exports of primary produce declined to less than 20 percent of the NICs' exports. These NICs diversified their manufacturing exports from their labor-intensive, light-manufacturing character (of the post-war period) to broader-range manufacturing composition such as chemicals, steel, machinery, and myriad of heavy-industrial goods. Most of these were exported to the developed countries (DCs), while the NICs imported mainly primary produce from the LDCs.

Table 1.1 indicates that, as of 1990, the NICs not only ranked among the top thirty leading exporters of manufactured goods in the world but also had achieved an average annual growth rate of exports (in manufactured goods) exceeding 15 percent (more than double the average world export growth rate of 7 percent). Table 1.1 shows that apparently the NICs in addition to China, India, Brazil, and Mexico were able, during the 1980s, to transform their industries from their hitherto inward-looking postures to an outward-looking and technologically-competitive orientation. Although this achievement did result in different levels of economic growth and development in individual NICs, an *OECD* (1988) report indicates that over the two decades 1964-1984 these NICs (except Thailand and Malaysia) were able to raise their share of total OECD imports of manufactured goods (total volume of manufactured goods that they exported to OECD countries) from a meager 1.6 percent level in 1964 to a significant level of 9.5 percent in 1985.

It is important that we observe why the NICs, and the Asian countries in particular, succeeded in maximizing the gains from international trade and were able to use it as the engine of growth during the twentieth century, while the other developing countries, such as those of Sub-Saharan Africa, failed to do so.

Table 1.1
Manufacturing Export Growth and Ranking of NICs, 1990

	Average Annual % Growth (1980-1990)	Rank (World Level)
Hong Kong	14	9
Taiwan	13	11
South Korea	14	12
China	16	15
Singapore	14	17
Mexico	18	20
Brazil	9	25
Malaysia	18	26
Thailand	20	27
India	11	28

Source: Adapted from Williams (1994, p.18),
as per: GATT. 1992. *International Trade 90-91* (Vol.II), Geneva.

The main reason lies in the abilities of the NICs to achieve and maintain significant levels of both micro and macro level competitiveness for their economies. In the immediate post-World War II period, most East Asian countries, especially Indonesia, Malaysia, and Thailand, or even South Korea, were prototypes of a typical LDC: agricultural, primary-product exporting, and low-income economies. Over the years, however, each of these countries was able to rapidly expand its primary-product-dominated exports through aggressive pursuit of competitive production methods. At the same time, they established complementary manufacturing industries across a broad range of export products, thereby diversifying their economic bases. They then simply reaped the benefits of the complementarity of industrialization and agricultural development, enabling them to easily succeed in the increasingly competitive world market.

Moreover, as indicated by the accounts of Sachs (1997b), Asian countries have undertaken credible steps to implement major economic reforms that have succeeded in establishing international competitiveness for their economies. Among such steps documented by Sachs are:

1. How South Korea was able to pull back sharply on excessive state spending when it overheated in 1979. This launched the country on a sound footing toward a reduced public sector, a factor that is essential for attaining macro level competitiveness.

2. How Malaysia pursued a policy of privatization and budget cuts after it went overboard with state enterprise investment during the early 1980s. This step resulted in increased productivity as private sector activity is driven by profit incentives and devoid of the massive corruption and inefficiencies that beset public sector activities and often impair productivity. This is crucial for the achievement of micro level competitiveness. The streamlining of the government's budget improved confidence in the country's fiscal management and raised its macro level competitiveness.

3. How Indonesia effected a determined program of market reforms that enabled it to steer out of its 1974 financial crisis. Much of this reform involved privatization, state divestiture, and deregulation, many of which yielded greater micro and macro competitiveness for the economy.

The East Asian NICs of South Korea, Taiwan, Hong Kong, and Singapore together earned the label of "Tiger economies" as they were able to raise their per capita income levels by more than six times during the three decades 1965 to 1995. Over this period, the other Southeast Asian high-performance but relatively less-growing economies of Malaysia, Thailand, and Indonesia, were able to raise their per capita incomes by more than three fold. These achievements mark an era of rapid economic growth propelled mainly by international trade and driven through maintenance of substantial levels of international competitiveness. The recent sudden currency and capital market crises that have beset these countries notwithstanding, there are grounds to expect that, provided they maintain their fierce and aggressive records of international competitiveness (coupled with continued encouragement of high domestic savings and attraction of capital, investment, and technology), the East Asian economies will recover and continue on the paths of high, if not rapid, levels of sustained economic growth, toward the status of *takeoff* onto economic development.

A few countries in Latin America have also attained the NIC label through their abilities to achieve relative degrees of success in growth through international trade. These include Mexico, Argentina, and Brazil. However, the debt crises of the 1980s severely hit these countries very hard, and their performances have suffered significantly as a result.

Lack of Competitiveness: Failure of Trade to Achieve Growth in LDCs

The massive development potential of international trade appears to have been severely limited, if not entirely lost, in present-day LDCs. Many economists argue that international trade has become one of the factors that have contributed to the ongoing impoverishment of LDCs. The main reasons for this argument are propounded in *structuralist* theory of economic development, and we highlight the key issues here.[12]

After the Great Depression and the two World Wars, confidence in the stability of the international economic order was severely shaken, and many economists began to question whether the international economy could be the engine of economic growth for developing countries in the twentieth century in the same way that it had been in the nineteenth century. The main question was whether the international economy could continue to provide expanding opportunities for trade in such a way that developing countries could not only benefit from it but also use it as a major instrument for sustained economic growth and development.

In the nineteenth century, for instance, the policies of the gold standard and international free trade created a world economic order within which international trade expanded much faster than world output, as the rapidly advancing economies of Europe provided growing markets for the expansion of primary products and manufactured goods produced by the then developing countries. However, during the 1930s, the gold standard was abandoned, devaluation of currencies occurred, and countries embarked upon rampant protectionist trade policies. As a result, the pace of international trade and international capital flows seriously slowed down. And so did the benefits and opportunities that accrued to nations through international trade.

The pace of world trade came to be dominated by the developed countries, to the increasing disadvantage of the developing countries. The prospects for expansion of trade by the developing countries in a world economy that was largely dominated by the developed countries seeking to maximize their individual advantages from trade were very dim indeed. Historical evidence indicates that, over time the developed countries have resorted to aggressive trade protectionism in response to the combined advents of productivity slowdowns and nationalism. On the whole, international trade has not yielded much benefits to the developing countries in the ways and magnitude expected. Empirical evidence supports the view that international trade has lost its engine of growth (Reidel, 1984).

The engine of economic growth that trade was in the nineteenth century has been totally lost to the twentieth-century LDCs. During the nineteenth century, rapid growth in Western Europe, particularly in England, was transmitted to other countries through international exchange. But the rapid growth of the DCs of the twentieth century has not been, and is not being, transmitted to the LDCs of the world. This failure is due mainly to the deliberate actions of the DCs through their attitudes, conduct, and designs, adopted in order to remain ahead in what they apparently have perceived to be a highly "competitive" world economic (dis)order in which "only the strong survive."

The *appendix* to this chapter presents the structuralist analyses and critique of international trade and its failure to be an engine of growth for present-day LDCs. It also offers some account of how the achievement of international competitiveness can enable a country to overcome the constraints and thereby utilize international trade's engine to achieve growth.

COMPETITIVENESS AS "FUEL" FOR THE ENGINE OF GROWTH

The international economy of the twenty-first century is far from anything resembling that of the nineteenth century in which most of the present-day developed countries operated as developing economies. It is even markedly different from the twentieth-century scene in which many of today's developed countries achieved their *takeoffs* into sustained economic development, or in which the emerging economies of East Asia were able to achieve remarkable successes. One major isolating factor is the explosively significant emergence of the Communications and Information Technology (CIT) revolution and its pervasive application into almost every aspect of economic undertaking, and its implications for maintenance of relative competitiveness in trade among nations (see chapter 6).

Another factor isolating the twenty-first century from the preceding two centuries is the prominent place given to the global *environment* and its related issues in most aspects of economic operations and policy decisions of various nations, which have significant bearing on relative competitiveness of countries (see chapter 8). Therefore, the relative international competitiveness parameter represents a unique factor in the ability to alter the economic prospects of a country as far as its trade circumstances are concerned.

International trade still has the potential to propel growth and development for any country. However, given the ongoing social and political arrangements that govern the various regions of the world, many countries, especially LDCs, could hardly achieve growth and development through trade that is based on the *goodwill and cooperation* of trading partners. The era of such goodwill and cooperation was gone with the nineteenth century.

To benefit from the potentially massive advantages that international trade could confer, countries must be capable of tapping into it. A country must be able to participate successfully as a player in the international trade arena. However, this success depends on the ability of a country to *create* and possess the crucial *necessary and sufficiency conditions* for sustained profitable trade. These necessary and sufficiency conditions exist in the achievement and maintenance of international competitiveness. To reiterate, the only chance that a country has of achieving growth through trade, exists only in form of achieving and maintaining international competitiveness.

Achievement and maintenance of micro and macro level competitiveness could enable a country to benefit immensely from international trade. Different levels of relative competitiveness appear to be what has made the difference between success and failure on the part of a country in being able to achieve economic growth through trade. As discussed above, the Asian NICs used their international competitiveness as a means of tapping the full benefits of the classical gains from trade. The growth engine that international trade is appears to merely represent a potential. This potential must be harvested. The means for applying the engine of growth to effect growth is to engage that engine. Without a country's exports and import-competing products being competitive, these products could not command a wide market demand, and therefore could not yield revenues, incomes, and employment. That is, the engine could not be sustained in motion, and therefore, would fail to effect growth.

International competitiveness may be regarded as the "fuel" for the engine of growth because it is the instrument that empowers the engine. It is the competitiveness of exports and import-competing products that cause them to command greater market shares in the domestic and world markets. These market shares sustain the levels of revenue, incomes, and employment created in the various sectors of the economy. The needed level of competitiveness must then be maintained (or even improved upon) in order to ensure that the market shares and their accompanying economic spinoffs (revenues, incomes, employment) are retained. In this way, competitiveness acts as an empowering fueling mechanism required to keep operational the growth engine that is international trade.

The evidence represented by East Asia's experience indicates that LDCs could use international competitiveness (at both micro and macro levels) as the tool for bypassing or even preempting the constraining effects of the factors that have hitherto mitigated against the growth-effect potentials of trade for them. These mitigating factors (see *appendix* to this chapter) also acted against the East Asian NICs, but were overcome with micro and macro level competitiveness strategies. The processes of these micro and macro level mechanisms are analyzed in the remaining chapters of this book.

COMPETITIVENESS AND STRATEGIC TRADE THEORY

In this section we provide some important background considerations of key related issues to the subject of international trade and competitiveness treated in the text chapter. We outline the basic ideas of the so-called *strategic trade theory* and its parent New Trade Theory, and also consider the issues of trade restrictionism, formation of regional trade blocs, and international financial transaction flows. Clear understanding of these topics are essential to a fuller appreciation of matters relating to international trade transactions, international competitiveness, and the economic growth of nations.

The New Trade Theory

The New Trade Theory (NTT) emanates from the New Growth Theory (NGT) that emerged within the international trade and economic growth and development literature during the early 1990s. The NGT emphasizes technological progress (and the determinants of technological progress) as well as the externalities that the development and application of new knowledge confers, as explicit variables that determine economic growth. Apparently, it posits that innovations take place more in some countries than others because of, among other things, differences in the development of science in the countries, the relative levels and quality of their research institutions, and the relative levels and quality of their educational systems.

The role of the diffusion of knowledge is another key parameter stressed by the NGT as central in determining growth. The model posits that knowledge that is acquired by one firm could not only yield greater productivity for that firm by empowering the workers engaged within the firm concerned, but also could lead to greater productivity in other firms as workers in those firms receive knowledge spillovers from the original firm. Thus, in the NGT, knowledge is given as a key factor of production. Therefore, the main essence of the NGT, and the main attribute that sets it apart, is its implication that firms should invest in knowledge, as much as they invest in other capital resources, in order to be productive or to maintain productivity.

The connection between the NGT and the NTT lies in their common emphasis of the importance of technology and the transmission of knowledge in the relative flow of the "gains from trade" to trading countries. These theories are regarded as "New" because they depart from the traditional (neoclassical) trade theories based on the principles of comparative advantage, which emphasizes the differences between nations (particularly in relation to relative resource endowments). As can be seen from the text, traditional trade theories work under the assumptions of competitive markets and posit international trade as the chief means through which countries could benefit from their differences in resource endowments.[13]

The NTT recognizes the possibilities and probabilities of product differentiation and specialization leading to quasi-monopolies in international markets. For instance, the existence of economies of scale, or massive technological leadership advantages, for firms in any country could result in those firms emerging as world monopolists in the world market. But then the rapid diffusion of technologies could cause firms in other countries to quickly copy the leading firms and emerge as competing rivals in the world market. The scenario then becomes analogous to the standard case of oligopolistic rivals engaged in strategic game settings in the world market stage, in which case the relative gains from trade accruing to a country would depend more on the successes of the trade "strategies" adopted than on the comparative advantage (which depends on competitiveness). This has been termed the Strategic Trade Theory (STT).[14]

The New (Strategic) Trade Theory holds important implication for an understanding of how a country could engineer its economy to achieve international competitiveness. A country could work to achieve greater comparative advantage for itself by devising and adopting some more effective strategic trade policies. Such strategic policies include subsidizing its domestic firms, or attracting more high-tech firms through, say, relaxation of environmental standards (see chapter 7). In this way, a country could attract firms that confer high levels of technological (knowledge) spillovers to others in the economy (see Krugman, 1986). However, some aspects of such "strategic" policies amount to the implementation of protectionist barriers or to straightforward anticompetitive measures. In either case, it interferes with the macro competitiveness drive of the economy and defeats the very essence of international competitiveness. Therefore, we must question whether the so-called strategic trade policies are really beneficial to a country, or, indeed, self-defeating. We shall discover in the remaining chapters of this book that apparently much of the policies of the so-called "strategic trade initiatives" are actually anticompetitive.

Trade Protectionism

Protectionism arises as countries adopt various trade restrictionist measures to protect their domestic markets, on behalf of domestic producers, against foreign competitors. The reasons generally given for such interventionist measures are discussed below. But it must be stressed that protectionist measures amount to implementation of uncompetitive actions (as we discover in chapter 2 where free-trade measures (trade liberalization) are classified under the macro level competitiveness parameters of *economic liberalization*. Thus, the adoption of trade protectionist measures are apt to reduce the relative international competitiveness of a country. Examples of each particular aspect are analyzed in turn.

Forms of Trade Protection

The various forms of trade protectionist measures include:

1. Trade embargo: Through this policy, a country simply bans the products of a potential trading partner within its markets. This is usually adopted as a punitive measure (referred to as trade sanctions) against a country, normally in response to a political situation. Examples are the trade sanctions that several countries imposed against South Africa because of its *apartheid* policy up until 1994, or against Iraq after the 1991 Gulf War. This measure simply destroys the international competitiveness of the country being punished, as the world market shares of its exports are effectively dropped to zero.

2. Trade quotas: This is the policy of restricting the quantity of traded goods and services. It may be used as a means of observing a bilateral or multilateral previous agreement, such as when some countries agree to limit their competitions in certain products in the markets of partners to enable the partners' producers to maintain a certain level of the share of their domestic markets. Trade quotas are also used for political reasons. The use of trade quotas impair the international competitiveness of the countries concerned as their export intensities (EIs) are limited; that is, their exporters are restricted on the extent of their marketing drives.

3. Trade tariff: Trade tariff is the most commonly used protectionist measure. It is the tax (import duty) that is imposed on goods imported into the country. Imposition of the tariff results in increases in the prices of imports and reduction in their quantities demanded. This effectively gives a competitive edge to domestic producers of similar goods. However, the kind of "competitive edge" that tariff protection gives to domestic (import-competing) producers is not an efficient "protection." It effectively shields them from market competition from international firms, as it allows them to operate with high-cost margins and yet remain in business, thereby rendering them inefficient. Such a situation amounts to an uneconomical utilization of resources and would not sustain a long-term economic health for the country. Tariff protection simply impairs a country's international competitiveness: at the micro level (as explained here), and at the macro level by interfering with, and restricting, trade liberalization.

4. Subsidies: This takes the form of grants or tax concessions extended to domestic producers to enable them to achieve overall lower unit costs of production, which effectively makes them more "competitive" relative to foreign producers. Subsidy grants amount to giving the firms artificial low costs of production, allowing them to operate under relatively low productivity conditions. It could also promote the tendency for corruption and misuse of productive resources. Subsidy grants could impair competitiveness in ways similar to the explanation given for the imposition of tariffs. But worse still, the granting of subsidies tends to render domestic firms highly dependent and unable to attain independent efficiency in operation.

5. Countervailing duties: A country would place special tariffs on incoming foreign products whose production were subsidized by their home governments. This is designed to protect the importing country's domestic producers from the supposedly "unfair competition" posed by the foreign producers. The consequences of this for competitiveness is similar to that discussed under subsidies. Further, such retaliatory actions often reduce the volume of bilateral and multilateral trade, and thus impede macro level competitiveness.

6. Nontariff barriers: There are several other forms of *nontariff barriers*. These

include different forms of import restrictions, product standard and quality regulations, environmental regulations, and health and safety standards. All these tend to negate international competitiveness in various ways.

Arguments for Trade Protection

The applications of trade protectionist measures go totally against the free-trade principles expounded in the comparative advantage doctrine. However, several arguments have been advanced to support trade protectionist actions. The major ones include:

1. Optimum tariff agreement: This argues that a country suffering from unfavorable terms of trade could improve its terms of trade by imposing a tariff in order to restrict the volume of imports.
2. Infant industry argument: Another argument for protectionism is the *infant-industry argument*. It advocates for measures to "protect" supposedly newly established (infant) industries that are not able to compete with well-established and mature foreign industries. These infant industries have not reached their maturity stages where they could reap scale economies and compete effectively.
3. Anti-dumping measure: The most-used *anti-dumping* argument is advocated as a legitimate means of preventing low-cost producers of inferior quality products from "dumping" these products in the markets of their trading partners.

Regional Trade Blocs and Integration

It is important to understand the prelude to the onset of the various aspects of regional integration and their historical trends in world international trade. Just as countries realized their economies' dependence on trade, they also realized that trade brought with it certain dangers that go with opening their economies up to the influence of the rest of the world. The virtues of free and unrestricted trade were so highly promoted in the world that it found its way into the economic development planning and policy making of every country that saw itself as a free-market-based economy. Nations based their trade policies on the driving force provided by the comparative advantage paradigm, namely, that each country's welfare would be greatest when each country specializes in the production and export of products in which it has comparative advantage over others, while importing from its partners those products whose comparative advantage are lower abroad.

Over the decades, however, countries gradually came to realize that totally uncontrolled international trade had certain problems associated with it, problems such as dumping, unequal factor prices, varieties of product qualities and standards across countries, health and environmental concerns, and the like. Therefore, most countries instituted various forms of trade restrictionist measures, on the one hand, to regulate and correct for these problems, and on the other hand, to protect their domestic economies from foreign competition. At the same time, certain world bodies and international institutions began to be formed to address the problems that are bound to arise with greater world trade. Further, countries began to realize the need to form free-trade alliances with their neighbors so as to take full advantage of their proximities to each other by forming regional trading blocs (or free-trade areas).

As the developed countries (DCs) vigorously embarked on trade protectionism, LDCs began to be increasingly frustrated as they realized that such attitudes severely threatened their capabilities of achieving growth and development through trade. The protectionist actions of the DCs simply set the clock back for world trade; it led to poor terms of trade for trading partners (especially LDCs) and resulted in slow growth of industrial specialization and exports for partners. As a result, countries advocated *economic integration* among regional neighbors. Through integration, countries reduce or abolish all trade barriers among them. The form of integration adopted could range from the loosest form of integration (such as a mere preferential trade agreement), to a deeper form (such as a completely free-trade area), or a customs union, a common market, an economic union, or even a total economic and monetary union.[15]

The formation of regional economic blocs is widely regarded as a potential threat to further expansion and development of multilateral and liberalized world trade. This is more so as the global economy increasingly polarizes around regional economic interests built mainly around the European Union (EU), the United States, and Japan. Hence, regional integrationism is on the rise worldwide, and it is fueled by the rise of concentrated (narrow) interests of groups who perceive that they would lose out if free trade were allowed to run its course. Such groups include owners and workers of various industries such as textiles, steel mills, automobiles, chemicals, or even agricultural produce. These pressure groups lobby their political leaders to enact strict protectionist laws to guard their respective industries against foreign competition—measures that act against international competitiveness.

Forms of Regional Integration

There are diverse forms of bilateral and multilateral trade agreements and blocs among nations. While some involve very mild trading arrangements, others extend to wider economic and even political cooperation. The various forms are as follows.

1. Preferential Trade Agreement (PTA): The PTA is an arrangement among countries whereby members adopt reduced tariff rates and extend preferential treatments to the imports of each other. This seems to be the loosest form of integration.
2. Free-Trade Area (FTA): The FTA is the form of agreement that removes trade protectionist barriers among the member countries, while allowing each country to retain these barriers against nonmembers.

3. Customs Union: This includes all the provisions of the FTA in addition to the stipulation that member countries retain common trade barriers against nonmembers.

4. Common Market: A Common Market provides for a much more involved form of integration. In addition to the provisions of the Customs Union, a Common Market involves the free movement of productive resources (such as capital and labor) between each other's economies.

5. Economic Union: The Economic Union is a much more complete and extensive form of economic integration. It not only provides for all the conditions of the Common Market but also goes further in integrating the monetary systems of member countries. The Economic Union, basically, unites member countries toward the formation of a political union.[16]

One of the most effective and modern regional integrations is the European Union (EU)..It began in 1957 as the European Economic Community (EEC), a Customs Union. It then converted to a Common Market in 1970, and now is becoming a complete Economic and Monetary Union. Among the LDCs, Latin America entered a Free Trade Association in 1960, while the Caribbean countries formed their Free Trade Area (CARIFTA) in 1968. In Africa, the East African Community (EAC) was formed in 1967, while the Economic Community of West African States (ECOWAS) was formed in 1975. A Preferential Trade Area (PTA) agreement was reached in 1984 among some Eastern and Southern African countries. In Asia, the Association of South East Asian Nations (ASEAN) was formed since 1967.

Generally, despite the widely recognized common interest in it, the history of regional economic integration is marked by failure to realize the economic aims and objectives to the extent that were initially envisaged. Regional integration has neither helped to promote rapid growth in intraregional trade nor led to massive economic benefits in the various countries in the ways expected. The main reasons this has been propounded in some recent studies (see, for example, Shiells [1995], or Asante [1986]). But the importance of regional trading blocs as means of promoting trade is currently being emphasized. Most countries have renewed their interests in regional integration, and many have pursued it vigorously and concluded major agreements. A major example is the North American Free Trade Agreement (NAFTA) between the two developed economies of North America (United States and Canada) and their developing neighbor, Mexico. The renewed efforts at regional integration among the developed countries since the 1980s is not unconnected to the relative successes of the NICs of Asia and Latin America, as well as the Japanese export dynamism, especially as these deeply penetrate and threaten to overwhelm the markets of the developed countries. This happens as the developed countries increasingly encounter the decline of their aging industries whose productivities now face aggressive competition in world markets.[17]

World Trade Agreements: The GATT

Such were the strengths of the forces against global free trade that world leaders realized that there was need to negotiate and safeguard mutual interests in world trade. The General Agreement on Tariffs and Trade (GATT) was established as a negotiating body that monitored and supervised global multilateral trade agreements. As the wave of protectionism raged during the 1930s (which may or may not have played a significant role in the Great Depression), international trade simply collapsed. The post-depression era, therefore, brought increasing efforts in the developed countries to seek for ways to forestall any such trade slumps in the future. Through a series of meetings and conferences arranged to discuss the need to lessen trade restrictionist policies among countries, the GATT evolved. The role of GATT (and its associated World Trade Organization) is examined fully in chapter 7.

GATT rules were enacted to govern tariffs and act as a supervisory mechanism among the world's trading partners. A very prominent GATT provision is the *most favored nation* (MFN) status that is accorded to a GATT member. MFN grants that every member of GATT automatically receive tariff reductions as long as such reductions have been extended to any member. Also, under the auspices of GATT, various global trade negotiations aimed at promoting more global trade liberalization are frequently pursued. One such attempt is referred to as the Uruguay Round of trade agreements, in which various countries sought to reach agreement toward simultaneous tariff reductions and lowering other forms of trade barriers.[18]

From its inception, GATT has generally resulted in significant tariff reductions through multilateral agreements. It is agreed that the level of tariffs facing member countries of GATT are much lower today than they have ever been. Nonetheless, any of the benefits of GATT's provisions, such as the MFN, have accrued solely to the developed countries relative to the developing countries, for many of its provisions are designed to be more favorable to the former. For example, tariff reductions on goods exported by the developed countries—industrial manufactured goods—far outweigh tariff reductions on goods exported by the developing countries, that is, primary products.

Although there exists a GATT principle of preferential treatment of the exports of LDCs, known as the *generalized system of preferences* (GSP), which provides for reduced tariffs on selected manufactured goods exported by the LDCs, the countries have not really benefited much from it. This is because many key industrial manufactured products exported from LDCs are exempted from benefits of the GSP: textiles and apparel, processed raw materials, and a wide range of industrial and labor-intensive products. It appears that the range of goods favored by the GSP are those that are exported by the Asian NICs; it is generally true that the benefits provided by this situation played a significant role in the relative successes of these Asian NICs. The increasing emergence of trading blocs is rapidly changing the world international economic order. These blocs are apt to usurp the global multilateral trading arrangements (provided for within the GATT), which have guided global trade and the world economy since the immediate post-World War II period.

International Financial Flows

Countries ordinarily acquire financial resources through sales of exported goods and services, or through transfers from other sources in the form of loans, grants, credits, or other forms of diverse payments. International debt is incurred through borrowing, as countries obtain credits from lenders in order to finance (balance-of-payments) deficits that they incur over the course of their development programs. As a country engages in international trade and trades its exports in the international market, it receives foreign exchange payments that it may then either spend immediately to acquire additional resources (capital, raw materials, or finished consumer goods), or save as foreign exchange reserves for future use. At any given time period, a country that spends more than it earns in terms of foreign exchange will have to finance such a deficit by borrowing from foreign sources or generating more goods and services in exports. Where this recourse becomes impossible, the country ends up taking foreign loans, thereby entering into foreign debt.

International capital flows could be in the form of *private capital* or *official government capital*. Government capital comes in the forms of foreign government lending or payments, and loans from international financial institutions, or financial aid and assistance (*bilateral loans and grants*) from foreign governments and other agencies. Private capital is in several different forms, such as direct capital investment made by private foreign investors, stocks and bonds purchases by foreign investors, cash loans or export credits from foreign financial institutions, and grants and other forms of aid from private sources.

The two main international financial institutions are the World Bank and the International Monetary Fund (IMF), both located in the United States. These bodies extend finances solely through official capital flows in form of multilateral loans and grants. When these institutions or foreign governments extend official financial flows to a country on *concessional terms*, it implies that such finances are either gifts, grants, or loans with liberal terms (soft loans), as compared to those available in the private international capital markets. Loans that are granted in this category for the express purpose of promoting the recipient's financial stability and economic development are ordinarily termed *foreign aid*, or technically referred to as *official development assistance*. This contrasts with loans extended on terms similar to those that obtain in the private international capital markets on *nonconcessional* (or commercial) terms.

Following the precedent set by the nineteenth-century and early-twentieth-century experiences of the "European offshoots," namely, the United States,

Canada, Australia, and New Zealand, which relied heavily on foreign capital for their economic growth and development efforts, many LDCs contracted significant private capital flows that grew very rapidly after the post-World War II period. Those of Latin America (especially Brazil, Argentina, Mexico), as well as India, received heavy capital flows. The trend of heavy indebtedness in LDCs continued into the 1980s, with the main creditors being the international financial institutions, the United States, Britain, France, and Germany.

The debt crisis was a global phenomenon involving both the developed and the developing countries. To the developed countries, it qualified the risks of loss to which their banks and lenders were exposed if the LDCs failed to repay their debts. To the LDCs, however, the debt crisis had much more serious ramifications. It implied the range of economic, social, and political consequences of being caught in a situation not only of heavy indebtedness but also of honoring the debt-servicing commitments of constantly generating substantial amounts of resources to make foreign payments. The debt crisis that arose during the early 1980s was precipitated by the nature of indebtedness itself: the interest compounding and the continuous need for servicing could only be sustained through further indebtedness.

APPENDIX

This appendix presents the structuralist analysis of how international trade lost its potency as an engine of economic growth for the developing countries during the twentieth century. It also gives an overview of how the achievement of international competitiveness can enable a country to benefit from the growth potential of international trade.

As the "engine of growth" actually stalled in the developing countries and regions of the world during the twentieth century, the question has arisen as to whether there are ways to restart the "engine." In this regard it is presumed that the achievement of international competitiveness could be the thrust that restarts the engine of growth for the developing countries of the twentieth and twenty-first centuries, namely, most countries across Africa, Asia, and Latin America and Caribbean.[19] Moreover, the achievement and maintenance of international competitiveness could be the factor that would sustain the engine of growth from losing its power and momentum for growth in the developed economies of Western Europe, North America, and Australasia where it has always been an engine of growth (see chapter 4).

The Stalled Engine of Growth

Many studies have shown that, when viewed in the light of the experiences of most twentieth-century LDCs, international trade did fail to be engine of economic growth and development. Economic development analysts and researchers have always puzzled as to what went wrong. Explanations as to why international trade failed to be the engine of growth to LDCs that it was for DCs, have been provided by eminent researchers and writers.[20]

Based on historical studies and analyses of the facts and economic performances of various LDCs, these writers propounded hypotheses, theories, and expositions to prove that international trade has lost its engine of growth mechanism for the LDCs. The most well-known three of these propositions are the *circular deterioration hypothesis*, the *lost interdependence (linkage) effects* paradigm, and the *impact of colonization*. These are briefly discussed below.

The Secular Deterioration Hypothesis

The secular deterioration hypothesis was advanced by Raul Prebisch who viewed the twentieth-century world as markedly different from the nineteenth-century world in which international trade played the key roles in the achievement of economic development takeoffs for most of the present-day developed countries.[21] The twentieth-century world is dichotomized into the economic Northern and Southern hemispheres—the *center (or metropolis)* and the *periphery (or colony)*. The center produces and exports mainly manufactured goods by utilizing raw materials acquired from the periphery which serves mainly as the source of cheap raw-material imports. The periphery also depends on the center as the market outlet of its primary produce. The center, therefore, essentially exercises a considerable degree of monopsony power and control in the global international trade arrangement.

The main argument, therefore, is that international trade has resulted in a one-sided flow of benefits to the center away from the periphery. This view was advanced by Hans Singer (1950) and Raul Prebisch (1959, 1964, 1984), who argued that the primary-product exporting countries, most of whom are still developing countries, do face the problem of *secularly deteriorating terms of trade*. They asserted that the primary product (raw-material) exports of the periphery are characterized by low price-elasticity of demand and low income-elasticity of demand. This price-inelasticity of demand means that any attempts by the producing periphery countries to raise output would amount to massive price declines and severe losses in export revenues. Moreover, the income-inelasticity of demand would mean that rising incomes in the center (consuming) countries do not lead to rising demand and rising prices for these raw materials. This situation has been referred to as the perpetual *terms of trade adversity syndrome* (Ezeala-Harrison, 1996a).

As a result of the perpetual terms of trade adversity syndrome (TOTAS) facing the periphery countries in their international trade relationship with the center countries, the center (buyers of raw materials) is often the sole beneficiary from the international trading of these products in the world. Gains from any productivity increases in raw-material production in the periphery accrue solely to the center. At the same time, output and productivity increases in manufactured products in the center remain in the center as these products have high income- and price-elasticity of demand. Thus, twentieth-century LDCs in the periphery could not raise sufficient foreign exchange to finance their capital needs for industrialization and development, as, say, Japan (who did not face the condition of TOTAS) did during the nineteenth century.

Lost Interdependence Effects

It was thought that the LDCs could escape the damaging effects of TOTAS by adopting a policy of processing their primary products and converting them to more durable semifinished products, with higher value-added, before exporting them. By so doing, the LDCs would:

(1) initiate industrialization within their economies.
(2) create additional employment avenues for their labor force.
(3) create additional value-added for their export products.
(4) earn higher prices for their exports as their terms of trade improved.

These benefits constitute what Albert Hirschman called the *interdependence effects* of primary-product processing policies.

The interdependence effects have been largely lost in the twentieth-century LDCs that have pursued the primary-product processing initiatives. This is because of the counter-policies and measures adopted by the center to thwart such initiatives. Hirschman believed that during the twentieth century, the center countries adopted the policy of *selective tariff bias* (STB) as a way of discouraging raw-material processing and exportation by periphery countries. The STB is a policy of imposing very high tariffs on imported processed or semifinished products from periphery countries, while at the same time imposing very little or no tariffs on unprocessed raw materials imported from the periphery countries.

To implement the STB, the center countries organized themselves as the *Organization of Economic Cooperation and Development* (OECD), and together with the periphery countries, formed the *General Agreement on Tariffs and Trade* (GATT). Through GATT, the voting power of the OECD (center) countries would be sufficient to operate and maintain their STB policies. As an example of the STB policy, in 1975, the United States had a 121 percent tariff on cocoa butter, but only a 0.06 percent tariff on raw cocoa beans.[22]

As a result of the counteractive attitudes and policies of the OECD center countries, the LDCs are denied the massive advantages that flow from the interdependence effects through international trade. The lost interdependence effects simply nullify the well-acclaimed classical gains from trade for LDCs during the twentieth-century. These effects made international trade the engine of growth that it truly was for the DCs. Developing countries of the nineteenth century, many of which are the developed countries of today's world, did not face as formidable an obstacle to their development as STB and TOTAS.

Impact of Colonization

Colonization was a nineteenth- and twentieth-century undertaking driven principally by the search for international trade expansion. It was a bid to access greater sources of industrial raw materials and market outlets for the manufactured produce of the center.

As discussed above, the development potential that international trade possessed and so generously spread across the "developing" world of the nineteenth century quickly evaporated by the turn of that century. By this time, colonialist and expansionist expeditions led by the countries of continental Europe transformed international trade from an "engine" of growth into a "weapon" of exploitation against the societies of Africa, Asia, and Latin America and the Caribbean.

Colonial domination meant a more complete and effective exploitation of the periphery, through which the center oversaw the continuous and uninhibited massive transfer of resources (raw materials and profits) from the colony (periphery) to the metropolis (center). By the time colonialism was dismantled, the economies of the colonized periphery countries had become strongly dependent on their colonial "masters." Their production structures had been fashioned on alien patterns as they produced mainly to satisfy the needs of the center's industries. They concentrated on production of cash crops, such as coffee, cocoa, tea, cotton, peanuts, and rubber, for export to the center; and imported manufactured consumer goods from the center. Such lack of diversity rendered many of these LDCs exclusively dependent on the economic moods and dictates of the center countries, thereby dislodging them prematurely and alienating them from their self-sufficient economic structures.

In the quest for even bolder economic gains, the colonizers also became settlers in many of the LDCs where the climate and environmental conditions were favorable. They selected the best and most fertile land (such as parts of eastern, central, and southern Africa) and established their own economic bases for even more thorough economic exploitation: they exploited the mines of these areas and utilized cheap local, and sometimes forced, labor. In such circumstances there could be no long-term commitments to the economic development of the colonies.

Colonialism doubtlessly disrupted production, distribution, consumption, savings, and investment aspirations in the affected LDCs. Colonies provided "captive consumers" for the center countries' expanding economies; many of the resulting center-periphery trade arrangements and special trade preferences still remain strong today.

Walter Rodney (1972) presented a candid and complete account of the legacy of colonialism for Africa. The bulk of the feedback effects of colonization (termed *neocolonization*) are still central in keeping most LDCs underdeveloped today. Many LDCs are still highly dependent and concentrate on the production of primary produce for export to center countries.

Restarting the Engine of Growth: Enter Competitiveness

International competitiveness provides the mechanism for restarting the engine of growth that is international trade. To reiterate, a major consequence of secular stagnation is that primary product producing and exporting countries inevitably face deterioration of their terms of trade. Two main factors, one from the demand side and one from the suppply side, are responsible for this situation, as follows.

1. On the demand side, growth in demand for primary (agricultural) products is small because of low income elasticities of demand.
2. On the supply side, if and when the growth in technological progress is applied to production, the resulting massive output increases would create a situation of excess supply and declining prices.

The pertinent ways in which the achievement of international competitiveness is able to overcome the constraints are as follows.

Competitiveness and Secular Deterioration

At the micro level, competitiveness involves rising productivity (see chapter 2). Higher productivity would result in higher incomes and greater effective demand for output, which would lessen the degree of dependence on foreign markets for the sale of the country's output.

At the macro level, a country's international competitiveness is affected by, among many other things, changes in its currency exchange rate. Maintaining a lower currency exchange rate would amount to reduction of the country's export prices. It will result in greater demand for the country's exports in foreign markets, leading to higher output and employment in the export-producing industries. That is to say that the country's exports have become more internationally competitive. And this is achieved without causing a deterioration in terms of trade because, under competitive conditions in which the typical export producing firm is a *price taker*, the profit-maximizing price of output would be equal to the firm's unit cost of production (proxied by P_x in equation 1.1). This is especially so if an overall (macro level) *competitiveness policy* is in place—removal of export duties, excise taxes, export licensing, and such restrictive factors. Thus, the secular deterioration problem would be countered because the terms of trade need no longer be perpetually adverse.

Moreover, should there be a reduction in foreign competitors' prices (proxied by P_M in equation 1.1), the country would stand to benefit in at least two ways: (1) the resulting higher TOT leads to rising relative incomes to domestic producers; (2) the effect would be similar to that of falling prices facing a representative firm in perfect competition, namely, it must produce and market its products at lower costs by operating more efficiently. To achieve this latter case, the firm must maintain higher productivity.

It must be noted, however, that despite this apparent ability to overcome the secular deterioration problem with greater competitiveness, the more formidable problems of price- and income-inelasticities of demand that lie underneath secular deterioration still persist. This raises the question of whether or not the achievement of greater international competitiveness can make a country's exports more price- and income-elastic. The answer to this is now considered as follows.

Competitiveness and Selective Tariff Bias

A wholesale adoption of trade liberalization would signal to the international trading community that a country is, indeed, willing, able, and ready to undertake profitable trade. This is especially so if such a stand is backed by a relatively moderate and stable level of the country's currency exchange rate, and more importantly by production of high-quality and competitively-priced products. To such a situation, the OECD countries are very likely to respond with a positive attitude toward trade. An example is the conferring of the most favored nation (MFN) status by the United States to certain trading partners.

Some countries (for example, China) are known to have received this coveted MFN trading status from the United States. This status has been accorded to China following a display of some level of commitment to trade liberalization (as well as certain political concessions, however). The result has been a general and significant reduction in tariffs levied on products imported into the United States from China. For China, this achievement amounts to overcoming the STB.

A primary product exporting country that achieves greater competitiveness would process its raw materials and convert them to more durable semifinished products, with higher value-added, before exporting them. The greater competitiveness could be achieved through the macro level policy of lower currency exchange rate, resulting in lower P_X, and greater demand for exports. By so doing, the country would reap the benefits of raising its level of industrialization, creating additional employment avenues for its labor force, and creating additional value-added for export products and thus earning higher prices for exports as its terms of trade improves.

International competitiveness achieved through increased productivity in primary product processing will not only make the primary products more competitive, but will also raise their quality and render them more durable and more price- and income-elastic. This will overcome the *elasticity problem* that is known to face most primary-product exporting countries. In this way, such a country will no longer be adversely affected by the perpetual terms of trade adversity syndrome that it often faces.

Competitiveness and Colonial Trade Legacies

One major legacy of colonialism that has important international trade implications is the legacy of making the colony a *monocultural export economy*. The country became a producer of cash-crops for "export markets" and food-crops for the domestic market. This simply rendered the country incapable of international trade diversification in terms of spreading its export products variety. As a result, the country is often vulnerable to unpredictable events in the world market for its primary product raw materials.

Domestically, the dependence on peasant-level agriculture for food production meant the limitation of the ability to generate the income base to support the demand for industrial output. The growth of industrialization is therefore hampered. At the micro (productivity enhancement) level, greater competitiveness would bring important gains to primary product exporting countries in ways discussed above. In addition to these ways, however, greater productivity in food products would greatly enhance the country's economic growth. It would result in significant benefits ranging from foreign exchange conservation to even greater competitiveness by way of lower domestic costs of food products. These would clearly help the economy overcome some of the constraints of colonial legacy.

At the macro (trade liberalization) level (including foreign exchange flexibility), greater competitiveness enables the country to reach more advantageous trading agreements with its former colonial power. It could use its familiarity with the colonial power's language, educational system, and culture to acquire and adapt any modern technologies that are developed within the economy of the colonial power. Besides, achievement of greater competitiveness would enable the country's exports to gain easier entry into the market of the former colonial power with lesser trade restrictions. Moreover, the country could gain the support of its former colonial power in international trade bodies such as the GATT.

NOTES

1. See some recent works such as Bliss (1989), Bruton (1989), and Lewis (1989) for good treatments of the various important issues of trade and economic growth and development.
2. See Brue (1994).
3. The comparative advantage doctrine was formulated by David Ricardo, a nineteenth-century British economist, and has been applied extensively since then in the development of international trade theories. This principle lies behind almost all free-

trade proposals that are advocated by free market proponents the world over.

4. Key related topics and issues of international trade that are important for international competitiveness are treated later in this chapter. These include the topics of trade restrictionism, regional integration, and international financial movements.

5. Some supporting evidence of the growth impacts of international trade is cited by Bryan (1994, p. 210), who reports a study indicating that over the three decades 1950-1980, those countries that adopted and implemented an outward-oriented trade policy achieved an average economic growth rate of 5.22 percent and total factor productivity (TFP) growth rate of 2.2 percent. This contrasted with the corresponding rates achieved by those countries that adopted an inward looking trade policy: 4.28 percent and 1.6 percent, respectively.

6. A country's BOP is analogous to an individual's monthly or yearly statement of personal account. The individual can spend more than she earns (a current account deficit) as long as she can either borrow (to create a capital account surplus) or draw from her savings (reserves) to finance the spending deficit.

7. This is because if either the country's imports or exports, or both, have inelastic demand, reduction in their prices (due to devaluation) would not result in any significant changes in the amounts traded, resulting simply in heavy revenue losses (for the country's exports) and heavier expenditures (on imports). Such a situation would only worsen any existing balance of trade deficits.

8. The Bretton Woods Conference of 1944 (in Britain) was organized to find ways to better organize the international monetary system. It established a system of fixed exchange rates for a country as long as such a country was not in "fundamental" BOP disequilibrium. A country in fundamental or chronic BOP disequilibrium should allow its exchange rate to depreciate.

9. The Organization for Economic Cooperation and Development (OECD) was formed originally under a 1960 Paris Convention with the policy objectives to: (1) achieve and promote the highest sustainable economic growth, employment, and living standards in member countries, while maintaining financial stability, and thereby contributing to the development of the world economy at large; (2) contribute to sound economic expansion in member countries; and (3) contribute to the expansion of multilateral world trade. Membership of the OECD is made up of the industrialized Western European countries of Austria, Belgium, Denmark, France, Germany, Greece, Ireland, Italy, Luxembourg, the Netherlands, Norway, Portugal, Spain, Sweden, Switzerland, Turkey, and the United Kingdom; the North American countries of the United States of America and Canada; and Iceland. Japan joined in 1964; Finland in 1969; Australia in 1971; New Zealand in 1973; and Mexico in 1994.

10. It is believed that among the main sources of the problem that has beset some of the NICs' economies (South Korea, Hong Kong, Thailand, Malaysia, and Indonesia) were some inappropriate economic management policies on the parts of these countries. In particular, these countries continued to peg their currencies to the U.S. dollar for too long despite the rising strength of the dollar. The consequence of such a situation for these NICs was a loss of (macro level) competitiveness for their exports, especially in the Japanese and European markets, which had been the mainstay of the NICs' export sales. As they lost their relative competitiveness in this way, China, which had since 1994 devalued its (Yuan) currency, gained these export markets. If these countries had allowed a free-market determination of their exchange rates, the appreciation of the dollar would have led to a relative reduction of the values of their currencies and thus

reductions in the prices of their exports (macro level competitiveness). With the resulting higher export sales, their currencies would have gradually gained strength over time with greater international confidence in their economies—a situation that would have largely averted the currency crises that they were subsequently plunged in.

11. Countries in this region have well-established records of bouncing back from economic woes. Sachs (1997b) suggest that East Asian countries have ample strengths in prudent economic management based on pragmatism and flexibility. Sachs credits Asia's leaders with knowing "how to read the markets and therefore how to trim their sails in stormy waters." This indicates the ability to quickly adopt and implement economic policies designed to immediately meet and address the economy's ongoing need. Apparently, this is what many LDCs (especially those of Sub-Saharan Africa) often fail to do.

12. Lewis (1980) offers a candid examination of the trend in the "slowing down of the engine of growth." Reidel (1984) also gives an empirical study of the relationship between trade and economic growth in LDCs. See also Ezeala-Harrison (1996a) for some in-depth presentation of the structuralist position on the potential of international trade in economic development of LDCs; the core analytical critique is presented in the *appendix* to this chapter.

13. The leading ideas regarded among "traditional trade theory" include the Ricardian comparative advantage paradigm discussed in the text; and the Heckscher-Ohlin theory of trade, commonly found within undergraduate courses in international economics, which applies differences in factor endowments to explain the profitability of trade. The Heckscher-Ohlin theorem simply states that countries would tend to produce and export those goods in which production they use the resources that they possess most abundantly. The difference between these two trade models is that the Ricardian comparative advantage model emphasizes the differences in technology under similar resource endowments, which results in different *comparative costs*. The Heckscher-Ohlin model assumes similar technologies across nations for whom resource endowments differ, resulting in different comparative advantages.

14. Deeper treatment of the New Trade Theory can be found in Krugman (1986) or Krugman and Obstfeld (1991).

15. For extended details on this, see Nafziger (1990) or Ezeala-Harrison (1996a).

16. The United States of America is an example of a political union that formed out of the formation of a strong Economic Union. The 1789 Constitution of the United States provided for a *complete economic and monetary union* among the initial thirteen states that formed it (see Nafziger, 1990).

17. Traditional European- and North American-dominated industries such as textiles, footwear, steel, automobiles, and chemicals now face increasing competition from cheaper, high-quality products of Asia and Latin America, whose lower wages enable their firms to operate with greater relative competitive advantage in the global market scene (see chapter 3).

18. Many countries, especially the developed countries, tend to disregard the GATT rules and simply carry out any trade practices that they presume will suit their economic interests and circumstances at any time. For a good account of this and other GATT operations, see Gillis et al. (1992, pp. 473-480).

19. Ezeala-Harrison (1997) gives the detailed analysis which also forms the main content of this appendix as well as chapter 4.

20. For more on this and other details of the structuralist positions on economic

underdevelopment, see Ezeala-Harrison (1996a).

21. Prebisch was the executive secretary of the Economic Commission for Latin America and the Caribbean (ECLAC) during 1948-1962. For a complete profile of Prebisch's structuralist ideas, see Prebisch (1959, 1963, 1964, 1984).

22. A good economic analysis of the impact of the OECD countries' STB structure on LDCs can be found in Balassa (1976). See also Boltho (1988) for a related account covering resources as a whole.

2

Conceptions and Misconceptions of International Competitiveness

What exactly is meant by the *international competitiveness* of a country (at the national level) or a firm (at the industry level)? This question has always been the first that comes to mind whenever one deals with the subject of the competitiveness of nations. In his well-known seminal piece on this subject, Porter (1990a) addressed the question by applying the concept of *competitive advantage*. However, one can assume a much more confining posture in confronting this question; namely, is international competitiveness a cardinal entity? That is, could it be measured? Or is it an ordinal entity? In other words, is international competitiveness a concept that can only be qualitatively construed, and not quantifiable?

As these are questions that are bound to be met by any country that attempts to raise its international transactions profile with the rest of the world, they raise some compelling issues indeed. What must such a country do to ensure that it maintains a relative edge in terms of the rate at which its traded goods and services exchange for those of its trading partners in the rest of the world? That is to say, what must a country do to ensure that it maintains relative competitiveness in its ongoing international trade transactions? This chapter will address these questions and many others that arise in relation to the issues of international competitiveness. And by the end of the chapter, a clear definition, complete formulation, and concrete specification of what constitutes *competitiveness* will emerge.

Relative to a country's trading partners, the maintenance of international competitiveness involves a range of factors ranging from increasing productivity and advancement of research and development (R&D) initiatives to obtaining high trade surpluses, advancement in high-technology products, and maintaining a highly trained labor force. These parameters suggest that a country's competitiveness status is a situation that could be achieved, retained, or lost, over time. And the ability to achieve and retain competitiveness would depend on the ability to effect the required and appropriate measures and implement the needed economic policy actions.

As this chapter is devoted to the complete exploration of the notion of competitiveness, the starting point is a discussion of the contemporary formulations of the term *competitiveness*. This will serve as a background against which is provided a step-by-step development and presentation of a complete specification, with a view toward a more concrete understanding of the concept.

CONTEMPORARY FORMULATIONS OF COMPETITIVENESS

Ordinarily, international competitiveness may be defined as the relative ability of a country's firms/industries to market their products cheaper (more competitively) in the global marketplace. Put is a broader sense, a country's international competitiveness is judged in terms of its ability to maintain a favorable relative position in its international (trade) transactions with its trading partners and the rest of the world. This ranges from having a low-cost export production base to attracting a large inflow of foreign capital. A number of studies assert that a country would be losing international competitiveness if it suffers from such factors as poor research and development (R&D) record, a growing trade deficit in high-tech products, an ill-trained labor force, and declining productivity. This would indicate an overall weakness in its ability to effectively compete with its trading partners.[1]

Whether or not a country is internationally competitive depends on how competitiveness is defined, and what indices are used to determine competitiveness. Of recent, there have been different approaches to the measurement of national competitiveness.[2] Among the most common indices of competitiveness are: (1) the Trade Performance criterion, (2) the Labor Productivity and Cost of Production criterion, and (3) the criteria based on Subjective Indices. We examine each of these in greater detail.

Trade Performance Criterion

By trade performance is meant the volume of total exports relative to total imports of the country, and their relative changes over time. Trade performance may be depicted at both the national (macro) level and the firm/industry (micro) level. At the national level, trade performance is a measure of the balance of trade (relationship between the volume of exports and the volume of imports) within the current account of a country's balance of payments situation.

A simple formula for determining a country's trade performance index (TPI) can be defined. We apply the following symbols:

X_i^j = total yearly exports of product i by country j
M_i^j = total yearly imports of product i by country j
i = 1, 2,... k
j = 1,2,... n
k = number of tradeable commodities in world trade
n = number of trading nations

Then, the trade performance index for the country, at the national (macro) level, can be defined as the ratio of the volume of aggregate commodity exports to the volume of aggregate commodity imports. This may be written as:

$$\text{TPI}^j = \Sigma_1^k X_i^j / \Sigma_1^k M_i^j \qquad (2.1)$$

Based on this index, the trade performance of the country in any given year could be determined according to whether the TPI ratio (equation 2.1) was greater or less than one. A country would have a favorable trade performance if

$$\Sigma_1^k X_i^j / \Sigma_1^k M_i^j > 1$$

and would have an unfavorable trade performance if

$$\Sigma_1^k X_i^j / \Sigma_1^k M_i^j < 1$$

At the industry/firm level, trade performance is a measure of the ratio of the shares of import and export in individual products (goods and services) transacted by the country. It can be measured as the ratio of a country's share of exports of a product in relation to the total level of world exports of that product. In this case, the TPI for a country at the firm/industry level is given by:

$$\text{TPI}_i^j = X_i^j / \Sigma_{j=1}^n X_i^j \qquad (2.2)$$

Based on this index, the trade performance of the country, at the micro level, could be determined according to whether the ratio (equation 2.2) was greater or less than one. A country would have a favorable trade performance if this ratio was greater than one and would have an unfavorable trade performance if this ratio was less than one.

The trade performance criterion cannot represent an effective index for measuring international competitiveness. It fails in several respects, the most important of which is the fact that the TPI does not contain the value of traded services. Moreover, the TPI is subject to wide fluctuations over time, as the volumes of exports and imports are often influenced by political factors. Again, the volume of a country's exports depends on the demand conditions of those exports in other countries where they are imported, over which the exporting country tends to not have much control. The TPI cannot adequately indicate the most fundamental forces behind the ability of a country to achieve and maintain a high level of productive efficiency and economic well-being over time in the face of a highly competitive and free-market oriented global environment.

Labor Productivity and Cost Criterion

This is the criterion adopted in the so-called sector definition of competitiveness (Bryan, 1994, p. 206). The two versions of this industry level definition are:

1. An industry would be competitive if it achieves (and presumably maintains) a productivity level that is equal to or higher than the levels of its competitors.
2. An industry (or firm) would be competitive if the level of its unit costs (average cost of production) are equal to or lower than the levels of its competitors (Markusen, 1992, p. 8).

The Productivity Criterion of Competitiveness

Productivity relates output to inputs, and represents the closest measure of the efficiency of the production process. Productivity is said to have increased when the same amount of input produces larger quantities of output than before, or the same output level as before is produced with smaller quantities of inputs. Specifically, productivity is defined as the level of output per unit of input used. In this specific sense, productivity represents the average product of resources. However, sometimes the marginal product of resources may be used to refer to productivity; the marginal product is the level of any additional output (to the total output level) resulting from the use of a unit amount of resources.

Labor productivity is the real value-added per unit of labor input utilized in production of output. It is measured as the average product of labor. Labor productivity is the real value-added per unit of labor input (labor time). Problems about the actual use of labor time in productive effort (which therefore affects what really constitutes labor productivity) arise when the question of labor effort as against labor time is considered. Studies in efficiency wage models of employment and productivity have dealt with such issues.[3] A simple measurement of the productivity of labor may be depicted as follows. Defining Q = total quantity of national output within the year, and L = total amount of labor employed in the economy within the year, then, the average product of labor is

$$AP_L = Q/L \qquad (2.3)$$

The relationship defined by equation (2.3) gives the *productivity* of labor. However, the *marginal productivity* of labor, defined as the additional (marginal) output contributed by any additional (marginal) unit of labor used, is given by:

$$MP_L = dQ/dL \qquad (2.4)$$

The labor productivity index is beset with problems ranging from accuracy of measurements to the actual use of labor time in productive effort (which therefore affects what really constitutes labor productivity), as well as the question of labor effort as against labor time. Labor productivity can be approximated to either the real GDP per employed person or the real per capita GDP in the economy. This would offer a practical yardstick for assessing relative overall productivity (bearing in mind that other factors of production are involved in the production process together with labor, and for which the appropriate allowances must be made).

The Cost Criterion of Competitiveness

The cost of production constitutes the key determinant of the relative competitiveness of firms. The unit (average) cost of output is the total cost per unit of output level produced and marketed. It determines the unit price at which the product may be sold, and thus determines the extent to which the product attracts demand in the market place relative to its competitors. To successfully compete, the product must retain some *standard level of quality dimension* that meets the satisfaction of consumers, and which they implicitly approve through their purchases of the product at the selling price. The relative unit production cost at which the product is marketed subject to meeting the standard quality dimension is an important determinant of competitiveness.

Just as labor productivity is sometimes used as an index of competitiveness, so is unit labor cost of output also used as an index of competitiveness. Labor cost means the *compensation cost* of the labor input used in production. Compensation cost encompasses all expenses incurred on workers (including wages, the firm's portion of employment or unemployment insurance contributions, retirement and pension benefits to workers, accident insurance, and all other aspects of such *payroll taxes*). The total compensation cost per unit of output gives the unit labor cost of production. International comparisons of unit labor costs are then used as the indicator of relative international competitiveness of countries.

On the basis of the unit labor cost criterion, it should be commonly expected that traditionally high-wage countries (such as Germany, Japan, and many Western European countries) would be less internationally competitive than traditionally low-wage economies such as Mexico, Taiwan, Singapore, Hong

Kong, or South Korea. But this is clearly an incomplete observation, because labor costs alone without their corresponding productivity levels cannot give an accurate picture of competitiveness. A high-wage economy in which the high wage reflects high productivity would result in a low unit cost of production; and a low-wage economy in which there is low productivity might end up with a high unit production cost.

Thus, a high-wage economy, such as Germany or Japan, can still achieve and maintain a greater level of competitiveness relative to a low-wage economy, such as Mexico or Indonesia, through a greater level of productivity, which allows the growth level of output to exceed the growth level of production cost. This point is borne out by the continued successes of high-wage economies (Germany, Japan, United States, Canada, Switzerland, Belgium, Netherlands, Sweden), in terms of their abilities to achieve and maintain international competitiveness on the basis of high productivity—high value-added production (subject to meeting the quality dimension) as against low wages. On the other hand, the very low-wage conditions of many countries in Asia, Africa, and Latin America have not enabled those countries to achieve and maintain high levels of relative international competitiveness on the basis of low wages.

Moreover, it must be realized that although labor (compensation) cost constitutes a major part of total cost of production, it is by no means the only cost. Other costs such as the cost of capital (interest costs), cost of land (rental costs and taxes), cost of raw materials, legal fees, and marketing costs (transportation, storage, and advertising costs—see chapter 3 for classification of these as *in-house* production costs and *overhead* production costs), also feature significantly in total cost of production. Therefore, the use of unit labor cost as an index of competitiveness is flawed.

The Subjective Indices

Various independent studies employ different methods and criteria based on subjective indices of measurement to determine the state of competitiveness of a country. Such indices are labeled as being subjective because they are based on impressions, perceptions, and conjectures regarding some trend (time series) or cross-sectional observations of certain macroeconomic indicators. Often, such criteria cannot be quantified or measured explicitly. Examples of subjective indices are:

1. The degree of openness, internationalization, or international orientation of a country's economy. This is used to judge whether or not the country's market is easily accessible to foreign producers who may wish to compete in it.
2. The size of the country's public indebtedness, especially foreign debt. This is used as an indicator of the flexibility of the country's financial system and its ability to withstand pressures arising from international transactions.
3. The level of government borrowing or size of budget deficit. This usually affects

the level of domestic interest rate and hence the currency exchange rate of the country.

4. The degree of diversification of export markets. A country that depends mainly on one or two export commodities tend to be more prone to foreign trade instabilities (arising from any unexpected fluctuations in international markets).

5. The country's attitude toward embracing "free-trade" policies and practices (measured by the level of protectionist trade barriers it imposes or removes).

6. The country's financial sector viability (measured by its relative interest rate levels, exchange rate, corporate bond issues, and level of confidence in its banking and financial institutions).

The agencies that adopt these criteria in determining the rank ordering of countries according to their relative competitiveness levels include the World Economic Forum (WEF) and the International Institute of Management Development (IMD).[4]

Other subjective criteria range from such factors as industrial efficiency to human resources and sociopolitical stability. Others are natural resource endowment, number of technology-intensive industries, manpower training, R&D, patent registrations, and number of engineers and scientists that the country has.

It is obvious that the ranking criteria employed in the above studies are not objective indices for assessing competitiveness. Therefore, any conclusions reached on the basis of these would be inconsistent over time and would lead to gross misconceptions. For example, as Luciani (1996) indicates, a 1990 WEF study ranked Italy eighteenth among twenty-four countries in sociopolitical stability, size of the national debt, and business confidence; while Germany and Japan ranked first and second, respectively. On this basis, one would expect a relatively very dismal performance by Italy in the international market. But rather, Italy ranked only after Japan as the world's fastest growing exporter. In fact, the U.S. Bureau of Labor Statistics (1989) report on *International Comparisons of Manufacturing Productivity and Labor Costs Trends* (1988) indicates that Italy not only had an extremely productive manufacturing sector but also had one of the fastest growing economies in Europe throughout the 1980s. Thus, the apparent contradiction in this example suggests that rankings and conclusions about competitiveness based on mere perceptions are prone to being misleading.

COMPETING NOTIONS OF COMPETITIVENESS

The particular way in which the term *competitiveness* is defined and measured would affect the result of any study on whether or not a country is "competitive." Competitiveness has always been a somewhat difficult and controversial concept. There is very little agreement regarding its precise definition. There is disagreement also about its measurement, the indices to be used in its measurement, and the interpretation of whatever results that would emerge from such measurements.

The contemporary existing different definitions of international competitiveness may be categorized according to their criteria bases. We group the various criteria according to their levels of application, that is, those criteria that apply at the firm/industry level of competitiveness are regarded as micro level criteria; and those criteria that apply at the national level of competitiveness are regarded as macro level criteria. Based on this approach, the various competing notions of international competitiveness may be represented as follows.

The Productivity-based Index (Micro Level)

Significant interest developed around the subject of the relative international competitiveness of nations since Porter (1987, 1990a, 1990b) drew attention to it, within both the academic and business circles. The issues raised at that time, basically centered around the question of how a country could effectively play the "strategic" trade game and succeed in being able to exact high levels of "gains from trade" relative to its trading partners, within the world market stage. This model simply amounted to the application of the so-called New Trade Theory (see chapter 1) in the formation of national and international trade policies. It offers an explanation of what makes some countries more successful than others in terms of their relative strategic trade positions and their relative abilities to outwit each other in the global market place. The various approaches taken to define competitiveness by using productivity as an index are as follows.

Porter's Innovative Advantage Index

In Porter's (1990a) proposals of the notion of international competitiveness based on company initiatives of innovation and upgrading, the most important parameter that is manipulated by trading countries in order to capture and maintain higher market shares from each other is productivity. Porter (p. 84) states that the only meaningful concept of national competitiveness is productivity. Thus, productivity is believed to be the crucial parameter of relative international competitiveness. Applying the standard notion of comparative advantage, Porter believes that trade and investment are among the key factors that increase productivity and incomes in a country: through specialization in the production of those goods and services in which its industries are more productive relative to international competitors, a country gains larger world market shares in them, while importing those products in which its industries are less productive.

The notion of competitiveness being advanced here makes it an institutional concept. This implies that a country's competitiveness would be determined by the ability of its institutions and infrastructure to perform. In turn, this ability depends on at least three institutional and infrastructural qualities (Economic Council of Canada, 1992):

1. Efficiency of institutions and infrastructure in meeting their goals.
2. Adaptability of institutions to quickly imitate superior techniques.
3. Innovative abilities of institutions.

These institutional qualities cause firms in both the private and public sectors to enjoy certain operational advantages that result in lower costs and higher production efficiency. In this way, a country's industries are able to gain international competitive advantage relative to its competitors.

However, it is important to note that competitive advantage need not necessarily imply competitiveness. For where competitive advantage represents a static potential that may or may not translate into competitiveness and that may or may not lead to economic growth, competitiveness represents a dynamic attribute that necessarily translates into economic growth (see chapter 3). But then, the achievement of competitive advantage is the key requirement for achieving competitiveness.[5]

WEF Product Characteristics

In its annual *World Competitiveness Report*, the World Economic Forum (WEF) depicts competitiveness as the ability of entrepreneurs to design, produce, and market goods and services, the price and non-price characteristics of which form a more attractive package than that of competitors. This approach to defining competitiveness also applies the New Trade Theory, based on productivity and strategic trade policies.

Productivity and Cost Base

Markusen (1992) advocates a definition of industry competitiveness based on industry productivity relative to that of trading partners—index of productive efficiency, which he sees as a more reliable guide to a country's overall standing than a definition based on, say, trade performance. Competitiveness is defined at the firm/industry level as the ability of the firm/industry to achieve and maintain a level of productivity that is equal to or higher than the level achieved by competitors. In terms of costs, competitiveness is the ability of the firm/industry to produce and market products at equal or lower unit costs relative to that of competitors.[6]

Trade Performance-Real Income Index (Macro Level)

Another approach depicts a country's competitiveness as a residual that would be evident in terms of the real income levels and living standards of its citizens. This posits competitiveness at the national level, referring to the performance of the country's economy. This is the approach taken by the U.S. Presidential Commission on Industrial Competitiveness, which defines competitiveness in terms of a country maintaining a growth rate of real income equal to that of its trading partners in an environment of free and long-run balance of trade (McCulloch, 1988). Competitiveness is explained as the degree to which an economy, under a free-market regime, could produce goods and services that withstand the test of international markets, while at the same time maintaining and expanding the real income levels of its citizens. This definition emphasizes the long-run growth of real incomes, and attempts to link competitiveness with economic growth and trade. But at this *macro* aspect of it, one other important factor does enter into the definition of competitiveness, namely, the country's currency exchange rate. The higher the exchange rate, the more expensive the country's currency would be in the international market, and hence the lesser would be the demand of the country's exports in foreign markets. Within this category would lie also the definition of competitiveness offered by Fagerberg (1988), in terms of the ability of a country to realize central economic policy goals, especially growth in income and employment, while maintaining stability in its balance-of-payments situation.

Inferences from the Competing Notions of Competitiveness

The above classifications clearly show the two levels of international competitiveness, namely, competitiveness at the *micro level* and competitiveness at the *macro level*. It is easy to see how a clear misconception of the term *competitiveness* could quickly emerge from a confusion of imprecise definitions. Most often, competitiveness (and a change in competitiveness) is associated with trade performance (Cas, 1988), for if a country loses export share (in a particular item or sector) or gets increased import penetration (in a particular commodity or sector), it is said to have become less competitive (Rugman and D'Cruz, 1989).

Studies on the topic have tended to use the term in ways that relate to various economic parameters such as trade performance and real exchange rates (Cas, 1988), terms of trade (Arndt, 1993), relative unit labor cost (Enoch, 1978, Rao and Lempriere, 1992); growth rate of GDP per capita (World Economic Forum, 1996), and productivity and total factor productivity growth (Porter, 1990a; Markusen, 1992; Dollar and Wolf, 1993; Ezeala-Harrison, 1995). Several of these studies have emphasized that trade performance measures do not adequately reflect the state of competitiveness of a nation. Despite these various approaches, however, most often competitiveness is associated with trade performance.

In a recent study, Markusen (1992) demonstrated that the meaning of the term *competitiveness* would change if it is equated with trade performance. Applying this study, Ezeala-Harrison (1995) shows why the connection between trade performance and competitiveness should not be made. Markusen (1987) showed how this misconception resulted in large current account deficits in the United States during the 1980s being interpreted as a loss of U.S. competitiveness, which it was not. In fact, a notion of competitiveness based on the trade performance definition may generate results that are virtually opposite to the results produced by the productivity definition.

On a theoretical plain, Markusen (1992) suggests three reasons why a definition of industry competitiveness centered on trade performance will conflict with one centered on productivity:

1. Technological factors: Technological progress, which transfers factors of production out of a sector X into another sector Y, will result in shrinking trade performance in sector X (increasing imports or decreasing exports) even though there has been no decreased productivity in the X industry.

2. External factors: A decrease in the world price of some commodity X (due to, say, more supply from new countries entering the world market, or deteriorating world market demand) will lower trade performance in X, even though productivity does not deteriorate relative to other producers.

3. Political factors: Domestic political pressures could cause the government of a country to adopt protective measures in favor of domestic producers. The resulting imposition of import barriers or provision of export subsidies may improve trade performance in a sector, but generally they do not increase productivity.

The use of trade performance, in particular, gives the term *competitiveness* a normative connotation (for example, more exports is better than more imports; or, more competitiveness is better than less competitiveness) and fails to differentiate between the micro and macro applications of the term. At a micro level, more competitiveness is perfectly sensible for individual firms within a given industry, but this does not mean that the industry is economically desirable.[7] This is because, with balanced trade in the economy, some industries will be exporters while others will be domestic-oriented and competing locally with imports. Global market changes that result in declining exports or increased imports would not necessarily mean a loss in competitiveness. Capital inflow (imports) that may be used for productive investment may lead to a balance of trade deficit or a current account deficit, but may constitute an investment for raising future productivity and competitiveness. On the other hand, when such deficit-creating capital inflow is used to increase or maintain current consumption, then its association with the loss of competitiveness may be valid.

A normative definition of competitiveness at the macro level that focuses on real income relative to trading partners is also used. In this connection, competitiveness is equated with real income performance. As noted above, the U.S. Presidential Commission on Industrial Competitiveness defines it in terms of a country maintaining a balanced trade performance and achieving a comparable growth rate of real income (McCulloch, 1988). It was in following this real income- and trade performance-based definition that Britain was deemed to be losing competitiveness during the 1960s and 1970s when its growth of per capita income lagged behind that of much of Western Europe (Markusen, 1992). The growth of competitiveness in the Far East during the late 1980s has been thought of in terms of rising income levels and current account surpluses.

Indeed, measures of trade performance for a country may move in directions opposite to measures of real income, thereby giving results that may conflict with each other. For example, consider two domestic industries X and Y, in a given country, where X is an import-competing industry and Y is an exporter. Assume that the world price for the product of industry X declines and that of industry Y increases. This is an improvement in the country's terms of trade (a positive outcome), but then industry X may be seen to have lost competitiveness (with lower world prices as against domestic unchanged prices). So, a gain in competitiveness (in terms of higher real income due to improved terms of trade) is clearly at odds with a loss in competitiveness (due to weaker trade performance).

So far, we have seen that there is very little agreement regarding the precise definition of international competitiveness. But it is totally unsatisfactory to have a concept of a national policy objective for which there can be no consensus as to its precise meaning. Given its overwhelming importance in national economic policy, it is necessary to specify an idea of international competitiveness in concrete and observable terms. We need a concept that can be quantified and for which a target objective can be set. In this regard, the rest of this chapter is devoted to determining the precise and measurable definition of international competitiveness.

CONCRETE SPECIFICATION OF COMPETITIVENESS

A more concrete specification of competitiveness is necessary in order to overcome the problems of misconception discussed above. Not only must a clear definition and measurement of competitiveness be adopted, but also a clear distinction must be made between the use of the term in a strictly positive sense (as when the declining X industry is referred to as "losing competitiveness") and its use in a normative sense (in which case the X industry's "losing competitiveness" may or may not be desirable). Considered are the following specific classifications of the various criteria for determination of international competitiveness, and then established are some concrete specifications and measurement criteria for the concept. The *qualitative* indices are first presented, and then the *quantitative* index is given in the *appendix* to this chapter.

Micro and Macro Level Competitiveness Parameters

The various parameters that determine the state of international competitiveness of a country apply either at the *micro* level or the *macro* level. The micro parameters are those that determine competitiveness at the firm or industry level, while the macro parameters are those that determine competitiveness at the national (and institutional) level. It is important to consider these concepts in greater depth.

Micro Level Parameters: Productivity (Technology) and Cost Base

Global competitiveness may generally be defined in terms of technology and scale: a country is competitive if its industries have an average level of *total factor productivity* (TFP) greater than or equal to that of its foreign competitors. As will be explained in greater detail below, the TFP is a measure of the level and growth rate of overall efficiency of the economy. It indicates the combined productivities of all factors of production and (socioeconomic) institutions and infrastructure at work within the country. A country's international competitiveness is then measured by the level and growth over time, in its TFP relative to those of its trading partners. This aspect of competitiveness may also be depicted in terms of costs: a country is competitive if its firms and industries have an average level of unit costs (average costs) lower than or equal to that of its foreign competitors.

In considering these notions of competitiveness, it must be recognized that a country can be competitive under the technological and scale definition but not under the cost definition. This is because its industries may be paying higher prices for their factor inputs relative to its competitors' industries (an example is the alleged higher labor costs in industrialized countries of North America and Europe relative to developing countries). Moreover, the technological and scale definition does have a normative connotation (higher productivity is good), but the cost definition does not (it is not necessarily undesirable that a country is not competitive in terms of unskilled and/or labor-intensive production). If a country loses market share in its export markets mainly because of the entry of new foreign competitors, this need not represent a loss of competitiveness. But where such a loss of market share is due to increased productivity of foreign competitors, then it could indicate a loss of competitiveness. Thus, productivity always plays the major role in the determination of a country's longer term (cost) competitiveness.

Therefore, the productivity criterion does provide a general index for determining competitiveness. The productivity index (based on technological parameters such as total factor productivity and unit costs of production) does not suffer from ambiguities and conflicting conceptual connotations. The use of costs, however, may suffer from international currency changes and global monetary instability, and the next section gives a discussion of the necessary adjustments in using this approach.

Productivity relates output to inputs and represents the closest measure of the efficiency of the production process. Productivity is quantifiable and measurable; its levels are unique, and they do not vary according to perceptions and impressions. Productivity trends could be consistently determined over time for cross-sectional and time series comparisons.

Total factor productivity is the measure of the relationship between output and its total factor input. The TFP measures the output of the weighted sum of all inputs, thereby giving the residual output changes not accounted for by total factor input changes. The TFP is a residual measure. Changes in TFP are not influenced by changes in the various factors that affect technological progress, factors such as the quality of factors of production, flexibility of resource use, capacity utilization, quality of management, economies of scale, and the like. Also, changes in TFP are not influenced by efficient factor substitutions induced by changes in relative factor prices and product demand conditions (Rao and Preston, 1984). Therefore, such changes are the measures of the efficiency (productivity) with which all factors are used in the production process.

The use of TFP in measuring national competitiveness overcomes the problems which, say, *dumping*, or lack of demand, may cause in assessing the state of competitiveness of a country that is highly productive in, for instance, raw materials. The occurrence of these phenomena would suggest a loss of competitiveness if trade performance criteria are used, but these do not indicate a true loss of competitiveness. Competitiveness must relate to overall economic efficiency of a country's use of its resources rather than to the skillfullness of its external trade negotiators.

Total Factor Productivity as Index of (Micro Level) Competitiveness

As TFP measures the relationship between output and its total factor input (that is, as already explained, the output of the weighted sum of all inputs), it gives the residual output changes not accounted for by total factor input changes. Thus, the TFP is a residual measure. Changes in TFP are not influenced by changes in the various factors that affect technological progress, factors such as the quality of factors of production, flexibility of resource use, capacity utilization, quality of management, economies of scale, and the like. Also, changes in TFP are not influenced by efficient factor substitutions induced by changes in relative factor prices and product demand conditions (Rao and Preston, 1984). Therefore, such changes are the measures of the efficiency (productivity) with which all factors are used in the production process.

In a 1992 study, Rao and Lempriere (1992c) examined labor productivity and unit labor cost performance of U.S. and Canadian industries. They concluded that TFP provided a more complete picture, even though labor productivity and labor costs are a usual way to measure how competitive a country is. As a result of the difficulties of productivity measurement, many studies have tended to focus on single factor productivity such as labor productivity, or capital productivity, and an index for observing "how productive" an industry or a country is. The danger with this procedure, however, is that individual factor productivity hardly captures all the gains in productive efficiency.[8]

It can be quite misleading if, say, changes in labor productivity are entirely attributed to changes in labor input because the output of any given amount of labor is affected (positively or negatively) by other co-operant factors independent of the labor input. For example, a labor-saving capital substitution may occur in response to falling capital costs and/or rising wages. As output levels remain unchanged after such a shift away from labor, the result would be a higher average product of labor, which could then give the erroneous impression that the efficiency of labor has increased, which is not the case.

The use of TFP in measuring national competitiveness overcomes the problems which, say, *dumping*, or lack of demand, may cause in assessing the state of competitiveness of a country that is highly productive in, for instance, raw materials. The occurrence of these phenomena would suggest a loss of competitiveness if trade performance criteria is used, but these do not indicate a true loss of competitiveness. Competitiveness must relate to overall economic efficiency of a country's use of its resources rather than to the skilfullness of its external trade negotiators.

Macro-Level Parameters: Economic Liberalization and Supportive Institutional Structures

At the macroeconomic level, the degree of "economic liberalization" and existence of adequate institutional and infrastructural framework are crucial factors that influence a country's state of competitiveness. These factors, however, hang largely on the political (and ideological) leaning of the country's authorities and policy makers—policies that usually remain fairly unchanged over time. The macro parameters are therefore considered as given (or constant) within the realm of international competitiveness consideration.

Economic liberalization is the package of measures designed to direct an economy away from "uncompetitive" regulatory and central control toward a free-market based system—a system based on competition, liberalization, deregulation, and enhanced private-sector. Among the conceivably several major parameters of economic liberalization, two of the most cogent ones are the country's: (1) trade liberalization (or free trade) policy, and (2) currency exchange rate regime (flexible but stable and moderate exchange rate level).[9]

The supportive institutional structures (including the institutional and infrastructural framework) of a country constitute another aspect of the macro level indices of competitiveness. Among these are the "subjective indices" discussed earlier. They include:

— The degree of internationalization (international orientation) of a country's economy.

— The size of the country's public indebtedness, especially foreign debt.
— The level of government borrowing or size of budget deficit.
— The degree of diversification of export products and markets.
— The level of protectionist trade barriers a country imposes (or removes).
— The country's financial sector viability (measured by its relative interest rate levels, exchange rate, corporate bond issues, and level of confidence in its banking and financial institutions).
— The quality of public infrastructure and utilities.

As already pointed out, some notable world agencies such as the World Economic Forum (WEF) and the International Institute of Management Development (IMD) adopt these macro criteria exclusively in determining the rank ordering of countries according to their relative competitiveness levels.[10] Conclusions about relative competitiveness of countries based solely on the macro level parameters are clearly inadequate, as the ranking criteria employed in such studies are not objective indicators of competitiveness.

Complete Formulation of Competitiveness: Necessary and Sufficiency Conditions

A specific and complete formulation of competitiveness is necessary in order to overcome the problems of misconception and misunderstanding that surround the use of inadequate notions of the concept. As far as it applies to a country's relative (global) performance, it is important that the term competitiveness be depicted in its correct and complete conceptualization. Such completeness must embrace the full aspects of the necessary and sufficiency conditions of competitiveness, namely, its micro- and macro-level parameters.

The nation's state of total factor productivity and relative costs of output, as the micro level parameters, represent the *necessary conditions* of international competitiveness. These are the quantitative indicators that could be monitored over time to indicate the nation's relative performance. These factors determine the country's ability to compete, in terms of achieving *export intensity* for its products in foreign markets, and containing the degree of *import penetration* of foreign products within its own domestic market (see chapter 1).

The *sufficiency conditions* for international competitiveness are given by the ability of the country's socioeconomic institutions and infrastructure to perform. The ability to perform depends on the three institutional and infrastructural qualities of:

1. efficiency of operation.
2. adaptability toward quick imitations of superior techniques, and
3. innovativeness.

It is these institutional and infrastructural qualities that enable the country's firms and industries to function under low-cost overhead conditions and facilities that give them some international *competitive advantage.* Among the institutions and infrastructure as outlined earlier are the country's openness, size of public indebtedness, level of government borrowing or size of budget deficit, degree of diversification of export products and markets, level of protectionist trade barriers, financial sector viability (measured by relative interest rate and exchange rate levels, bond and stock price levels, etc.), and quality of public infrastructure and utilities.

On the basis of the foregoing, it is stressed that competitiveness involves both micro and macro level dimensions. For purposes of its measurement, competitiveness may be regarded as essentially a micro level phenomenon, under given states of the macro level parameters. Thus the following specific formulation may be stated:

International competitiveness may be defined as the relative ability of a country's firms to produce and market products of standard or superior quality at lower prices.

This definition indicates that the state of a country's competitiveness is subject to changes in either or both of the micro- and macro-level packages of parameters. It is these parameters that play the crucial role in the country's export performance in foreign markets, import-competing performance in domestic markets, and the overall macroeconomic performance over time. The productivity parameter would affect the cost of production, and hence the ability to market the products (subject to standard or superior quality) at relatively lower prices. Productivity is quantifiable and measurable. Productivity levels are unique; they do not vary according to perceptions and impressions; productivity trends could be consistently determined over time for cross-sectional and time series comparisons.

APPENDIX

This appendix presents the procedure for generating a specific quantitative measure for index of national competitiveness. This would complement the approach for firm/industry level competitiveness presented in chapter 3, where the concept of competitive advantage (of a country's firms/industries) is developed and applied to model the state of relative international competitiveness of the country.

In this appendix we present a model of how competitiveness can be quantified and measured. The model is developed from first principles, by application of the basic definition of competitiveness within the structural framework of the economy. This would yield the appropriate index for measuring competitiveness, an index that is determined through a simplified formulation of the workings of the economic system.[11]

Framework for Measure of National Competitiveness

The generalized implicit production function linking total output to the set of inputs used is of the form:

$$y_i = y_i(L_i, K_i, R_i) \tag{A2.1}$$

where subscript i denotes the ith sector, and
   y = quantity of output
   L = labor input
   K = capital input
   R = natural resource input

Over time, the growth rate of output in each sector of the economy is made up of the sum of the products of each input's marginal productivity and the rate expansion of the input. That is,

$$dy_i/dt = \partial y_i/\partial L_i \cdot dL_i/dt + \partial y_i/\partial K_i \cdot dK_i/dt$$
$$+ \partial y_i/\partial R_i \cdot dR_i/dt \tag{A2.2}$$

This expresses the output potential of each sector of the economy under its given set of inputs and given technological know-how. But we need to assume a specific technology in the economy in order to isolate the role of the combined effects of the inputs, the TFP.

For simplicity, we assume that each sector of the economy is characterized by a production function of the Cobb-Douglas type:

$$y = \lambda L^\alpha K^\beta R^\gamma \tag{A2.3}$$

where:
   λ = the TFP index[12]
   α = the factor share of capital in total output
   β = the factor share of labor in total output
   γ = the factor share resources in total output

The economy's TFP growth over time is given changes λ, given for the ith sector of the economy as:

$$d\lambda_i/dt = dy_i/dt - (\alpha_i dL_i/dt + \beta_i dK_i/dt + \gamma_i dR_i/dt) \tag{A2.4}$$

Substituting (A2.2) into (A2.4) we obtain:

$$d\lambda_i/dt = \partial y_i/\partial L_i \cdot dL_i/dt + \partial y_i/\partial K_i \cdot dK_i/dt + \partial y_i/\partial R_i \cdot dR_i/dt$$
$$- (\alpha_i dL_i/dt + \beta_i dK_i/dt + \gamma_i dR_i/dt)$$

That is,

$$d\lambda_i/dt = dL_i/dt[\partial y_i/\partial L_i{-}\alpha_i] + dK_i/dt[\partial y_i/\partial K_i{-}\beta_i] + dR_i/dt[\partial y_i/\partial R_i{-}\gamma_i]$$

As α_i, β_i, and γ_i are factor shares, it follows that

$$\alpha_i = [\partial y_i/\partial L_i]/[y_i/L_i]$$
$$\beta_i = [\partial y_i/\partial K_i]/[y_i/K_i]$$
$$\gamma_i = [\partial y_i/\partial R_i]/[y_i/R_i]$$

Therefore:

$$d\lambda_i/dt = dL_i/dt[\alpha_i y_i/L_i{-}\alpha_i] + dK_i/dt[\beta_i y_i/K_i{-}\beta_i] + dR_i/dt[\gamma_i y_i/R_i{-}\gamma_i]$$
or
$$d\lambda_i/dt = \alpha_i \cdot dL_i/dt[y_i/L_i{-}1] + \beta_i \cdot dK_i/dt[y_i/K_i{-}1]$$
$$+ \gamma_i \cdot dR_i/dt[y_i/R_i{-}1] \tag{A2.5}$$

This gives the measure of TFP growth for any given sector of the economy. For the n sectors of the economy, where $i = 1,2,3...n$, the aggregate TFP change is:

$$\lambda' = d\lambda/dt = \Sigma_1^n\{\alpha_i \cdot dL_i/dt[y_i/L_i{-}1] + \beta_i \cdot dK_i/dt[y_i/K_i{-}1]$$
$$+ \gamma_i \cdot dR_i/dt[y_i/R_i{-}1]\} \tag{A2.6}$$

This gives the national measure of TFP growth, which we posit as the most appropriate index for measuring competitiveness.[13]

This TFP growth as given in equation (A2.6) is the weighted sum of individual input growth rates and their productivities. It can be used to show that the growth in any particular factor's productivity depends, in turn, on the growth of the TFP. For instance, labor productivity growth is:

$$dL_i/dt[\partial y_i/\partial L_i{-}\alpha_i] = d\lambda_i/dt - \{\beta_i \cdot dK_i/dt[y_i/K_i{-}1]$$
$$+ \gamma_i \cdot dR_i/dt[y_i/R_i{-}1]\} \tag{A2.7}$$

It indicates that labor productivity growth is influenced not only by TFP growth but also by the growth in the substitution of other inputs for labor.

Empirical Significance of the TFP Model

Based on the foregoing results, the appropriate time series and/or cross-sectional data may be employed to compute the trend values of:

1. *A country's sectoral TFPs*, λ_i (using equation [A2.5]), to obtain a picture of its intersectoral TFP performance. This may then be used to ascertain the relative competitiveness of the various sectors of the economy.

2. *A country's aggregate TFP growth over time*, λ' (using equation [A2.6]); this would

not only give an indication of the country's potential competitiveness profile, it would also indicate whether or not, and at what particular points in time, the economy might or might not be losing its hold on relative competitiveness.

3. *The aggregate levels of TFP growths*, λ', of various countries (using equation [A2.6]); this enables an international comparison of competitiveness through employing cross-sectional data on various countries to compute trend values of λ' for each country, which may then be compared to determine international relative competitiveness of the countries.

NOTES

1. It is important to stress the difference between competitiveness and productivity, as these two distinct concepts should be clearly understood (see Moon and Peery Jr., 1995). Productivity is the measure of the average level of output per unit of resource employed and refers to the internal capability of an organization (a firm, industry, or nation). Competitiveness is the relative standing of the organization against its competitors and trading partners. Examples of some recent studies can be found in *World Competitiveness Report* (1995), Warda (1990), or Rugman and D'Cruz (1989). Some of these formulations emphasize the micro level criteria of "high growth and high value-added industries" (such as the telecommunications industry).

2. See Ezeala-Harrison (1995).

3. For examples of these, see Lazear and Moore (1984), or Medoff and Abraham (1981). More recent examples can be found in Weiss (1990).

4. Luciani (1996) indicates that the studies for the rankings that are published in the annual *World Competitiveness Report* employ methods such as surveying about 20,000 business managers who are asked to give their "views on national and international prospects" of each country in the areas of "domestic economic strength, internationalization of the economy, finance, infrastructure, and government."

5. See chapter 3, and also Mahmood and Ezeala-Harrison (1997).

6. Apparently, in defining international competitiveness, this approach also stresses the ability of a country to maintain a growth rate of real income that is equal to or greater than that of its trading partners, in an environment of free and balanced trade.

7. It is certainly preferable for firms in an industry to be efficient, productive and profitable, and able to procure higher market shares. Therefore competitiveness at the level of the firm is perfectly desirable.

8. Practical measurements of productivity are difficult because measuring the output of a firm or industry often involves combining different types of output into a single output measure by means of weighting them by their relative importance in the total production of the firm or industry. The different types of inputs have to be combined in a single input measure by weighting them by their relative importance in the production process, and obtaining the accurate price measures for each component (used for the weighting purposes) often proves to be difficult. Also, the difficulties of measuring changes in the quantity of inputs and outputs, over time, compound the problems of measuring changes in productivity trends.

9. The other parameters of economic liberalization such as degree of privatization, deregulation, and centralization are equally important, and various indices could be employed to measure their levels to assess the degree of economic liberalization. The use

of only two of these (namely, trade liberalization and exchange rate) has been selected here on the basis of their being relatively easy to keep track of explicitly.

10. Also included in this criterion are factors ranging from industrial efficiency to human resources and sociopolitical stability. Others are natural resource endowment, number of technology-intensive industries, manpower training, R&D, patent registrations, and number of engineers and scientists that the country has. Luciani (1996) indicates that the studies for the rankings that are published in the annual *World Competitiveness Report* employ methods such as surveying about 20,000 business managers who are asked to give their "views on national and international prospects" of each country in the areas of "domestic economic strength, internationalization of the economy, finance, infrastructure, and government."

11. This section is based on Ezeala-Harrison (1995 and 1996a).

12. The parameter λ is simply the Hicks-neutral technical change coefficient on the production function.

13. Based on equation (A2.6), the appropriate national time series data could be employed to compute the trend values of the competitiveness parameter λ', which would then indicate competitiveness profile over time.

3

Competitive Advantage and Competitiveness

Competition is the norm surrounding trade and all international business relationships in a world that has opted to carry out its transactions under a "free-trade banner." Under the assumption of *purchasing power parity* (see chapter 1) in such a competitive world, the "survival of the fittest" is, indeed, the actual rule of the game.[1] The game involves players made up of firms from various countries, and the field of play is the world market. However, to survive and remain in the game, each player must maintain fitness—the ability to sustain production and marketing of its products in the face of the competition from other players. The ability to maintain fitness in this setting is termed the competitive advantage of the firm, and by extension, of the home country from which the firm operates. For in the final analysis, "the competitiveness of a society is doubtless a reflection of the competitiveness of each of the institutions of which it is comprised" (Economic Council, 1992, p. 19).

Porter (1990a, p. 74) observed that companies succeed in international markets by acting to achieve competitive advantage through innovation, carried out by adopting new methods and new technologies for product design, production processes, marketing, and general operations. And once competitive advantage has been achieved through innovation in these areas, companies can strive to sustain that advantage only through improvements upon the preceding achievements in a relentless fashion. This is because, as Porter points out, almost any advantage that any firm achieves at any time can be imitated, so that global competitors are apt to eventually overtake any firm that relents upon improvements and further innovation—the dynamic process of *upgrading*.

The activities involved in the competitive market include both the production and marketing of the goods and services; marketing covers both domestic and export venues and is important because it involves the transportation, insurance, storage, advertisement, distribution, and financial transaction costs of marketing the products. In fact, these aspects of the firm's business activity are very crucial in shaping its state of (international) competitiveness. The total cost of operation is made up of the sum of the *in-house* (or factory outlet) production cost and the *overhead* production cost. The in-house production cost is the cost of the actual creation of the products (covering the total resource costs, namely, cost of raw materials, wages and salaries, administrative and personnel costs, interest charges, and rental costs). The overhead production cost is the cost of marketing the products (as explained above), as well as taxes, licenses, and other overhead expenditures.

The situation governing the production and market structure of firms engaged in constant competition in the world market can be likened to that of a standard *oligopoly* model in which a number of firms exist and compete in the industry (world market) as rival competitors, in the production and marketing of products that are close substitutes. Each country's products may be differentiated in terms of brand names and other physical attributes, but they are very close or perfect substitutes for the products of the other countries; therefore there is a continuous state of competition among these various brands (of the same product).[2] Each competitor strives to achieve and maintain or even increase its *market share* (proportion of the total market sales that the firm has) in the world market. If possible, a firm will try to gain absolute control (over price and output levels) in the world market. Gaining and retaining competitive advantage is the means by which firms (from any country) may succeed well above their rivals and become the *dominant firms* in the world market.[3]

THE PROCESSES OF COMPETITIVE ADVANTAGE

The overriding objective of firms involved in business activities is to maximize profits and remain profitable in all business endeavors. This is assumed always to be an immediate (short-run) objective of the firm, within an overall long-term policy of sustaining productivity and all other operations at the level that would ensure a steady-state growth rate of the firm's desired (or projected) profit level. The scenario can be represented as a model of a typical firm operating for ongoing profitability: it needs to market its products widely enough to attract greater market share to raise revenue. The total profit it can earn per time period is given by

$$\pi_i = R_i(q_i) - C_i(q_i) \tag{3.1}$$

where

π_i = profit level of a representative firm i
R_i = total revenue of firm i
q_i = the firm's output level
$C_i = C(q_i)$ = total cost of production of firm i

The necessary conditions for the firm's *optimal* operation require that maximum profit occurs at the point of production where

$$\partial \pi i/\partial q_i = R_i(q_i) - C_i(q_i) = 0 \tag{3.2}$$

This yields

$$\partial R/\partial q - \partial C/\partial q = 0$$

or

$$\partial R/\partial q = \partial C/\partial q \tag{3.3}$$

But, by definition, the term $\partial R/\partial q$ stands for marginal revenue (MR), and the term $\partial C/\partial q$ stands for marginal cost (MC). Thus, equation (3.3) simply indicates that the firm's marginal revenue must equal its marginal cost at the level of output where its profit is maximized. This means that, assuming that the production level of firm i where its MC equals its MR is q_i^*, then the firm cannot perform better at any other level of output except q_i^*. Therefore, it must set its operating plans (by operating plans is meant employment of resources, marketing (supply and sales), plant size, etc.) on the production of the output level q_i^*. It therefore produces and markets q_i^* level of output and reaps the *maximum* level of profit π_i^*.

However, we must understand how the profit level π_i^* is realized: it is the residual given in equation (3.1):

$$\begin{aligned}\pi_i^* &= R_i(q_i) - C_i(q_i) \\ &= p.q_i^* - c_i^*.q_i^*\end{aligned} \tag{3.4}$$

where

p = market price of the output
$c_i^* = C_i(q_i)/q_i^*$ = cost per unit (or *average cost*) of the output

It must be realized that the firm operates in two dimensions: the supply (or production) dimension, where it deals with the production parameter c_i (the cost per unit of production), and the demand (or marketing) dimension, where it confronts the market parameter p (the going market price of the product). Apparently, the firm could directly influence only the production parameter c_i, which it is capable of controling through its ability to adopt and implement efficient operational measures and policies. As for the market parameter p, it is ordinarily beyond the control of a firm within a competitive setting. However, where a firm is able to achieve a *dominant firm* position in the (world) market, it could be able to influence the level of p and hence operate with much more expanded relative market leverage in relation to its competitors. But, again, the ability of a firm to attain this fit rests on its capacity to manipulate circumstances in its production dimension, that is, its micro level competitiveness (see chapter 2).

State of Efficiency and Competitive Advantage

The critical question regarding a typical firm's competitiveness concerns the parameter c_i^*, and specifically, regarding the magnitude of c_i^* relative to p. That is, a firm's ability to achieve some competitive advantage (and hence its competitive condition) depends on whether or not its operating unit production cost is lower than the market price of output, according to the following decision rules:

1. If $c_i^* < p$, the firm has (unit) competitive advantage, given by the magnitude $p-c_i^*$.

The magnitude $p-c_i^*$ signifies the firm's competitive leverage—it defines the firm's ability to absorb price reduction and yet remain in business, allowing it to capture greater market share. The *competitive leverage* is an indicator of the degree of relative competitiveness among competitors. Should any firm fail to achieve a positive level of competitive leverage, it would lack the ability to withstand any unexpected market-induced price reduction (known as downward price shock). The situation of such a firm is illustrated as follows.

2. If $c_i^* > p$, the firm lacks competitive advantage and is uncompetitive.

This situation means that the firm does not cover its operating unit cost and would be operating at a loss per unit of output (given by the magnitude c_i^*-p). With a total output level of q^*, the firm's total loss (per time period) would be $q^*(c_i^*-p)$, which must be financed through some subsidy, grant, past accumulated profit, or other form of support, or the firm would have to shut down and go out of business.

The above illustrations indicate that the achievement of competitiveness calls for a clear relative cost advantage (which is the inverse of productivity advantage). It means that the firm must be able to maintain a revenue premium over its costs. This implies some level of economic profit, which really is the factor that confers a competitive leverage to the firm.

Ordinarily, however, in a competitive market a firm would be competitive if it is able to cover its cost, even if it is only in a *break-even* situation. That is:

3. If $c_i^* \leq p$, the firm is competitive, although it may lack competitive leverage.

In this latter case, if the firm only breaks even ($c^* = p$), it means that it reaps no economic profit and has no leverage whatsoever in its market. Any situation that arises and causes either the market price to fall or the unit production cost to rise would create an uncompetitive situation ($c^* > p$) and ultimately create a *loss* situation for the firm. An operating loss situation cannot possibly be sustained in the long run, meaning that either the firm would then have to be helped out by the government (by way of subsidy grants to cover the losses), or the firm would shut down.[4] In either case, the economy is worse off, and its state of competitiveness suffers.

It is important to note the difference between the firm's competitive advantage or competitiveness as analyzed above, and its efficiency of operation. The firm's efficiency relates to its economical use of resources. The firm would be operating efficiently if it would be operating with a plant that yields q_i^* and c_i^* at the *minimum level* of c_i^*. Achieving such a production situation would not only create sustainable relative competitiveness for the firm, it would also ensure the conditions for sustained profitability. It means that the firm is producing and marketing its output at the minimum level of unit cost, and thus, is *optimizing* its production activities. It could not perform any better than this; it is operating at its *exact capacity* (as against an excess capacity). It is competitive and efficient.

Competitive Advantage and Competitive Leverage

A firm's ability to survive and operate with long-term profitability in a competitive setting is determined by how much *relative competitive advantage* it holds within that given business environment. A firm's competitive advantage relative to its rivals in the market place can be easily measured by the *competitive leverage*. Consider the two conditions given by

$$c_i^* \leq p \qquad (3.5)$$

and

$$c_i^* < p \qquad (3.6)$$

Inequality (3.5) is equivocal regarding the firm's ability to obtain a clear margin of price over unit cost. Inequality (3.6), however, is clearly unequivocal: the firm has an absolute premium over cost. The reason for this distinction is obvious.

The *competitive advantage* that a firm may have over its rivals in the market place is represented by the ratio of its *competitive leverage* to the market price; it is the ratio of the margin over (unit) cost to the market price. Thus, a firm's competitive advantage may be depicted as

$$\xi_i = (p - c_i^*)/p \qquad (3.7)$$

where

$$\xi_i = \text{firm } i\text{'s competitive advantage}$$

and

$$1 > \xi_i > 0$$

The parameter ξ_i simply defines the ratio of competitive leverage of firm i to the market price of the product; therefore, by definition, it stands for firm i's *competitive advantage* in the market place—it measures the relative advantage that firm i has regarding its ability to function (compete) in the market in a *profitable capacity.*

Thus, the firm's competitive advantage is given by the magnitude of ξ_i as given in equation (3.7). For example, a break-even (equivocal) condition $p = c_i^*$ would fail to sustain (or even yield) competitive advantage. To verify this, substituting $p-c_i^* = 0$ into equation (3.7) gives

$$\xi_i = (p-c_i^*)/p = 0/p = 0$$

indicating a state of zero competitive advantage, $\xi_i = 0$. This implies that the country's firm(s) have no competitive advantage whatsoever; and it means that although the country may not have lost competitiveness *per se* (firms are able to break even), there is virtually no competitive leverage under which they could manoeuvre. Under such circumstances, the country has a weak state of competitiveness and cannot effectively compete in the world market place. In such a condition, the state of competitiveness is impaired because any domestic microeconomic shock that raises c (weakens micro level competitiveness) or any uncontrollable world market fluctuation that lowers p, or any macroeconomic shock (that creates a macroeconomic instability), would create a competitiveness crisis for the country. Such a situation would devastate whatever little competitive ability that may remain for the country, and the economy cannot sustain any pace of positive growth.

From equation (3.7), we are able to easily assess the various determinant factors of competitive advantage and their respective natures of influence. Application of simple comparative statics analysis shows:

$$\partial\xi_i/\partial p = c_i^*/p^2 > 0 \tag{3.8}$$

and

$$\partial\xi_i/\partial c_i^* = -1/p < 0 \tag{3.9}$$

Equations (3.8) and (3.9), respectively, demonstrate that:

1. An increase (decrease) in the (world) market price of the product would enhance (impede) the competitiveness of the exporting country.
2. An increase (decrease) in production cost would impair (enhance) the competitiveness of the exporting firm (and country).

Hence, for a typical firm i, the size of its *leverage (p-c_i*)* indicates the extent to which it could survive any given unexpected *shock* such as a sudden price decline (due possibly to a fall in market demand) or a cost increase (due possibly to an increase in in-house costs, such as the cost of inputs, or overhead costs such as taxes, levies, or marketing expenditure).[5]

International Competitiveness as Dynamic Competitive Advantage

Given the definition of competitive advantage as the relative advantage that a country's firms and industries have regarding their ability to operate profitably within a competitive environment, this concept can be extended to define the international competitiveness of the country. The only important distinction between competitive advantage and competitiveness is that competitive advantage is a *static* concept of a firm's relative performance, while competitiveness is a *dynamic* concept. International competitiveness refers simply to a *state of ongoing maintenance of competitive advantage*. In this dynamic sense, the state of *competitiveness* for a country j, would be given by:

$$\xi_j = \partial(\Sigma_1^n \xi_i)/\partial t > 0 \tag{3.10}$$

where t = time.

This implies that an ongoing state of competitiveness would mean that a country's n number of firms/industries must maintain a *positive rate of growth of aggregative competitive advantage*, over time. In other words, a country achieves international competitiveness if and when its firms/industries have a positive growth rate of aggregative competitive advantage. A country loses competitiveness whenever

$$\xi_j = \partial(\Sigma_1^n \xi_i)/\partial t \leq 0$$

Thus, a country's state of competitiveness cannot be static. Competitive advantage may be gained or lost at any time by any number of firms in the economy, according to those firms' respective operational efficiencies, as well as the economy's ability to control the micro and macro level parameters of competitiveness discussed in chapter 2.

To reiterate, the international competitiveness of a country is given by the aggregative competitive advantages of its firms and industries, $\Sigma_1^n \xi_i$. The country achieves competitiveness if the time growth rate of its firms' aggregative competitive advantage is positive.

To enable us determine the pertinent factors of national competitiveness, we need to express international competitiveness in terms of the individual firms' competitive leverages (equation 3.7). International competitiveness would be:

$$\xi_j = \partial/\partial t\{\Sigma_1^n (p-c_i^*)/p)\} \geq 0 \tag{3.11}$$

Equation (3.11) enables us to identify the key parameters that determine international competitiveness. It is clear that the two major parameters that determine international competitiveness are the same ones that determine competitive advantage at the firm/industry level, namely, the unit production cost of firms, c_i^*, and the market price of the product, p.

Although it may not seem obvious at first glance, these two parameters are similar to the factors discussed in chapter 2, where the parameters were identified as *productivity* (micro level parameters) and *institutional settings* (macro level parameters). However, by definition, productivity is the inverse of production cost, while institutional arrangements, such as the role of infrastructure, exchange rate, the socio-economic regime, and financial sector situation, are the actors that combine to shape the terms of trade—the world market price of the country's exports.

Thus, as identified in chapter 2, a country's state of international competitiveness is shaped by the same micro and macro level parameters discussed in that chapter. The micro level parameters are represented by the production costs that are under the control of firms/industries. The macro level parameters act through the market price of the product (which is beyond the firms' control, but may be influenced by the institutional factors in the country).

Public-Sector Activity and Competitive Advantage

The central role that the government sector plays in a country's economic activity often proves to be far more influential than the role of the private sector. The government sector does have very significant impact upon a country's state of international competitiveness. In most countries, government economic activity is omnipresent. The public sector is large and all encompassing, and it not only determines and shapes the extent of the economic activities of the private sector but also largely affects the economic and business lives of all citizens in many respects. In particular, government decisions and policies in the areas of revenue, expenditures, economic stabilization, public debt, regulation, and income maintenance influence the levels of productivity, competitive advantage, and competitive position of firms and industries that operate within the country.

The government is the provider of a wide range of services and infrastructural facilities (social overhead capital and infrastructure). The government also establishes and oversees a range of regulatory framework (such as the interest rate, tax rates, the currency exchange rate, money market instruments, and regulatory control legislation) that are used to stabilize the country's key business and economic indicators (such as the national income level, the rate of inflation, and employment and unemployment levels). The effectiveness and efficiency with which these state services are provided are crucial in the country's state of international competitiveness. This is because these services often enter as inputs in the production activities of private sector firms that operate within the country. (As analyzed in the text, the firms' total production activities are made up of their in-house or factory outlet activities and their overhead activities.)

In chapter 2 we learned about notions of competitiveness that are based on the operational qualities of a country's (socioeconomic) institutions and infrastructure. A country's international competitiveness is simply given by the resultant state of competitiveness of each of the socioeconomic institutions and infrastructure within that country. This implies that a country's competitiveness would be determined by the ability of its institutions and infrastructure to perform. In turn, this ability depends on the three institutional qualities of: (1) efficiency of institutions and infrastructure in meeting their goals; (2) adaptability of institutions to quick imitation and application of superior techniques; and (3) overall innovative abilities.

Chief among a country's institutions and infrastructure is the greatest one of all: the government institution. It is the institutional and infrastructural qualities of the government together with all the other socioeconomic institutions (see chapter 2) that combine to enable both private and public sector firms and industries to achieve low cost operations that give them competitive advantage. This is a major factor that makes one country more competitive than another.

Role of Government in Economic and Business Activity

With an overall economic objective of ensuring the attainment of the most optimal economic well-being of the society, the government acts as a supervisor, regulator, or overseer of the economy. In free-market economies, the political success of the government often depends on the degree to which it achieves or fails to achieve this economic objective. A country's government performs certain traditional economic functions. We discuss four of these functions, as they relate closely to the influence of the government on international competitiveness. The four major economic functions of government are:

1. Administration: The government undertakes the day-to-day adminstration and record-keeping of all issues concerning the citizens of the country. In carrying out this function the government uses the civil service for performing its administrative duties; and uses the legislative assembly (legislature) to devise laws, rules, and regulations that govern society's economic activities. The government has taxing powers to obtain finances and other resources for funding its functions.

2. Maintenance of Security and Defense: For internal order and security within the country, the government uses the police, national guard, and the judiciary to maintain social order. For external security, the government employs the national armed forces (army, navy, air force) to deter foreign aggression against the country and to protect the the country from foreign attack.

3. Economic Stabilization: The government takes action to promote the achievement of the *economic goals* of the country, namely, the goals of *efficiency* and *equity*. To achieve the goal of efficiency, government undertakes economic policy actions to promote economic growth, create jobs to reduce unemployment, fight and reduce the rate of inflation, maintain fiscal balance (avoid high budget deficits), and maintain strong balance-of-payments position. To achieve equity, the government acts to promote more equitable income distribution and reduce poverty levels. In carrying out this function the

government applies progressive taxation and transfer payments (subsidies, employment insurance, income support, and social assistance payments).

4. Provision of Public Goods: Public goods are goods (and services) that are characterized by the *free-rider* problem and *non-excludability*. This their distinguishing characteristic (as compared to private goods) implies that they may be consumed by several individuals at the same time without rivalry. Examples of public goods are national defence, environmental protection, (police) security provision, street lighting, etc. The government must be the provider of these goods/services because a private sector provider cannot effectively market such products due to the products' nature of free-ridership and non-excludability in consumption. As a result of this condition, it is said that there is *market failure* in the provision of public goods. Therefore, the government must be the sole provider of such goods, financed through public expenditure, and then made available to the society.

Linkages of the Public Sector and Competitiveness

The relative competitiveness of a country is shaped, to a significant extent, by the relative efficiency of its government in carrying out these functions. A country's firms and industries derive various advantages through *linkages* that connect government services to the business (private) sector. The most important among these linkages can be identified as:[6]

1. The provision of key public infrastructure to the business community. This includes reliable and efficient legal framework, banking and insurance sector, health care and educational facilities, capital (social overhead) infrastructure (such as adequate land, rail, air, and sea transportation facilities, water and sewerage, and post and telecommunications), and access to natural resources. The availability of these facilities is crucial for effective operation of industries. These facilities largely determine the magnitude of individual firms' competitive leverage parameter of competitive advantage. Often the crucial question surrounds how to most efficiently deliver and price key infrastructural products (such as hospitals, electricity, or telecommunications); in particular, should these industries be made to function under competitive regimes or under state regulatory controls? The choice seems to be whichever regime would yield the maximum (economic) efficiency; and it seems to be the competitive regime. (See chapter 5).

2. The regulatory activities of the government. This is constituted of two types: micro and macro policy regulations. Macro policy regulations are the regulation of factor markets (such as natural resources; and labor, including the government's role in supporting or not supporting labor unionization and collective bargaining processes); the environment; and financial sector regulation. Micro policy regulations are the regulations of prices and quantities, as well as quality, of products (such as product standards), the degree of competition in product markets, and rates regulations (such as rates of return on profits, interest rates, and exchange rates). Generally, stringent regulations tend to be detrimental to the achievement and maintenance of competitive advantage and impair competitiveness. The lesser the level of regulatory controls in an economy, the more competitive its firms would likely become.

3. The distributional (equity) role of government. The government supervises certain income maintenance programs such as employment insurance, pension plans, worker

compensation, and wage-subsidy programs. These programs are *payroll taxes* that impose significant costs on firms and impair their international competitiveness. There also are the levels of profit and excise taxes. The degree of intensity and extensiveness of these programs in an economy is a major factor that affects relative competitiveness: the impact of taxes on competitive advantage tends to be negative. However, as the tax revenues are used to finance social spending that improves redistribution of income, there could be positive longer-term impacts on productivity and hence competitiveness.

4. Government's direct services to businesses. There are substantial levels of services that the government provides to business that have very high international competitiveness effects. These include such services as: research and development incentives and subsidies, grant and protection of patent rights, protection for intellectual property, and bankruptcy laws. These services play major roles in promoting a country's corporate competitive advantage and international competitiveness.

5. The government's international negotiations and obligations. These are the negotiations through which a country's government enter into certain international treaties and obligations regarding such things as trade volumes (such as quotas), investment flows, product standards, environmental quality levels, tax rates, and financial movements (such as loans, grants, and profit repatriations).

Overall, it may be stated that the efficiency with which a country's government performs its economic functions, and the intensity of the linkages between public sector services and industries, is the indicator of the government's own state of efficiency. This state of government (or public sector) efficiency is determined by the government's structure of governance and policy processes and procedures (particularly regarding whether or not there are effective ways in which the government could be held accountable for its actions, policies, and programs).

APPENDIX

This appendix presents the long-run model of national level international competitiveness, by utilizing a *first principles* approach that depicts (micro level) competitiveness as the nation's relative ability to make efficient use of its resources. In this regard, Porter (1990a, p. 78) maintains that nations succeed in creating international competitiveness in industries where they are "particularly good at factor creation." A nation's relative international competitiveness is *created* from the efficient allocation, rather than *inherited* through the abundant acquisition, of resources. This is even more so because the existence of abundant resources (such as the abundant supply of cheap labor or raw materials) is often met with a lax reliance on the advantages of such abundance, resulting in their inefficient deployment. However, if firms are faced with an inherent disadvantage of relative scarcity problems of high costs of land, labor, or raw materials, they would have no other choice than to *innovate* and *upgrade* (Porter, 1990a, p. 78) in order to survive in a competitive global market environment. It is in the course of this continuous innovation that the firm may enhance its competitive advantage.

Competitive Advantage and Competitiveness in the Long Run

A simple model can be applied to analyze long-run competitive advantage and national competitiveness. This model would be akin to the one presented in the appendix to chapter 2.

Consider an aggregate production function:

$$Y = \psi . Y(L,K,R) \tag{A3.1}$$

where:

    Y = total output (GDP)
    L = available labor force
    K = capital resources
    R = amount of natural resources
    ψ = the state of technology[7]

Following the *Solow-Dennison growth accounting model*, growth in the production function may be depicted as:

$$(\partial Y/\partial t)/Y = (\partial \psi/\partial t)/\psi + \alpha.(\partial L/\partial t)/L + \beta.(\partial K/\partial t)/K + \gamma.(\partial R/\partial t)/R \tag{A3.2}$$

where:

    α, β, γ, are respectively the factor shares of labor, capital, and natural resources.

Equation (A3.2) represents the time growth path of national output, in terms of the growth rates of the various inputs and their productivities.[8] In pursuit of competitiveness, firms seek to effectively utilize resources (the components of the production function) in the most efficient manner relative to others. That is, factors at play are:

1. the available factor endowment in the economy,
2. the level of utilization of those factors (resources), and
3. the efficiency with which the existing endowments are allocated.

We define the following terms:

    μ_f = index of factor endowment
    μ_u = index of factor utilization (*the employment effect*)
    μ_e = index of level of efficiency with which the available factor endowment is allocated (*productivity effect* or *competitive advantage*)

ϕ_d = index of the drag effect brought about by such reallocative activities as rationalization and other actions designed to improve macro level competitiveness.

Using these parameters, the production function may be written as:

$$Y = \psi. Y[(\mu_f,\mu_u,\mu_e,\phi_d)L, (\mu_f,\mu_u,\mu_e,\phi_d)K, (\mu_f,\mu_u,\mu_e,\phi_d)R] \tag{A3.3a}$$

which, upon assumption of linear homogeneity, becomes:

$$Y = \{(\mu_f,\mu_u,\mu_e,\phi_d)L, (\mu_f,\mu_u,\mu_e,\phi_d)K, (\mu_f,\mu_u,\mu_e,\phi_d)R\}. \psi Y(L,K,R)] \tag{A3.3b}$$

This expression indicates the usual causality between resource endowment and national output; and in terms of these parameters, the growth equation (A3.2) may be written as

$$\begin{aligned}(\partial Y/\partial t)/Y = {} & (\partial\psi/\partial t)/\psi + (\partial\mu_f/\partial t)/\mu_f + (\partial\mu_u/\partial t)/\mu_u + (\partial\mu_e/\partial t)/\mu_e \\ & - (\partial\phi_d/\partial t)/\phi_d + \alpha.(\partial L/\partial t)/L + \beta.(\partial K/\partial t)/K \\ & + \gamma.(\partial R/\partial t)/R\end{aligned} \tag{A3.4}$$

This relationship highlights the potential sources of growth through comparative and competitive advantage these are shown as the economy's national competitiveness (total factor productivity), resource discovery (a comparative advantage factor), factor utilization rate, efficiency of factor utilization (rationalization, upgrading, and innovation—competitive advantage factor), and the factor growth rates and their productivities.

To determine how comparative and competitive advantage phenomena relate to national competitiveness, the expression for the growth rate of total factor productivity (competitiveness) may be written as

$$\begin{aligned}(\partial\psi/\partial t)/\psi = {} & (\partial Y/\partial t)/Y + (\partial\phi_d/\partial t)/\phi_d - \{(\partial\mu_f/\partial t)/\mu_f + (\partial\mu_u/\partial t)/\mu_u \\ & + (\partial\mu_e/\partial t)/\mu_e + \alpha.(\partial L/\partial t)/L + \beta.(\partial K/\partial t)/K \\ & + \gamma.(\partial R/\partial t)/R\}\end{aligned} \tag{A3.5}$$

Close inspection of equation (A3.5) reveals that:

1. $\partial\mu_e/\partial t)/\mu_e$ is time growth rate of productive efficiency, indicating *competitive advantage*,
2. $\partial\mu_f/\partial t)/\mu_f$ stands for the rate of resource discovery, indicating *comparative advantage*, and
3. $\partial\mu_u/\partial t)/\mu_u$ represents the effectiveness of resource utilization, indicating *comparative advantage*.

Thus, total factor productivity growth is the residual of the economy's growth rate net of the negative drag factor, the rate of resource discovery and rate of factor utilization (both of which are comparative advantage factors), and rate of efficiency of factor utilization and the factor growth rates and their productivities (competitive advantage factors).

It is important to realize not only how important the rate of economic growth is for national competitiveness (see chapter 4), but also the crucial influence of the drag factor as well. First, it is untenable to expect that a nation could achieve national competitiveness in times of recession, *ceteris paribus*. Second, the drag effect features strongly as a factor to reckon with regarding a nation's competitiveness (indicating that in pursuit of competitiveness, a country must make allowance for such negative side effects as adverse terms of trade, institutional rigidities, corruption, political instability, and flawed economic policies). Clearly, the drag factor, among other things, appears to account for the differences in competitiveness among different countries (for example, why the Newly Industrializing Countries of Asia and South America are more competitive than countries in sub-Saharan Africa or south Asia).

The prominent roles of resource endowment, factor utilization, efficiency of utilization, and factor growth rates and productivities, as depicted in equation (A3.5), are of particular interest since they emphasize these same parameters as discussed in chapter 2. It also shows how strongly competitive advantage at the firm level affects competitiveness at the national level. Further, the complementarity (rather than substitutability) of competitive and comparative advantage is evident by the relationship expressed in equation (A3.5).

To explore the pertinent determinants of competitiveness, we proceed to isolate indices of competitive advantage, comparative advantage, and their drag effects in a country. These parameters are identified as:

1. competitive advantage parameters:
   $(\partial\mu_e/\partial t)/\mu_e$, $\alpha.(\partial L/\partial t)/L$, $\beta.(\partial K/\partial t)/K$, $\gamma.(\partial R/\partial t)/R$
2. comparative advantage parameters:
   $(\partial\mu_f/\partial t)/\mu_f$, $(\partial\mu_u/\partial t)/\mu_u$
3. *drag* factors: $(\partial\phi_d/\partial t)/\phi_d$

Denoting the *combined effects* of these parameters on national competitiveness as

Δ_p = combined effects of competitive advantage
   $= (\mu_e/\partial t)/\mu_e + \alpha.(\partial L/\partial t)/L + \beta.(\partial K/\partial t)/K + \gamma.(\partial R/\partial t)/R$
Δ_m = combined effects of comparative advantage
   $= (\partial\mu_f/\partial t)/\mu_f + (\partial\mu_u/\partial t)/\mu_u$
Δ_d = combined drag effects
   $= (\xi\phi_d/\partial t)/\phi_d$

equation (A3.5) may be decomposed further; the respective combined effects are obtained as

$$\Delta_p = (\partial Y/\partial t)/Y - [(\partial \mu_f/\partial t)/\mu_f + (\partial \mu_u/\partial t)/\mu_u + (\partial \psi/\partial t)/\psi]$$
$$+ (\partial \phi_d/\partial t)/\phi_d \tag{A3.6a}$$
$$\Delta_m = (\partial Y/\partial t)/Y + (\partial \phi_d/\partial t)/\phi_d - \{(\partial \psi/\partial t)/\psi$$
$$+ (\partial \xi_e/\partial t)/\xi_e + \alpha.(\partial L/\partial t)/L + \beta.(\partial K/\partial t)/K + \gamma.(\partial R/\partial t)/R\} \tag{A3.6b}$$
$$\Delta_d = (\partial \psi/\partial t)/\psi - (\partial Y/\partial t)/Y + \{(\partial \mu_f/\partial t)/\mu_f + (\partial \mu_u/\partial t)/\mu_u + (\partial \mu_e/\partial t)/\mu_e$$
$$+ \alpha.(\partial L/\partial t)/L + \beta.(\partial K/\partial t)/K + \gamma.(\partial R/\partial t)/R\} \tag{A3.6c}$$

These expressions show how a nation's growth is closely tied to competitive and comparative advantage. They also give the measure of the various impacts of growth and competitiveness on each of these parameters themselves. Further, they reveal the crucial role that the "drag factors" play in a nation's ability or inability to achieve competitiveness.[9] Further details on this aspect of international competitiveness are considered in chapter 4.

NOTES

1. Throughout the discussions in this chapter and indeed the remainder of the book, the assumption of purchasing power parity applies. This assumption enables us to view competition between firms from different countries in the correct and proper perspective, without the complicating implications of unequal national currency strengths among countries in the world.

2. Yet each firm is, indeed, a quasi-monopolist in the production and marketing of its own (country's) brand of the product. It is in the sense of the two conditions (product differentiation and quasi-monopoly) that this market structure is referred to as *monopolistic competition*—state of ongoing competition among monopolists—in industrial organization studies.

3. The term "dominant firm" is used in industrial organization studies to describe a firm that is the undisputed leader in an oligopoly industry. The dominant firm is the "price leader" whose price (and output levels) are followed by the remaining fringe of rivals with whom it competes in the industry, in setting their own price and output levels. The dominant firm is "dominant" mainly because it usually holds a market share greater than the combined market share of its competitive fringe of rivals in the industry.

4. Countries adopting the so-called strategic trade policy tend to implement measures designed to help such losing or loss-prone firms (see chapter 7).

5. An example of a hidden overhead cost that could strongly affect competitiveness in this manner is payroll taxes.

6. This follows from three of such linkages that are outlined in Economic Council (1992).

7. ψ also represents the state of knowledge and institutional settings; it encompasses technological know-how, the states of socioeconomic and political institutions, and other *human factor* parameters. And as the index of *total factor productivity* in the economy, it is a measure of the economy's state of competitiveness (see chapter 2).

8. Note that the factor shares of the respective inputs are defined by the ratios of their

marginal productivities to average productivities: $\alpha=[\partial Y/\partial L]/[Y/L]$, $\beta=[\partial Y/\partial K]/[Y/K]$, $\gamma=[\partial Y/\partial R]/[Y/R]$.

9. Appropriate data could be employed toward an empirical analysis that computes the trend values of Δ_p, Δ_m, *and* Δ_m, thereby obtaining the measurable values of these parameters. These may then be used for cross country competitiveness comparisons.

4

Growth Impact of International Competitiveness

This chapter considers the degree of causal links between international competitiveness and economic growth in a country. The world is increasingly becoming a "global trading village" due to massive technological advancements that have given rise to rapid pace of communication and transportation mechanisms. Economic globalization has set off a wave of global struggle whereby all countries find themselves facing fierce competition from not only their traditional competitors but also emerging new ones. In this struggle to capture a larger market share for its products, a country's most important watchword is "competitiveness." Therefore, attainment and maintenance of international competitiveness has become a very crucial concern facing any modern society that wishes to achieve and sustain positive rate of economic growth. The extent and pace of economic growth and development in every country has come to be dictated by the extent and pace of the country's ability to maintain relative competitiveness in all facets of its economic transactions with the rest of the world. The records of achievement of the East Asian Newly Industrializing Countries (NICs) represent remarkable evidence of this link demonstrated during the later half of the twentieth century.

The World Economic Forum (WEF) in Geneva, Switzerland, publishes an annual survey, the *Global Competitiveness Report*, which ranks various countries annually on a number of (international) competitiveness determining factors (discussed in chapter 2). The 1997 WEF ranking for the ten "most competitive" countries according to the criteria adopted is presented later in this chapter (Table 4.2). It turns out that the criteria used in the WEF ranking fall under the concept of *macro level* competitiveness parameters discussed in the preceding chapters. These are exogenous parameters that are supposed to provide the background for a nation's achievement of international competitiveness. And it must be stressed that while these macro level parameters are *necessary* for a nation's achievement of competitiveness, they are not *sufficient* (see chapter 2).

The sufficiency condition for competitiveness is the micro (firm/industry) level parameter of productivity (and cost efficiency).

The most competitive countries are apt to be the ones with the highest levels of (relative) factor productivities. Studies indicate that Singapore, Hong Kong, the United States, and Canada truly have high levels of factor productivities. There clearly exists an important causality between micro and macro factors of international competitiveness. The line of causation is likely to be that the existence of the macro parameters would provide the conditions for the achievement of the micro level parameters, namely, higher productivity. But it is possible for a country to have the macro level conditions and yet fail to achieve the level of total factor productivity growth that would result in international competitiveness. This explains why all countries do not have the same level of competitiveness.

Economic performance of countries are correlated with their relative levels of international competitiveness. Countries with the highest levels of international competitiveness are the most economically developed in the world. This evidence is further indicative of a close association between international trade and economic growth and development. It is important that the nature of such a close association be thoroughly examined in order to further understand its underlying factors.

INTERNATIONAL TRADE AND ECONOMIC GROWTH

To better access the big picture in which to view the subject of how international competitiveness impacts economic growth, it is important to once more consider the international trade and economic growth linkage. Clearly, the route by which international competitiveness could translate to growth is by means of international trade. In chapter 1, the classical and neoclassical analogies regarding the role of trade in growth and development are presented. The general idea supports the notion that free and unrestricted trade among nations opens up opportunities for people in all countries to improve their welfare. International trade is advocated as a powerful *engine of economic growth* for countries. This is because, as nations are inherently self-insufficient, (free) trade offers immense advantages to a country. The question is: what are the true mechanisms through which international trade transmits growth? Could a country achieve growth by mere participation in trade *per se*, or are there necessary prerequisites surrounding the nature of the transactions?

Today's global economic environment involves an ongoing highly competitive arrangement between countries interacting and transacting in the New World Economic (Dis)Order. To survive in it, a country must be competitive in the following spheres:

Availability of Market

Mass export of output creates foreign exchange. International trade simply removes the constraints that limited market demand might place on a country's ability to expand production of its industries. A country must be able to have stable demand for its exports. This would enable it to expand the domestic output and create/expand employment opportunities within its borders. The lack of effective demand for exports would restrict the growth of output and employment within a country, resulting in unemployment and probably economic recession.

To be competitive in this regard means that the country's products must not only meet or exceed international quality standards, but also be priced at more affordable prices in the export/world markets relative to those of its trading partners. In this regard, the country needs to achieve a favorable *terms of trade* in its international trade transactions with the rest of the world.

Capital Acquisition

International trade opens up opportunities for a country to acquire needed financial and physical capital and equipment for production in its firms and industries as well as for investment in its infrastructural needs. This enables an economy to be able to apply diversified machinery, tools, equipments, and semifinished products in its everyday economic activities without being restricted to only those equipments that it alone could produce domestically.

A country is able to receive loans, grants, trade credits, aid, and the like from its richer international trading partners. Such resources are crucial to a country's growth as it could apply them toward importation of capital or other development needs. Moreover, a country could access borrowing and aid facilities available in international financial institutions such as the International Bank for Reconstruction and Development (IBRD) or the World Bank, and the International Monetary Fund (IMF).

Technological Acquisition and Benefits

A country could apply advanced technologies that it acquires (copies or imitates) through involvement in international trade, in order to enhance its own production systems and methods. Such ready-made technology that is available through the constant interaction that only international trade allows, would otherwise be unavailable or very slow and expensive to develop and apply. Further, international trade enables an innovating firm within a country to capitalize on its application of new knowledge (innovation). If a firm's marketing horizon is restricted by the size of its domestic market for the marketing of its new products, the returns that the firm could reap from its innovation before rival firms begin to copy it would not be as high (and sufficiently compensatory) as it would be if the firm could market its products globally. Thus, trade encourages the development of invention (Research and Development [R&D]), innovation, and further advancement of technology.

Skilled Labor and High-tech Specialists

Highly skilled technical, professional, managerial, and administrative personnel could be attracted into a country to involve in its economy. This would promote the pace of R&D initiatives, inventions, innovations, and the growth of technological progress.

Miscellaneous Spheres

International trade transactions could enable a country to attain other economic benefits that would promote growth. Such benefits include the promotion of tourism, which could raise demand in the country and increase foreign exchange earnings.

International friendship and sociocultural exchanges among countries are promoted through trade. Through the constant and frequent interaction among countries in the course of international trade, international good-will and friendly relations develop among them. They learn each other's consumption patterns, other institutional and organizational arrangements, values, ideas, and lifestyles. International cultural exchanges through sports and the arts flourish. This promotes world peace and harmony, enabling development to occur.

The foregoing section has given a brief presentation of the role of international trade to indicated that the channel by which international competitiveness could transmit growth and development to a country is international trade. But it is important also that we have a firm understanding of the precise meaning of economic growth and development, in order to better appreciate the ultimate goals to which a country may set itself in its pursuit of international competitiveness.

DEFINITION OF GROWTH AND DEVELOPMENT

The concepts of *economic growth* and *economic development* are closely related, although they are quite different. While economic growth involves an increase in an economy's real gross domestic product (GDP) and income over time, economic development involves economic growth itself in addition to the process of broad structural changes and transformation of the economy. Economic growth must precede and usher in economic development.

Real GDP is the economy's total output of goods and services, usually measured over a period of one year. The amount of achievable economic growth depends on the human resource acquisition of the economy, technological improvement, amount of capital investment, natural resource endowment and degree of its exploitation, and the managerial know-how existing in the economy.

In its closest association to the concept of economic development, economic growth is defined in terms of increases in per capita real output or per capita income. Economic development is the *process* through which the economy raises its per capita output and income by improvements and increases in productivity, and how these translate into per capita economic well-being in the society.[1]

Development involves *growth plus structural changes*. That is, for economic development to occur, there must be positive economic growth accompanied by *structural transformation* in the economy. Achievement and maintenance of economic growth is the necessary condition for development. Achievement and maintenance of structural transformation is the sufficiency condition for economic development.

Measurement of Growth and Development

Economic growth can be measured either with a view to an *absolute quantity* (internally) or as a *comparable quantitative measure* (externally). As an index of the overall economic well-being of a country's population, the GDP, as well as its per capita level, has traditionally been used. The GDP is an appropriate index of internal measurement of an economy's economic performance, namely, economic growth. The per capita income is used as the index of inter-country comparison of economic well-being, and therefore, measures much more than mere economic growth.

Internal Measurement of Growth

Growth in an economy reflects increases in the productive capacity (expansion of GDP) and changes in the rate of utilization of this capacity (percentage increase). Letting the GDP be Y, and regarding the productive capacity as the potential national (output) income, Y_p, the rate of utilization (denoted in percentage form) is given as Y/Y_p. Capacity utilization is different from increases in the total capacity itself.

It is important to avoid a great deal of confusion by specifying whether the rate of capacity utilization (short-term growth rate) is being measured, involving the calculation of the growth trends of Y, or whether the growth rate of the economy's productive capacity (long-term growth rate) is meant, involving the calculation of the growth rate of Y_p. The former, measuring the GDP and its growth rate, appears to be easier in terms of practical measurement.

The national income of a country provides the basis for measuring the total volume of (output) goods and services in that country. The GDP measures the total output of final goods and services produced by the residents of the country over a given period of one year. The GDP (Y) may be defined in terms of the annual gross national expenditure of the economy. The economy's total gross national expenditure is made up of its total domestic expenditure and its net foreign (balance of trade) transactions. The total domestic sector expenditure comprises the individual and household private-sector expenditure (consumption, C), the total business-sector expenditure (investment, I), and the total public-sector expenditure (government spending, G). The net foreign trade transactions is the total volume of exports (X) minus the total volume of imports (M). The GDP is then expressed as

$$Y = C + I + G + X - M \qquad\qquad\qquad (4.1)$$

Economic growth would occur in accord with growth in each of the sectors indicated in equation (4.1). The combined growth effects of all sectors would show in GDP growth rate over time.

External Measurement of Growth

For purposes of international comparisons of economic performance, a growth index that takes into account a nation's ability to expand its output relative to (or, rather, at a rate faster than) the growth rate of its population is often used. In this connection, levels and rates of growth of "real" per capita GDP are normally used to measure the population's overall economic state of being. The term *real* indicates the nominal or monetary value minus the rate of inflation. This index suggests how much of real goods and services would be available to the nation's average citizen. By using this index, it is easy to carry out a straightforward comparison of economic "well-being" or "welfare" across nations, a parameter that gives a quantitative measure of standards of living.

A measure of growth in productive capacity per capita (output per man-hour, or average output per man-hour employed) is generally referred to as *productivity*. However, the most widely used measure of economic growth is output (GDP) per capita. This approach focuses on the growth of material living standards rather than on the growth of productivity. The per capita income (PCI) is given as:

$$PCI = GDP/population \qquad\qquad\qquad (4.2)$$

The PCI gives a proxy measure of the average living standard of a citizen of the country. Its accuracy in depicting the true standard of living is only as good as the income distribution is equitable, and the GDP represents the true measure of national income. The PCI must be used with caution; but it is the closest parameter that is available to us for measuring the well-being of a representative citizen of a given country.

Measurement of Development

Given the qualitative (rather than quantitative) nature of economic development, it is not easy to measure it at any point in time. In fact, there is no
universally accepted standard for measuring economic development. The term
"development" itself involves a great deal of value judgment. Therefore, only
a proxy consensus might be possible if we must be able to assess the pace of
development within a nation or across nations.

For purposes of its measurement, development may be viewed as the process
through which, over time, a nation achieves sustained increases its per capita
real income (output), accompanied by significant structural changes that allow
for more equitable income distribution and significant increases in individual
economic well-being. This implies that economic development must be
associated with the general masses of the country's population benefiting from
the changes it brings, rather than just a small portion of the population being the
beneficiaries.

In assessing development, the rise in income must be evident through such
changes in basic living conditions as improved nutrition and high nutritional and
clothing standards, improved (modern) housing, improved health and health
care, low infant mortality rates, higher literacy rates, and a general environmental face-lift from a predominantly rural to an increased metropolitan
environment. In a broader sense, development would include the effectiveness
and reliability of social institutions, political freedom, efficiency of governments,
and government (officials') accountability to the public.

This opens up a quality aspect in the definition and measurement of
development that is not practically measurable. How development or lack of
development affects the "quality of life" has come to be regarded as crucial in
determining whether or not progress is made in economic development.
Therefore, the yardstick for assessing development is now termed the human
development index (HDI) and the physical quality of life index (QLI). The key
parameters that are used in the applications of the HDI and QLI are:

Equity in Income Distribution. The foremost economic indicator in the
measurement of economic development is the pattern of the *distribution* of
output and income: the shares of total income received by high-income, middle-
income, and low-income individuals and families. This indicator is referred to
as the size distribution of income and is used as a direct measure of economic
well-being. It is calculated from average income levels of individuals and
families covering several years. The data are ranked in order of magnitude,
corresponding to the cumulative percentage of the recipients.[2]

Consumption Index. The quality of life can be measured by the average level
of consumption of goods and services in the country. This includes the
consumption of durable goods such as housing (average number of persons per

room), clothing, transportation facilities (number of vehicles per capita or cars per household or number of cars per 1000 households or number of households that have cars), or, say, number of radios per capita; and nondurable goods such as quantity and quality of food (caloric or fibre) intake per capita. Also considered are the consumption of services, such as communication services (number of telephones per capita, newspaper circulation per capita), and per capita energy consumption. At the national level, the quality of life can often be assessed using the level of consumption of basic industrial products; for example, quantity of steel consumption or quantity of cement consumption.

Level of Literacy. The literacy rate is also used as a measure of the level of development. This measure would be correlated with the level of educational achievement. School enrollment in primary, secondary, postsecondary, and vocational and trade school levels could be used as a proxy for literacy achievement. This index also lends itself to comparison with other countries and is relatively easy to measure.

Nutrition and Health. Included in this index are such *physical quality of life* components as the number of physicians per capita, life expectancy at birth, death rate, and, say, level of protein consumption per capita. Based on the percentage of literacy, infant mortality, and life expectancy, the physical quality of life index (PQLI) is calculated. Scores ranging from 1 to 100 are assigned in each category of the parameters, and an average PQLI is calculated for each country. The main advantage of the PQLI is that it permits easy comparison across countries.

Industrialization and Occupational Patterns. Levels of development can also be measured by considering the occupational distribution of the country's labor force, such as the percentage of the economically active population engaged in agricultural employment as against the nonagricultural sectors. In addition, the level of wage and salary workers as a percentage of the entire labor force is considered. Other related indices are the manufacturing share in total GDP, or the percentage of the population that lives and works in the urban sector relative to the rural sector.

Overall development cannot be judged without these important qualitative criteria that indicate the *quality of life index*, listed above. If and whenever these qualitative indicators are declining or worsening, then even a very high growth level of the GDP and per capita GDP cannot really imply development.

ROLE OF COMPETITIVENESS IN GROWTH AND DEVELOPMENT

Now we consider the importance of international competitiveness in a nation's economic growth and development, which is the ultimate goal of any country.

We recall the specific definition of international competitiveness as given in chapter 2. A nation's competitiveness is determined by its productivity performance (at the micro level), under a given (constant) state of its economic liberalization profile (at the macro level). Thus, the state of a country's competitiveness depends on changes in either or both of the various parameters of productivity and economic liberalization. The questions addressed here are:

1. What is the exact nature of a possible growth-competitiveness linkage?
2. Given any existing link between international competitiveness and economic growth, how close could such links be?
3. Are there any common parameters that link the dual phenomena of international competitiveness and economic growth of a nation?

Beginning with the issues of causality between competitiveness and growth, the above questions are examined with a view to establishing the potential impact (as well as magnitude) of international competitiveness upon economic growth. We also examine the possibility of a cross-causality between these two phenomena.

Micro Level Growth-Competitiveness Linkage

In chapter 2 we considered the various parameters that constitute the measurement indices of competitiveness. It is shown that the most prominent economic parameter that determines a country's competitiveness is the (micro level) *productivity* of resources, given the (macro level) parameters (economic liberalization and infrastructure).

Table 4.1 presents the relative micro level competitiveness of various regions and countries of the world. It indicates a close correlation between micro competitiveness (TFP growth rate) and economic growth (GDP growth rate). And in this regard, it shows that East Asia and Western Europe achieved the highest competitiveness and economic growth among all the regions of the world.

The analytical illustration presented in the *appendix* to chapter 2 gives the details of the various aspects of productivity, and how they feature in the structural component of national competitiveness. To recap, an economy's total factor productivity (TFP) growth rate—the micro level index for the measure of national competitiveness—is depicted as the weighted sum of individual factor (resource) productivities and growth rates.

In the *appendix* to this chapter, a structural model that develops the components of economic growth from first principles is presented. There again, we see that the most prominent structural parameters that determine economic growth are productivity-related, namely, the levels of resource productivities and the pace of resource exploration and exploitation.

Table 4.1
Micro Level Competitiveness: World Regional Resource and
Productivity Growth, 1950-1990

Region	Average Annual % Growth			
	GDP	Labor	Capital	TFP
East Asia	6.8	2.6	10.2	1.9
South Asia	4.4	2.1	7.7	0.6
Sub-Saharan Africa	3.3	2.2	6.3	0.0
South America*	3.6	2.6	6.3	0.0
All LDCs	4.2	2.3	7.2	0.6
Europe, Middle East and North Africa	5.0	1.7	7.6	1.4
France	3.9	-0.2	4.8	1.7
West Germany	3.1	-0.6	4.2	1.4
United Kingdom	2.4	-0.2	3.1	1.2
United States	3.0	1.8	3.4	0.5
All OECD	3.2	1.6	4.4	1.8

* Including Central America and Caribbean.
Source: Calculated from: World Bank: *World
         Development Report* (Various Issues).

Clearly, then, resource productivity is a central parameter in determining an economy's pace of economic growth and state of international competitiveness. Therefore, any policy measures implemented to promote international competitiveness would necessarily result in growth as well. And as seen so far, such measures must be *micro (level) policies* that focus on resource productivities as well as the pace of resource exploration and rate of exploitation within a country.[3]

Macro Level Growth-Competitiveness Linkage

At the macro level, a country's international competitiveness is measured by the quality of its socioeconomic institutions and infrastructure (see chapter 2). Prominent among the institutions is the state of economic liberalization. The term "economic liberalization" is used to refer to the state of the economy characterized by the free-market system based on competition, deregulation, privatization, trade liberalization (free trade regime), dismantling of controls, and exchange rate stability. In other words, economic liberalization encompasses the package of measures designed to direct an economy toward a more competitive free-market system based on international (and domestic) trade liberalization, exchange rate stability and flexibility, deregulation, and greater private sector activity.

According to the World Economic Forum's (WEF) 1997 annual *Global Competitiveness Report*, the key parameters of international competitiveness for a country are: trade liberalization, size of government (state interventionism), financial liberalization, level of infrastructure, level of technology, level of managerial know-how, labor market liberalization, and levels of social/legal institutions. These WEF parameters still fit into our macro level classification of socioeconomic institutions. Table 4.2 indicates the importance of these macro level parameters in the competitiveness of nations and suggests that the role of these parameters in economic growth could be, indeed, varied.

The macro parameters are the *sufficiency conditions* required for international competitiveness of a country. To illustrate the importance of these, we can consider the role of trade liberalization and how it could contribute to growth:

1. Through trade liberalization, the economy could import some goods at lower prices relative to producing them domestically. Thus, resources are more efficiently used as they are no longer used to produce such goods but rather channeled to other uses.

2. The country would have greater access to diverse products, resources, and technologies, which it could adapt for its own use for greater productivity. Technology could be licensed (imported explicitly) or embodied in imported capital goods, and their availability could lead to the application of superior processes and methods of production. Certain intermediate (semi-finished) products could be obtained at lower prices for domestic use, leading to greater efficiency. By importation of appropriate intermediate inputs, the country could become an exporter of labor-intensive activities (such as assembling services), reaping massive *value-added*. In fact, in recent studies, both Dornbusch (1993) and Romer (1989) assert that access to a variety of cheaper intermediate inputs from abroad would shift an economy's production function outward—directly resulting in economic growth.

Table 4.2
Ranking the World by (Macro Level) Competitiveness, 1997

	A	B	C	D	E	F	G	H	J
Singapore	1	3	1	1	2	1	7	2	9
Hong Kong	2	1	2	4	1	21	13	1	19
United States	3	6	17	3	3	2	1	7	15
Canada	4	4	24	5	4	4	3	15	8
New Zealand	5	24	7	12	11	9	12	5	12
Switzerland	6	25	9	8	12	11	5	16	10
Britain	7	10	27	2	14	15	16	12	3
Taiwan	8	12	8	11	28	17	182	3	28
Malaysia	9	16	6	6	8	23	0	20	26
Norway	10	28	16	10	6	13	8	17	7

Key: A = *Overall competitiveness*
     B = *Trade Liberalization*
     C = *Size of Government (State interventionism)*
     D = *Financial Liberalization*
     E = *Level of Infrastructure*
     F = *Level of Technology*
     G = *Level of Managerial Know-how*
     H = *Labor Market Liberalization*
     J = *Levels of Social/Legal Institutions*

Source: Adapted from World Economic Forum:
     World Competitiveness Report, 1997.

3. The economy could access larger markets of its trading partners. This enables domestic firms to better utilize *economies of scale* and *economies of scope*, resulting in *capacity utilization*, and leading to greater output and employment.[4]

4. The country's domestic firms/industries are exposed to competition from foreign counterparts. Besides forestalling the growth of inefficient monopolies and oligopolies (since protectionism simply creates market power for domestic firms), foreign competition gives domestic firms incentives to devise better and more efficient and cheaper production methods, and better quality products, for sustained growth.[5]

The ways through which exchange rate stability could contribute to growth are by allowing for international free flow of transactions in both final products as well as intermediate goods. Importation of intermediate goods would allow for the permeation of technological know-how as discussed in number 2 above.

Cross-Causality between Competitiveness and Growth

It is apparent that the relationship between the international competitiveness and economic growth of a nation could be likened to that between the "chicken and egg." There can be no clear line of causality between these. Their relationship is that of a *cross-causality*.

Cross-causality indicates a constant interplay of cause and effect relationships between two or more entities. Competitiveness and growth are two such entities, and their cross-causality is demonstrated in the theoretical models provided in *appendices* to chapters 2 and 3. In these, it is expressly shown that economic growth is determined by the level of productivity of resources and the rate of discovery and effective utilization of these resources. The level of national competitiveness is also determined by the growth rates of productivity and utilization of resources.

Based on the common relationship that both competitiveness and growth have with productivity, would the line of causation between them be that competitiveness promotes growth, or that growth promotes competitiveness? It can be seen that, ordinarily, productivity promotes competitiveness, and competitiveness promotes growth; but growth further promotes productivity, which promotes competitiveness and further growth, and so on. This is the cross-causality relationship.

However, the cross-causality phenomenon goes beyond the simplified growth-competitiveness linkage illustration offered here. Economic growth and development in a society depends largely on the combined use of the resources and atmosphere provided by the political, social, cultural, and environmental circumstances of that society. If a country effectively utilizes its human resources (labor force and organizational and managerial know-how), natural resources (available in its land and waters), and material resources (capital stock and equipment), relative economic development is apt to be achieved. If these resources are not effectively utilized, development may not occur. The combined effects of human and material resources in creating productivity is the principal factor underlying the dual forces of international competitiveness and economic growth for a nation. These then determine relative economic performance levels among nations and the different regions of the world.

World Regional Growth-Competitiveness Links

In chapter 2 we saw that the measure of the combined effects of all resource inputs together in the creation of output in a country, is the TFP index. The TFP captures the efficiency with which all resource inputs are used in the production process, and to a very large extent affects (and even mainly determines) the productivities of individual resource inputs.

The TFP is, in effect, the difference between the growth in total factor input and the growth in output. For example, assuming a real GDP increase of 5 percent due to a total resource input increase of 3.5 percent, then subtracting the 3.5 percent increase in total resource input from the 5 percent increase in real GDP yields 1.5 percent growth attributable to TFP. In other words, of the 5 percent increase in real GDP, 3.5 percent is attributable to increases in resources, and 1.5 percent is the result of factor productivity: a measure of the *efficiency* of resource utilization. In this illustration, what must be stressed is that the increase in TFP does have a dual effect of increasing the economy's international competitiveness and economic growth.

The evidence in Table 4.1 highlights the importance of the growth-productivity link and shows the existing differences between the various regions of the world in terms of economic growth achievements and states of competitiveness (TFP levels). It indicates how uneven development can be explained by differences in degrees of resource utilization among the various regions of the world. It gives the growth rates of GDP, resource inputs, and TFPs in both the developed countries (DCs) and the less developed countries (LDCs) over the period 1960-1990. The data reveal that while Sub-Saharan Africa and South America show zero annual increase in TFP (lack of competitiveness), East Asia and Western Europe record relatively high levels of TFP growth (high competitiveness). We also see the differences in capital utilization.

Table 4.1 indicates a high correlation between the TFP, capital use, and GDP growth (economic growth). The poorest regions of the world, namely, Sub-Saharan Africa, South Asia, and South America, consistently show low TFP growth and relatively lower GDP growth. The uneven level of growth and development among the various regions of the world is therefore largely explained by differences in the efficiency of resource utilization as measured by the TFP, indicating differences in competitiveness, of various countries and regions of the world.

APPENDIX

In this appendix we develop and analyze the proposed complementary relationship between international competitiveness and economic growth that is the main subject of the chapter. The main question addressed is whether there is any causal relationship between competitiveness and growth. That is, does greater international competitiveness cause greater economic growth, or does greater economic growth cause greater competitiveness?

Following the argument advanced in the so-called New Growth Theory in its development of the *endogenous growth models*,[6] growth can be explained as largely a residual that is caused by technological change; that is, growth in TFP. It is important to not confuse the role played by TFP in determining the difference between what constitutes economic growth, on the one hand, and the process through which economic growth materializes, on the other. The TFP level and its growth rate considerations need not be involved in defining economic growth itself, rather, the TFP growth is central in the determination of competitiveness. And these two issues are distinct and separable.

Thus, we emphasize here that growth in TFP does not necessarily lead to economic growth directly. Rather, TFP growth determines *micro level* competitiveness, and thereby establishes the *necessary conditions for competitiveness*; and then, depending on whether or not the *macro level* competitiveness exists within the economic environment of the country concerned, which would establish the *sufficiency conditions of competitiveness*, economic growth may or may not take place.

As we discover here, there is a complementary and causal relationship linking growth to competitiveness, and it is important that the nature of this complementarity be fully expounded and understood. The analysis is presented in two stages: (1) first, a dynamic competitive advantage model is used to verify that international competitiveness and economic growth are analogous, and then (2) a theoretical formulation of economic growth is developed from *first principles* and used to demonstrate the hypothesized close correlation between competitiveness and growth.

Growth-Competitiveness Complementarity

It is important to examine more thoroughly the nature of causality between international competitiveness and economic growth. A one-way causal relationship between these two phenomena would be a case where, say, competitiveness causes growth to occur, or *vice versa*. However, if there should be a reciprocal causality, that is, if competitiveness affects growth and growth also affects competitiveness, then it means that there is a complementary causality between the two. A theoretical model that explores such a complementary cause and effect relationship is as follows.

The TFP-Competitive Advantage Model

The framework for the measure of competitiveness developed in the appendix to chapter 2 may be applied to generate a relationship depicting international competitiveness. The economy's generalized implicit production function is

$$y_i = y_i(L_i, K_i, R_i) \qquad\qquad\qquad (A4.1)$$

where

   $i = 1, 2...k$ are sectors of the economy
   y = quantity of output
   L = labor input
   K = capital input
   R = natural resource input

Sectoral growth rate of output over time is made up of sum of each input's (marginal) productivity and the rate of growth of the input:

$$dy_i/dt = \partial y_i/\partial L_i.dL_i/dt + \partial y_i/\partial K_i.dK_i/dt + \partial y_i/\partial R_i.dR_i/dt \qquad (A4.2)$$

that is, a general expression of the output potential of each sector of the economy under its given set of inputs and given technological know-how.

Assuming a specific technology in order to isolate the combined effects of the inputs, that is, the TFP, a Cobb-Douglas function may be used:

$$y = \lambda L^\alpha K^\beta R^\gamma \qquad\qquad\qquad (A4.3)$$

where

   λ = TFP index
   α_i = factor share of labor
   β_i = factor share of capital
   γ_i = factor share of natural resources

That is:

$$\alpha_i = [\partial y_i/\partial L_i]/[y_i/L_i]$$
$$\beta_i = [\partial y_i/\partial K_i]/[y_i/K_i]$$
$$\gamma_i = [\partial y_i/\partial R_i]/[y_i/R_i]$$

The economy's state of *competitive advantage*, its TFP growth over time, is:

$$d\lambda_i/dt = dy_i/dt - (\alpha_i dL_i/dt + \beta_i dK_i/dt + \gamma_i dR_i/dt) \qquad (A4.4)$$

Equation (A4.2) into equation (A4.4) gives:

$$d\lambda_i/dt = \partial y_i/\partial L_i . dL_i/dt + \partial y_i/\partial K_i . dK_i/dt + \partial y_i/\partial R_i . dR_i/dt$$
$$- (\alpha_i dL_i/dt + \beta_i dK_i/dt + \gamma_i dR_i/dt)$$

that is,

$$d\lambda_i/dt = dL_i/dt[\partial y_i/\partial L_i - \alpha_i] + dK_i/dt[\partial y_i/\partial K_i - \beta_i]$$
$$+ dR_i/dt[\partial y_i/\partial R_i - \gamma_i]$$

Hence,

$$d\lambda_i/dt = dL_i/dt[\alpha_i y_i/L_i - \alpha_i] + dK_i/dt[\beta_i y_i/K_i - \beta_i]$$
$$+ dR_i/dt[\gamma_i y_i/R_i - \gamma_i]$$

or

$$d\lambda_i/dt = \alpha_i . dL_i/dt[y_i/L_i - 1] + \beta_i . dK_i/dt[y_i/K_i - 1]$$
$$+ \gamma_i . dR_i/dt[y_i/R_i - 1] \tag{A4.5}$$

Equation (A4.5) measures TFP growth for the ith sector of the economy, that is, *competitiveness* at the firm/industry level.

For the k sectors of the economy, the aggregate TFP growth is:

$$\lambda' = d\lambda/dt = \Sigma_I^n \{\alpha_i . dL_i/dt[y_i/L_i - 1] + \beta_i . dK_i/dt[y_i/K_i - 1]$$
$$+ \gamma_i . dR_i/dt[y_i/R_i - 1]\} \tag{A4.6}$$

Equation (A4.6) gives an expression for the measure of competitiveness at the national level. This equation is the weighted sum of individual input growth rates and their productivities. It can be used to show that the growth in any particular factor's productivity depends, in turn, on the growth of the TFP. For instance, labor productivity growth is:

$$dL_i/dt[\partial y_i/\partial L_i - \alpha_i] = d\lambda_i/dt - \{\beta_i . dK_i/dt[y_i/K_i - 1]$$
$$+ \gamma_i . dR_i/dt[y_i/R_i - 1]\} \tag{A4.7}$$

That is, labor productivity growth, say, is influenced not only by TFP growth but also by the growth in the substitution of other inputs for labor.

Growth-Competitiveness Structural Links

As explained in the text, *economic growth* is regarded as a steady increase in national income and per capita income of the society over time. An in-depth structural model of determination of growth and its components may be depicted as follows.[7]

Growth is consistent with steady increase in GDP and per capita GDP over time, given by

$$g_t = \Delta Y/Y_t = dY_t/Y_t > 0 \tag{A4.8}$$

where

Y_t = GDP at time t
g = growth
$\Delta Y = Y_t - Y_{t-1}$

Applying an augmented production function (similar to equation A4.1, augmented by including entrepreneurial resources, E):

$$Y = Y(N,L,K,E)$$

A change in Y is defined by a total differentiation:

$$dY = \partial Y/\partial N.dN + \partial Y/\partial L.dL + \partial Y/\partial K.dK + \partial Y/\partial E.dE$$

with growth rate given by

$$dY/Y = \partial Y/\partial N.dN/Y + \partial Y/\partial L.dL/Y + \partial Y/\partial K.dK/Y + \partial Y/\partial E.dE/Y$$

Multiplying through the Right Hand Side (RHS) by a form of one, that is, respectively by N/N, L/L, K/K, and E/E, we obtain

$$dY/Y = \partial Y/\partial N.N/Y.dN/N + \partial Y/\partial L.L/Y.dL/L + \partial Y/\partial K.K/Y.dK/K$$
$$+ \partial Y/\partial E.E/Y.dE/E \qquad (A4.9)$$

Denoting the respective input-elasticities as follows:[8]

$\xi_N = \partial Y/\partial N.N/Y$
$\xi_L = \partial Y/\partial L.L/Y$
$\xi_K = \partial Y/\partial K.K/Y$
$\xi_E = \partial Y/\partial E.E/Y$

and the respective growth rates as

$g_N = dN/N$
$g_L = dL/L$
$g_K = dK/K$
$g_E = dE/E$

and substituting into equation (A4.9), we have

$$g = \xi_N g_N + \xi_L g_L + \xi_K g_K + \xi_E g_E \qquad (A4.10)$$

or the compact form:

$$g = \Sigma_i^j \, \xi_i g_i \qquad\qquad\qquad\qquad\qquad (A4.11)$$

The RHS of equation (A4.10) indicates the sum of the products of the input-elasticities of output and the growth rates of the various inputs. Equations (A4.10) and (A4.11) depict *economic growth* expressed as the summation of the products of input-elasticities of output and the inputs' growth rates. These stipulate that growth is made up of the total contribution of each resource weighted by that resource's own rate of discovery and utilization. In other words, economic growth is deduced as the aggregation of the products of the productivities of inputs and the relative sizes of the value of each input in national output.

Inspection of equation (A4.6) which depicts *competitiveness*, and equation (A4.9) which depicts *economic growth* shows that these two phenomena are determined by the same microeconomic parameters, namely, input-elasticities of output (the economy's *productivity growth rates*) and growth rates of inputs (the economy's *rate of resource utilization*). This establishes the phenomena of *growth-competitiveness complementarity* proposed in the text.

NOTES

1. Sometimes the necessary condition of higher output and rising levels of income (economic growth) for development need not hold. For example, rising productivity might lead people to prefer increased leisure rather than increased income; in that case a doubling of productivity, say, may result in people cutting their daily or weekly hours of work by half. This would represent a case of economic development being achieved while not accompanied by growth (no increasing real income). For extensive details on the concepts of growth and development, see Ezeala-Harrison (1996a).

2. The degree of equity in income distribution is usually analyzed and measured by application of the *Lorenz Curve*, a graphical model showing the percentage of total GDP received by any given cumulative percentage of the country's population. For a detailed example, see Ezeala-Harrison (1996a).

3. Generally, micro (level) policies are policies that are centered on specific and particular (micro) sectors of the economy. Where *macro* (level) policies provide short-term "fine-tuning" of the economy as it progresses along the desired directions, *micro* policies are long-term policy frames that shape and expand the growth and development paths themselves along those directions.

4. *Economies of scale* are the long-run advantages of larger output produced by (spreading over) the indivisible inputs that are employed. This would result in lower unit (average) cost of output. (For some exposition on the standard method of determining the presence or otherwise of economies of scale, see the *appendix* to chapter 3). *Economies of scope* are long-run advantages that result in lower unit costs as two or more product types are produced by one (multiproduct) firm rather than by separate specializing firms. In so doing, the firm achieves economies of scope by increasing its *scope* of (output) production activities. *Capacity utilization* occurs when the firm is able to fully utilize its plant's capacity by operating and producing its output level at *minimum average cost*.

5. It is important that we maintain the clear distinction between micro and macro level parameters, and to point out that some studies have suggested that trade liberalization, a macro level factor, could lead to growth in total factor productivity, a micro level factor. Dornbusch (1993, p. 89) cites the works of Chenery et al. (1986), Harrison (1991), Salvatore and Hatcher (1991), and World Bank (1991), as recent examples.

6. The New Growth Theory is discussed in chapter 1. See Romer (1986; 1994) or Grossman and Helpman (1994) for more in-depth analyses. See also Bryan (1994) for some informative account on the determinants of long-run growth drawing from the Solow Growth Accounting model and its decomposition that defines total factor productivity. The model decomposes growth in national output into its constituent parts of growth in the aggregative inputs plus growth in technological change (TFP growth).

7. This portion is based on chapter 1 of Ezeala-Harrison (1996a).

8. The input-elasticity of output measures the degree to which a proportional change in the level of the input would affect the level of total output. It simply measures the input's relative contribution to total output and is equal to the input's share (or factor share) in total output.

PART II

POLICY ISSUES OF INTERNATIONAL COMPETITIVENESS

5

The Path of Structural Reform to Competitiveness

In this chapter we explore the issues of structural economic reforms that may be pursued at both the firm/industry and national levels in order to achieve and maintain international competitiveness. Ordinarily, most countries that operate free market economies have tended to pursue economic policy initiatives that bear upon carefully directed and controlled government intervention, albeit where the government might only play more of a monitoring role rather than a controlling role. But then, the extent to which the free market is left alone to determine the pace and direction of the economy is often limited by the tendency for the country's authorities to intervene and "set things right" because of the inherent *market failure* whose ramifications tend to cause economic distortions.

FIRM-LEVEL RESTRUCTURING

At the firm (or industry) level, companies recognize the need for occasional (if not constant) structural reforms designed to enhance the firm's competitiveness. The most common forms of restructuring are *downsizing* and *reengineering*, both of which almost always result in reduction of the number of workers employed.

Downsizing involves such measures as layoffs, early retirements, buyouts, or attrition—designed to reduce labor cost. For most firms, labor cost constitutes the largest proportion of total cost of operation. Total labor cost is made up of the wage bill and non-wage costs known as *quasi-fixed* labor costs (including such costs as recruitment and training costs, employee benefits, payroll taxes, and worker-compensation premiums). Therefore, the firm's most effective way of cutting the level of its operational costs would be to reduce the size of its labor force—the restructuring measure known as downsizing.

Reengineering involves such measures as directing investments in new technologies, changing the labor-capital ratio, retraining workers, or reassigning workers and personnel to alternative job approaches and procedures. These actions are aimed at cost reduction and productivity improvement. Like downsizing, reengineering tends also to result in the reduction of the number of workers employed. Certain job skills and occupations might no longer be needed as reengineering occurs, and workers are displaced as the firm reassigns job tasks and implements new technologies that are usually capital-intensive.

Although firm-level restructuring eliminates jobs in the short run, it would result in creating more jobs in the long run. Restructuring raises the micro level competitiveness of the firm, enabling it to capture larger market shares for its products (globally), and to be capable of creating new positions to meet expanded market demand. Empirical evidence that supports this analysis has been found in a recent Industry Canada survey of the restructuring experience of Canadian companies since the mid-1980s.[1]

The study involved a survey of 568 firms (out of 10,000 approached) that underwent some form of restructuring during the period 1994-1995. It found (contrary to the general view that restructuring always eliminates jobs) that, "on the average, restructuring has created relatively more jobs than it has eliminated", apparently as it led to "numerous openings for new jobs and occupations." The study concludes that the competitiveness problems of Canadian firms are due to their inability to undertake "enough restructuring, particularly of the right kind, including investing in the efficiency of core operations."

RESTRUCTURING AT NATIONAL LEVEL

Unlike firm-level restructuring, structural reform at the national level is economy-wide and macroeconomic; but it has microeconomic as well as macroeconomic results in view. National level structural reforms would involve such measures as privatization of public-sector firms and public utilities, efficient operation of social overhead infrastructure, maintenance of appropriate monetary, fiscal, and tax rate targets, and overall dismantling of rigid prices and quantity controls.

It is evident that since the post-World War II period those countries (especially in Asia) that had effected less economic controls and had their economies function upon free-market forces were the ones that have experienced remarkable economic performance. This scenario has underlined strongly the need for immediate implementation of structural reforms on the part of countries (especially developing countries) whose economic structures are less than conducive for international competitiveness.[2]

Many countries are still engaged in the task of *reforming* their economies. The aim is to implement greater use of, and reliance on, the free-market mechanism in resource allocation and distribution of income and wealth in their societies. In chapter 2 the term *economic liberalization* is used to label the package of measures designed to direct an economy away from central planning and control toward a well-functioning free-market system based on competition, trade liberalization, deregulation, privatization, and dismantling of direct *command and control* systems in the economy. Where a country recognizes the importance of these conditions and initiates and promotes the various policy procedures and actions to achieve them, the country is said to have embarked upon the path of structural reform toward competitiveness. This chapter presents the detailed analysis of some aspects of structural reforms and the ways by which they lead to greater competitiveness.

The Economy's Structure

The structure of the economy constitutes the various sectors of which activities together make up the economy. These include nature, size, and compositions of the economy's production and consumption, employment, distribution, commerce and exchange, as well as its geography, environment, and resource acquisition. The term, *economic structure* (of a country), is a blanket reference encompassing such important sectoral aspects as the occupational and geographical distribution of the population and labor force (the proportion of the population that depends on *primary sector* occupation relative to *secondary- and tertiary-sector* occupations for their livelihood, and the proportion that lives and works in the rural areas relative to urban sectors), the relative states of agriculture and industrialization, the proportion of the country's GDP that is made up of agricultural (primary) production relative to industrial (secondary) and services (tertiary) production, the degree of mechanization relative to the degree of labor intensity involved in production activities, the level of technological sophistication, and the like.

The primary sector of the economy constitutes the agricultural activities of farming, fishing, hunting, handicraft, and petty trade and local commerce; the secondary sector is made up of manufacturing and processing industrialization; and the tertiary includes the services sector (including distribution) and infrastructural utilities (including transportation, communication, banking and finance, education, health services, and entertainment). The structure of the economy would also encompass the degree of foreign trade dependence and "openness" of the economy, as well as the composition of the country's items of trade (imports and exports). Whether or not the country is monocultural (depending on a single commodity export for much of its foreign exchange earnings), and whether or not the country's economy is susceptible to external trade and international market shocks, are also important aspects of economic structure.

The economic structure of a country is determined by the country's size, resource endowment, and population. Combined with the resource endowment, the level of technological know-how shapes the nature and pace of development of the country's agriculture, mining activities, construction, and industry. From these, the economy's international trade commodities emerge, defining the commodity compositions of exports and imports, and the relative importance of these in the country's economic activity and GDP.

Over time, the economy's structural compositions often change, depending on the pace of growth and development and the state of technological progress. For example, during the early stages of development, the agriculture sector usually occupies the largest share of the economy (in terms of proportion of total employment and proportion of GDP). Commerce and distribution usually follows, and then manufacturing. However, as the economy grows and attains greater development (see chapter 4), the secondary and tertiary sectors (manufacturing industry and services) tend to expand more rapidly to become greater than the primary sectors (agriculture and small-scale commerce), such that the economy's structure would assume a different composition. Such a relative decline in the share of primary economic activities (particularly in terms of relative employment of the labor force, productivity and incomes, and exports) is an example of the *structural changes* that the economy requires in order to attain and remain competitive.

The economy's international trade situation, and the state of its international competitiveness relative to its trading partners, are largely determined by the mix of structural factors of productivity (micro level) and institutional parameters (macro level) whose sizes and effects are determined by the economy's ability (or inability) to perform. These would influence the level and relative compositions of exports, imports, volumes of trade, financial flows, terms of trade, and balance-of-payments.

Sectoral Targets of Structural Reform

In the bid to redress economic policy inadequacies that have tended to impede their international competitiveness, most countries undertake structural reforms, albeit often reluctantly. However, while the reform programs have succeeded in some countries, they have not been successful in others. The reasons for the different experiences range from the inability of various countries to implement the reforms in a sustained fashion to the unwillingness of others to adhere strictly to the tenets of economic liberalization in full.

It is important to understand what exactly needs reforming in an economy in order to promote its international competitiveness. Different countries have different economic structures depending on their resource endowments and regional differences. However, there are major economic sectoral reforms that are common to most countries. Among these are the agricultural sector, industrial policy, the public sector, infrastructure, and financial management reforms. Activities in these sectors significantly affect and even determine the state of a country's international competitiveness. Sectoral reform in these areas means effecting the necessary and appropriate positive changes needed to raise productivity in these sectors. We examine each of these in turn.

Agricultural Reform

Agricultural sector reform is more crucial for developing countries in whose economies the agricultural sector is usually dominant. The labor markets of these countries indicate the overwhelming relative dominance of agricultural occupation in the labor force (on average about 76 percent), as against the relative smallness of nonagricultural activities (on average about 19 percent). Such an economy is referred to as an *agrarian* economy.[3]

Agricultural sector competitiveness is demonstrated by evidence of, say, self-sufficiency in food production, or by being the leading exporter of some agricultural produce in the world market. Some developing countries have retained strong competitiveness in this regard, while others have lost it. The loss of competitiveness in agriculture has contributed to economic declines in many developing countries. This occurred as some of these countries adopted policies that apparently favored the urban and industrial sectors of the economy, thereby creating rural-urban and agricultural-industrial imbalances in investment, infrastructural development, employment, productivity, and earnings. Continued neglect of the agricultural sector, while the policy of industrialization was prioritized, amounted to misplacement of emphasis in such *agrarian* economies.

The economy loses competitiveness as the policy results in unceasing waves of agricultural-industrial and rural-urban migration, and massive open and disguised unemployment. The severe manpower losses for the agricultural sector, as the agricultural-industrial (rural-urban) income disparity widens, manifests into huge shortfalls in domestic food and raw material supplies. This phenomenon has been a major factor that has contributed to making the (agrarian) economies of many developing countries highly vulnerable to incessant global shocks and international commodity price fluctuations. It simply destroys their competitiveness in the world raw material export markets.

Another factor that impairs agricultural competitiveness has been the heavy taxation imposed on the agricultural sector. Agricultural taxation is often carried out through the operations of produce Marketing Boards. Marketing Boards are state statutory monopolies that buy cash crops below market prices from domestic producers, for export at higher world market prices. They are simply used as mechanisms whereby governments could effectively tax agricultural producers. Farmers in developing countries are, on average, taxed about 70 percent more than farmers in the developed regions of the world. Such heavy taxation of agriculture results in massive "abandonment" of the farms, and results in low agricultural output. A recent study by Khan and Khan (1995) on African agriculture indicates that agricultural output grew at an average of only

1.9 percent per year during 1965-1980, and 1.7 percent during 1980-1992 (compared to, say, China's 3 percent and 5.4 percent for these two respective periods, in which case agricultural taxation was less severe).

Industrial Reform

The policies of industrial development in most countries are aggressively pursued. Many countries operate inward-oriented import-substitution or quasi-import-substitution policies of industrialization. Such a policy is driven by widespread tariff and import/export license barriers. This basically eliminates external competition, especially in manufacturing, and encourages the operations of weak and technically inefficient industries, and seriously impairs international competitiveness.

In most countries, state-owned industrial projects are established and operated under tariff protection. Direct foreign ventures are subjected to rigid controls, and even in some countries (especially developing countries) many foreign-owned enterprises are nationalized. As countries came to regard industrialization as the primary program to be pursued to achieve rapid economic growth and development, the first attempts were to set up import-substitution industries to produce previously imported manufactured goods. The potential economic benefits of this were obviously enormous: domestic employment expansion and market demand for locally produced raw materials, saving foreign exchange.

It turned out, however, that many of these industries came to be dependent on imported raw materials as domestic sources proved inadequate. Moreover, in developing countries in particular, the market demand for the industries' produce was limited in the face of the low income character of the general population. Consequently, the industrialization effort proved disappointing as these industrial policies impeded international competitiveness and saddled the countries concerned with balance-of-payments problems. However, most countries (mainly the developed ones) that adopted a free-market-based industrial development policy, succeeded in achieving rapid industrialization and growth. Such economies achieved and maintained high levels of competitiveness, and have applied the relative competitive advantage to sustain growth and development.

Public-Sector Reform

The public sector includes all direct economic activities of the government such as taxation, transfer payments, government expenditures, state enterprises, and public utilities. All these activities bear significant effects on the economy, with major implications for the economy's state of competitiveness. The size of taxation in an economy is a key factor in competitiveness. High direct tax rates such as income tax, property tax, and profit tax, have disincentive effects on the supply of work effort, entrepreneurial risk initiatives, and savings. Thus, it impairs an economy's productivity and hence its micro level competitiveness. High rates of indirect taxes, such as excise duties, sales taxes, purchase taxes, or import (tariff) duties, either raise production costs and prices (as firms pass them on as price mark-ups) or discourage demand as consumers curtail purchases on taxed products. These effects simply reduce competitiveness of the economy relative to other economies of lower tax rates.

Transfer payments impair competitiveness in many ways. Where governments grant subsidies to firms, the firms are artificially shielded from competition as their operating costs are subsidized. The incentives of such firms to apply the most efficient production methods are compromised, with the result of reduced micro level competitiveness. Moreover, financing the grants would raise government expenditures and even create budget deficits. The effect of large government budget deficit is to create reduced international confidence in the economy, which might cause capital flight and weakness of the exchange rate of the country's currency.[4] This may be compounded by larger resource losses that go to the servicing of high government debt.

Public-sector enterprises include the provision of socioeconomic infrastructure and direct public-sector investment in economic ventures. In most countries, the governments tend to commit themselves to public-sector provision of social overhead capital (infrastructure and public utilities such as postal and telecommunications services, roads and highways, water and sewerage, electricity, education and health services, and air and sea-port facilities), which are necessary requirements for economic development. This policy is normally supported by sound economic justification. However, as *natural monopolies* (characterized by *economies of scale* and *economies of scope*),[5] their operation under deregulated settings would yield inequitable outcomes, although the results might be economically efficient and competitive. On the other hand, their operation under regulatory control with a view toward greater equity, would require huge government subsidies, with their attendant consequences discussed above.

The overwhelming economic importance of the social overhead infrastructure industries requires that they be maintained at highly efficient and adequate levels. The level of social overhead infrastructure constitutes a significant aspect of the macro level parameters of an economy's international competitiveness. It is essential that this sector be efficient and competitive itself as a means of achieving overall competitiveness for the economy. Structural reforms aimed at fostering greater competitiveness must begin with deregulation and privatization of the social overhead infrastructural sector. (An extended theoretical analysis illustrating the competitiveness implications of operating natural monopolies is provided in the *appendix* to this chapter.)

Apart from the social overhead capital sector, state enterprises in other sectors such as transportation, banking, insurance, and even manufacturing industries cannot be economically viable and must be wholly privatized and deregulated. Operated as government companies, often devoid of profit incentives and rife with corruption and inept management, these enterprises promote gross inefficiency and misallocation of resources. A structural reform policy is required to massively deregulate and privatize these sectors as a prelude to enhancing the international competitiveness of a country.

In manufacturing, many of the state enterprises are established as import-substituting industries: mainly domestic monopolies shielded artificially from foreign competition, with high tariff protection. Under such market leverages, these firms produce high cost goods from inefficient, ill-equipped and over-manned factories. In some instances (especially in developing countries), the industries lack the requisite managerial skills, and their operations are shored up through state adoption of controlled prices, often resulting in disequilibrium conditions in the markets for these manufactures. Overall, state enterprises in the manufacturing sector fail to ever operate efficiently. Massive structural reform programs are required to deregulate and privatize such industries.

Financial Sector Reform

The banking sectors of many countries are dominated by huge government presence. Real interest rates are usually fixed, and the Central Banks exert considerable influence on the trading of a country's currency and the determination of its international exchange rate. Over-valuation of the national currency often occurs, fueling over-importation through undue cheapening of foreign goods. These conditions greatly impair the international competitiveness of a country.

Massive government borrowing and overspending (as well as support of inefficient public sector enterprises) tend to create big budget deficits, often cumulating into huge domestic and foreign public debts, jeopardizing the inflow of foreign investment while encouraging capital flight. Inflation usually ensues in the domestic economy, and the country seriously loses international competitiveness.

Financial sector reform would take the form of government divestiture in all financial institutions. The Central Bank would assume solely its traditional roles of broad monitoring of the economy and exchange rate supervision. In this position, the Central Bank promotes the economy's macro level competitiveness through maintenance of competitive levels for the exchange and interest rates, without necessarily interfering in the determination of the levels of these rates.

STRUCTURAL REFORMS AND COMPETITIVENESS

At both the micro and macro levels, it is important to determine the pertinent structural parameters to be targeted for reforms in order to enhance competitiveness. It is easy to carry out major reforms of macro level parameters such as deregulation of industries or financial sector liberalization, but it is more involving to bring such reforms down to the micro level. Micro level reform, as discussed earlier, include the measures of downsizing and reengineering at the firm level. Exmaples are productivity-enhancing measures, cost-cutting actions, product quality improvement, and administrative revamping, all of which can be tackled only at the firm/industry level. Macro reforms involve national level parameters, most of which have major social and political ramifications.[6]

Micro Competitiveness Reform

At the firm level, international competitiveness can be sustained through a determined effort to operate firms and industries with maximum efficiency. This goal calls for restructuring measures designed toward the following conditions.

Optimal Resource Use: Resources must be employed at economical proportions. Labor, equipment, and raw materials must be combined in such a way to avoid redundancy; this implies that their (factor) prices must be determined solely according to their (free) market conditions. Institutional influences on factor markets (for example, labor unions and government interventions in setting wages and payroll taxes) that cause disequilibrium outcomes and higher than market-clearing prices, must be at a minimum. Then would resource use be efficient with maximum productivity effect.

Capacity Utilization: Firms and businesses need to operate at full capacity utilization, ensuring that idle capacity in industries is minimized. This determines plant sizes, and therefore, operation costs: optimal capacity plant for firms means that output is produced at minimum cost (as firms operate at the minimum points of their average cost curves). With outputs produced and marketed at their minimum unit costs, the economy would be set for a state of relative competitiveness in the international market.

Cost Efficiency: Industries need to maintain maximum efficiency in technical and administrative operations. This means the elimination of bureaucratic excesses and costly institutional obstacles. For example, the use of nonmarket criteria in determination of price and output levels, employment levels, location decisions, marketing procedures, and other aspects of business transactions results in less than optimal efficiencies. They do not allow for the most convenient outcomes in terms of least cost options of highest productivity choices.

Institutional Setting: The choice of the institutional settings in which industries operate is a crucial determinant of the state of micro competitiveness. In particular, the market system governing the economy would determine the attitudes adopted by the economic agents that operate in it. To ensure maximum competitiveness, productive outlets (firms/industries) should be operated under private-enterprise-based *profit incentives*, to ensure management efficiency. This can be contrasted with the situation of centralized *command and control* system, whereby industries are *regulated* because they are state enterprises, and in which case there would be no profit incentives (and therefore no incentives to maintain maximum efficiency).[7]

Effective micro level reform would involve employment and human resource development, such as education and training, infrastructural development, and raising productivity of resources through liberalization measures (such as agricultural sector development and land redistribution), and, most importantly, the dismantling of high-tax regimes. These measures are vital to the enhancement of international competitiveness in the short-term, as well as long-term economic growth.

Studies by Jones and Kiguel (1994) indicate that the agricultural sector in particular has responded most favorably to reforms in African countries: total agricultural value added in the restructuring countries that implemented tax cuts on their major export crops jumped by about 2 percentage points. Countries that failed to sufficiently review "tax penalties" on their farmers experienced about 1.6 percentage point declines in their agricultural output. Agricultural sector restructuring allows rural-urban migrants from smallholder agriculture to automatically benefit by putting an end to their forcibly having to sell their farm produce at low *official* prices. School-leavers benefit from privatization and deregulation that allows for small-scale enterprise development through expansion of self-employment opportunities coupled with greater demand in the informal sector. Exchange rate adjustments that bring national currencies to their true market values enable local food producers to become more competitive against previously artificially cheap imports. Further, dismantling price controls on food prices and removing food subsidies act as incentives for rural farmers to raise food production and earn higher incomes.

Macro Competitiveness Reform

As seen in chapter 2, the main component of *macro level competitiveness* is the parameter broadly labeled as *economic liberalization*, which represents the spectrum of parameters which drive the economy away from the uncompetitive command and control posture toward a well-functioning free-market system based on a competitive environment, privatization, (trade) liberalization, deregulation, and a stable exchange rate regime. However, macro level issues involve a broader degree of socioeconomic and political parameters. Included in this are national economic policy instruments such as monetary and fiscal policies, budgetary management, taxation, infrastructural management, institutional liberalization, exchange rate policies, and financial sector management. The role of these factors in determining competitiveness is pervasive. It is important that some of these factors be discussed in greater depth.

Monetary Policy

Monetary policy is the manipulation of the money supply by the Central Bank to influence the interest rate in the desired direction with a view to stabilizing the economy upon a steady growth path (that is, avoid deep recessions and unemployment or high inflation rates). In the *monetarist* doctrine of macroeconomic policy, an economy should formulate and maintain a steady rate of growth of the money supply at all times as a way of smoothing out any fluctuations in the economy that may be imminent due to the *business cycle*. This is because controlling the money supply is thought to be a means of regulating economic activity and controlling inflation. Higher interest rates lead to higher savings in the economy, while lower rates lead to increased investment, employment, and income. In this way, a freely functioning money market enables scarce resources to be allocated most efficiently and productively. Applied wisely, the use of monetary policy is an effective means of "fine-tuning maintenance" of the economy over its course of growth and development. Through the appropriate monetary policy, the economy would operate an interest rate level conducive for maximum investment, savings, and aggregate demand levels required for maximum rate of growth and competitiveness, on the one hand, and minimum levels of *(demand-pull) inflation* rate and exchange rate, on the other. In this way, monetary policy reform could be effected to achieve and maintain international competitiveness.

Subject to the existence of *purchasing power parity* among nations (see chapter 1), a country that has a higher inflation rate relative to its trading partners would be at a major disadvantage in maintaining international competitiveness. For starters, inflation would raise the relative prices of the country's exports (which may reduce the level of export demand) and reduce the relative prices of imports (which may raise the level of demand for imports), creating a potential balance of trade deficit. Further, inflation may lead to capital flight as investors take their resources elsewhere; and with inflation, the real rate of interest would fall (higher price of bonds), reducing the level of inflow of foreign investment (although the nominal interest rate would rise, reducing the levels of domestic investment and consumption). All these outcomes are damaging to micro and macro level international competitiveness.

Fiscal Policy

Fiscal policy involves the use of taxation and government expenditure to influence economic variables toward desired target levels; fiscal instruments can be relied upon to not only stabilize the economy but also to effectively mobilize the resources for economic growth. The two sides of fiscal management are taxation and government spending. Taxation is the source and means of resources needed to finance the traditional government functions of administration, law and order maintenance, defence and national security, and infrastructural development (including public utilities, social overhead capital, education, health services, and the like). Achievement of relative competitiveness, as well as the pace of economic and social progress, depends largely on the economy's ability to generate sufficient revenues to provide these nonrevenue-yielding public facilities. However, the nature and operation of the taxation system may severely impair the ability to achieve and maintain competitiveness, in the following important ways.

1. Public Revenue: Direct and Indirect Taxes. Direct taxes are taxes that fall directly on personal or corporate incomes. They include income taxes, profit (corporate) taxes, property taxes, and payroll taxes. As a means of ensuring greater *equity*, especially in developed countries, rates in these taxes are usually high and *progressive*. However, such a situation impedes competitiveness. High income taxes act as disincentives to savings, work effort, and risk taking in entrepreneurship. High payroll taxes deter enterprise formation, employment creation, and attraction of investment.

Indirect taxes are those that do not fall directly on personal income. The most important of these taxes are custom duties (import taxes levied as tariffs, and export taxes levied on goods bound for the export market) and excise duties (taxes placed on domestically produced goods). Indirect taxes impair an economy's competitiveness at both the micro and macro levels. For example, import and export duties reduce the volume of trade; excise duties are considered by firms as added production costs and thus raise prices; sales taxes simply raise prices and reduce the level of market demand for the products.

Tax policy reforms could be effected by way of minimizing the variety and rates of direct and indirect taxes. In particular, payroll taxes, import/export duties, and excise duties are most damaging to international competitiveness, and at worst, need to be operated at their most benign levels, and at best, need to be eliminated. In fact, as a means of enhancing an economy's state of international competitiveness, as well as stimulating private investment and attracting foreign investment (measures required to expand the potential for greater economic growth), tax concessions are necessary to be granted to firms and industries. High-tax economies would be relatively uncompetitive economies.

2. Government Spending and Deficit Financing. Most countries face the problems of fiscal deficits. That is, the amount of public revenues they collect usually falls far short of their public expenditures. Over time, however, the accumulation of annual budget deficits gives rise to serious problems of huge public debts—both internal and external debts—for the country. The adverse effects of such debts include severe balance-of-payments adversities, capital flight, weakening of the international exchange rate of the country's currency, and undermining of international confidence in the country's economy. Nothing could be more damaging to the state of the country's international competitiveness than these outcomes.

The weights of servicing and accommodating public debts, especially the external debts, exert financial pressures tending to make the country to resort to incurring even more debt in order to service the existing debt, leading to yet heavier indebtedness. This gives rise to a *debt crisis* (as this cycle of the indebtedness syndrome came to be known during the 1980s and 1990s), often resulting in adoption of drastic *structural adjustment* measures required to restore fiscal health for the economy. The "adjustments" are often designed to enable the government to balance its budget and better manage its debt—measures that are critical toward achievement and maintenance of international competitiveness.

Deficit financing is the act of using an expanded money supply (that is, by increasing the quantity of money in circulation) to finance a government budget deficit. Many countries tend to resort to this method of fiscal expansion to finance development projects. This is also referred to as inflationary financing because it almost always increases the rate of inflation in the economy. However, in addition to their expanded spending ability, such inflationary financing may have some other positive side effects, which the authorities may wish to see take place.[8] But the inflationary consequences of deficit financing could prove to be far more destructive than constructive to the economy. Hyperinflation is often the actual result of unguarded deficit financing, and could set the economy into severe recession and stagflation. As hyperinflation erodes all confidence in the country's currency and the economy as a whole, savings for long-term investment and growth suffers, capital flights occur, and serious balance-of-payments problems arise, while severe economic hardships descend on the economy, together with their adverse social and political repercussions for competitiveness.

Therefore, in order to not jeopardize competitiveness, a country should not adopt deficit financing except as a very short-run measure designed to quickly enable the government to implement a key infrastructural development initiative. And even then, it must serve as a very last resort. The experiences of many countries (especially developing countries) have shown that once deficit financing is embarked upon as a means of raising government spending, it tends to be overdone, with severe consequences in the interim.

Institutional Reform

As mentioned earlier, an economy's institutional setting bears a critical dimension of its macro level international competitiveness. The major institutional parameters include privatization, deregulation, trade liberalization, and financial sector arrangement. A crucial starting point of reform is the enhancement of the private sector of the economy. The private sector possesses the main attributes that are most conducive to competitiveness. Among such attributes is the drive for profitability; the profit incentive lies behind the reason why the private sector is usually more productive than the public sector; also the profit incentive is largely responsible for the creativity of the private sector, which contributes largely to its competitive traits.

Dornbusch (1993) explains three reasons why privatization is a very important and useful step in economic restructuring, and through which, by implication, it promotes the international competitiveness of a nation. He argues:

1. The public sector lacks the managerial capacity and incentives to administer major sectoral enterprises in a cost-effective fashion. This means that a public enterprise cannot achieve the kind of level of efficiency and cost-consciousness that a private enterprise could achieve.
2. The public sector does not have the requisite level of investment resources that are needed for adequate provision of all public services. This implies that the government

cannot raise sufficient amount of investment to provide the adequate level of social overhead infrastructure and public utilities. Apparently, this is because the government has a limited source of stable revenue, namely, taxation; and it cannot rely on borrowing because of the problems of budget deficit and public debt management (see above).

3. The government needs reliable sources of (tax) revenues in order not to engage in (destabilizing) deficit financing and public debt creation. A public enterprise cannot expand fast and adequately enough to be capable of generating enough revenue (directly through taxes levied on itself, and indirectly through income taxes levied on those it employs) that can raise sufficient funding to finance government activities.

In their study of the rising unemployment problems in the transitional economies of Eastern Europe, Blanchard, Commander and Coricelli (1994) observed that in the process of economic restructuring, unemployment may be expected (initially) as the natural outcome of the process of massive resource reallocations that are involved. This is because the introduction of economic restructuring amounts to administering macroeconomic shocks upon the economy. Job losses through layoffs, attrition, early retirements, and job-sharing are the necessary results of the processes of privatization of state enterprises, deregulation of public utilities, and removal of state subsidies and tariff protections. However, these "short-term pains" are envisaged to yield greater "long-term gains" as the economy gains greater competitiveness through the restructuring.

The World Bank's (1994a) and (1994b) studies of the restructuring experience among twenty-nine African countries examined two major facets: the degree to which these countries' originally intended restructuring drives were actually carried out (intensity and extensiveness of reform), and the relative macroeconomic impacts over the two periods of reform, that is 1981-1986 and 1987-1991. The study found that only six of these countries achieved relative successes in terms of enhanced competitiveness, and that the degrees of success achieved were limited during the second period (1987-1991) when the commitments to reform appeared to have waned. Jones and Kiguel (1994) reveal that those countries who instituted the most far-reaching macroeconomic reforms during the period 1986-1991 generally appear to have achieved some concrete payoffs, albeit a rather moderate one, in the form of per capita GDP increases of about 2 percentage points, in addition to growths in exports and industrial expansion. Those that did not seriously undertake reforms suffered GDP growth declines of about 2.6 percent.

APPENDIX

In this appendix, we consider a simple model to analyze how an economy can operate its *infrastructure* and *public utilities* efficiently with a view to international competitiveness. These services referred to collectively as *social overhead infrastructure* belong in the class of *impure public goods*, of which specific examples include the class of *commercial merit goods*, such as electricity, postal service, telecommunications, gas supply, and railways transport; and *pure merit goods*, such as education, health care services, roads and highways, and air and sea-ports.[9]

On the demand side, these services involve very high *externalities* (in consumption), but are easily *excludable*. Therefore, the nature of their demand curves reflects this peculiarity. The total market demand is made up of the following two special characteristics.

1. The **revealed** private demand is represented by the going market demand curve. This demand level is referred to as "revealed" in the sense that it indicates the amounts that buyers are willing to purchase at the going prices.

2. The **spillover** social demand is the level of positive externalities (social benefits) that the production and marketing of the product yields to the society. They are not reflected in the market prices and are not captured by the going market demand curve.

On the supply side, production is characterized by *economies of scale*. The nature of production is such that increasing returns to scale occurs because of the relatively high proportion of fixed inputs in operation. Therefore, the cost per unit (average cost) of output tends to decline continuously as larger amounts of output are produced (see Figure A5.1 and Figure A5.2 below). The existence of *economies of scale* character of production is commonly determined in a firm by the use of a technical parameter known as the *function coefficient*, as follows.

The function coefficient (f) is the ratio of the average cost (AC) to the marginal cost (MC) at any given level of output. That is:

$$f = AC/MC \qquad\qquad (A5.1)$$

such that, if

$f > 1$, it implies the existence of *economies of scale*.
$f < 1$, it implies the existence of *diseconomies of scale*.
$f = 1$, it implies the existence of *constant returns to scale*.

The characteristics of the nature of production costs is the major factor that differentiates between private goods and public goods. The cost characteristic of public goods is the *subadditive* phenomenon (and the cost characteristic of private goods—increasing marginal cost—is the *superadditive* phenomenon).

Production under economies of scale displays the subadditive cost phenomenon apparently because of the relatively high proportion of fixed inputs and the capital-intensive nature of the production process. Therefore, the cost per unit (average cost) of output tends to continuously decline as larger amounts of output are produced. The subadditive cost phenomenon implies that it is cheaper (more efficient) to produce a given level of output by a single firm than by two or more firms. And a firm (or an industry) where this condition exists is known as a *natural monopoly*. Thus, most public utility industries involve natural monopoly operations.

Competitive Operation of Commercial Merit Goods

Figure A5.1 illustrates the possible operational scenario of commercial merit goods (such as electricity or telecommunications services). The quantity of the product (say, the number of telephone services connected) is measured on the horizontal axis, and the price P, as well as production costs, are measured on the vertical axis.

On the production side, as (impure) public goods, production of a commercial merit good is characterised by economies of scale; that is, its production is characterized by continuously declining average cost, labeled as AC, with the corresponding marginal cost MC.

Figure A5.1
Output and Pricing of Commercial Merit Goods

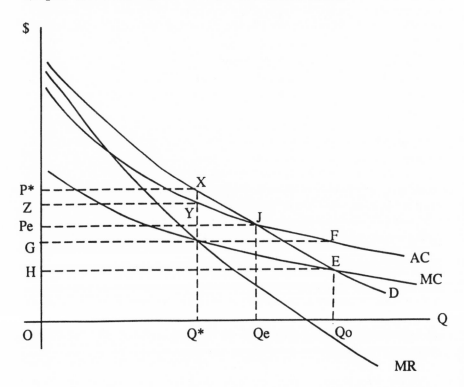

On the demand side, the market demand curve is D; the curve MR is the corresponding marginal revenue curve. These services command high levels of market demand in the economy, as members of the society desire the high levels of needed socioeconomic services that these facilities provide.[10] Moreover, commercial merit goods are excludable; that is, it is possible to effectively exclude a consumer who does not buy the product from consuming it.

Unregulated Private-Sector Profit Incentive

Under a totally private-sector *unregulated* setting, the firm would choose to maximize its profit, setting production level at the point where MC equals MR, and thus would produce and market the amount of the product Q* and charge the unit price P*. The firm then makes a total economic profit represented by the area P*XYZ, during the period. However, it is clear that the profit-maximizing level of output of this service being made available to the market by the producer, may be inadequate and uneconomical, for at least two reasons:

1. The available market output level (Q*) may just not be high enough to satisfy the market's level of desire for this service; thus, under this setting, the society is being unjustly and uneconomically "denied" of this *merit good* (service), which, by definition, is an essential good (service) toward society's economic growth and development.

2. The product's market price (P*) at which it is being made available to the society, is considered "too high" to make the service affordable to the generality of potential users. This means that the product is being priced out of reach; and moreover, with this price, the economic profit accruing to the firm is far above the opportunity cost of the resources that have been committed to producing the good (service), and therefore amounts to *economic rent*, which is a payment over and above what is necessary to compensate the productive resources.

Given these outcomes which result in uneconomical *deadweight losses* to the economy, it is ordinarily believed that the *merit goods* industry, being a natural monopoly, should not be allowed to operate under a private-sector profit-incentive market setting, as the deadweight losses are indicative of *market failure* in such industries.

The free-market *fails* to yield the desired economic goals of society, namely, *efficiency* outcomes (in society's resource use), and *equity* in income distribution among the members of society. It fails in efficiency because the level of output is far short of the amount that would optimize society's welfare (the level of output Q_o at which the *marginal social valuation* of the product, as measured by the unit price P, equals the *marginal social cost* of the product, as measured by the marginal cost MC)—indicated by the point E in Figure A5.1. It fails in equity because of the economic rent accruing to the firm. The existence of deadweight (welfare) loss involved in the operation of this industry is the evidence of market failure.

Regulated Social Welfare Maximization Setting

The common practice is to turn the commercial merit goods industry into a state enterprise under government regulation, with the mandate to operate in such a way as to ensure that the social welfare of citizens is optimized in their use of the product. However, even if this industry is operated under this seemingly noble objective, as is usually the case in many countries, the outcome would still be uneconomical and result in deadweight losses. This is because, should the firm then produce and market the social welfare maximizing output level Q_0 in Figure A5.1 (determined at the point where marginal cost equals price), charging the market unit price P_0 (*marginal cost-pricing* option), the firm would incur economic losses as the unit cost of production (average cost) exceeds the market price P_0. There would therefore be an economic loss per unit of output represented by the height HG, yielding a total loss in the amount represented by the area HGFE. Thus, in order to keep the firm to remain in operation, the loss HGFE must be subsidized by the government; a practice that is as popular as it is equally inefficient and uneconomical.

The usual policy and practice in many countries is for the government to operate the enterprise under the *optimal social welfare* option and support the firm continuously with annual grants of subsidies.[11] However, the practice of granting subsidies to cover operational losses of public companies, and thereby sustain them on a long-term operational basis, involves very serious negative economic situations. First, granting subsidies discourages profit incentives, adoption of cost-cutting measures, and efficiency drives, all of which result in inefficiency and perpetual dependence on subsidy "hand-outs. Second, the government would need to raise the funds required for the subsidies through one of three ways, each of which involves some negative economic results and its own type of deadweight losses: raising taxes, borrowing, or printing money; or a combination of them. The effects of these measures manifest in the following manner:

1. Raising taxes. Direct taxes are distortionary to savings, work effort, and entrepreneurship; indirect taxes impair market demand and micro competitiveness.
2. Government borrowing. Borrowing creates budget deficits and public debt, with potentially adverse effects on interest rate, exchange rate, and higher taxation.
3. Printing money. Printing money and using it to finance the subsidization of state enterprises might result in damaging inflationary consequences and exchange rate instability.

Clearly, then, it is neither economical nor competitive to operate a natural monopoly industry under either the private-sector profit-maximization setting or the social welfare maximization setting. The question then remains as to which other option might exist under which to operate the commercial merit goods industry in a free-market economy. Such an option may be the deregulated break-even competitive setting.

Deregulated Break-Even Competitive Setting

The commercial merit goods industry could be operated under a deregulated competitive option allowing firms to operate in such a way as to cover their operating costs (break even), with the possibility of even making economic profits if attainable. Under a deregulatory regime, two or more firms could be allowed to operate and *compete* in the natural monopoly industry. However, it is believed that because of the *subadditive* nature of the cost conditions in this industry (which makes it a natural monopoly), only one firm is economically justified in the industry, because it is cheaper for a single firm to produce and supply a given level of market output than it is for two or more firms.

It is possible, though, for two or more firms to compete in this industry and yet operate with lower unit costs of output than under a single firm. As more firms come into the industry, the competitive environment would mean that each of them would set production and price at the point J in Figure A5.1, where the demand curve intersects the average cost curve—the break-even objective ($P = AC$). The firm produces and markets the output level Q_e, and charges the price P_e. In this setting, there is still some deadweight loss (since output still falls short of the social welfare maximum level), but the competitive situation and profitability incentive is apt to give rise to the adoption of innovative cost-cutting measures, productivity-enhancement techniques, and other measures that enhance efficiency of operation in the industry. Success in such pursuits would cause downward shifts of the AC curve of a typical firm in the industry, thereby enhancing competitiveness.

Competitive Operation of Pure Merit Goods

The pure merit goods industry is similar in many ways to the case of commercial merit goods analyzed above. The only difference between the two lies in the demand side—the nature of the market demand (revealed preference) for a pure merit good is normally low due to the high externality component of its demand. As a merit good, a service such as education or health care has immense potential social benefits, but if left to themselves, the members of society do not take these high potential social benefits into account when planning their demands for them. Therefore, the actual level of demand for education or health care would be far smaller than the level that would yield the most total benefits to society, a level that society "merits." Thus, the total *private demand* for it and the total the *social demand* for it tend to diverge.

Figure A5.2 illustrates the various conditions surrounding the provision of a pure merit good such as education or health care in the economy. The quantity of the product Q (in, say, the number of school places or hours of health care) is measured on the horizontal axis, and the costs of production (average cost, AC and marginal cost MC) and price (P) are measured on the vertical axis. Both the AC and MC curves are continually downward-sloping as a result of economies of scale in production. The market demand curve is the *average revenue* curve labeled AR, which is assumed to lie below the AC curve because, as explained above, education is a merit good. The curve MR is the marginal revenue curve.

Under private-sector production, the producer would choose to maximize profit, setting production at the point where MC equals MR, and thus would produce the amount of education Q^* and charge the unit price P^*. This firm will not charge the price P_1 on the demand curve, which is the price that the buyers would be willing to pay for the quantity Q^*. This is because the price P_1 does not cover the unit cost indicated by the point A. The producer of education, therefore, would charge the price P^* which covers the cost of production. However, at this price the market demand would be only the amount Q_a corresponding to the demand curve at the price P^*. And at the amount Q_a, the unit cost of production is on the point C, and so on. This shows that the production of education or health care under the private sector would not be efficient in the economy, as the private-sector producer(s) would not only charge relatively very high prices but would also limit production at levels that would not yield the most benefits to the economy.

Figure A5.2
Output and Pricing of Pure Merit Goods

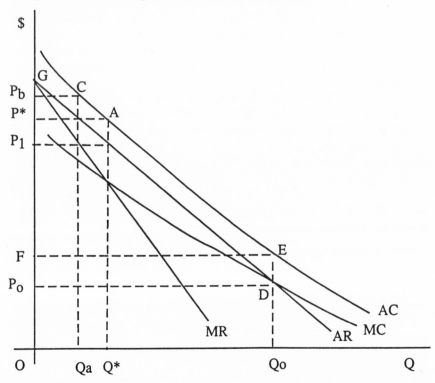

The social welfare maximizing level of the service would be the level at which marginal cost equals price. This obtains at the point D, at the unit price P_0 and production level Q_0. At this level, however, the unit cost, indicated by the point E, exceeds the price P_0, resulting in total losses equivalent to the area $FEDP_0$, to the producer. The private sector would not operate under this condition. However, the government could grant subsidies to cover these losses; and again, the question arises regarding the deadweight losses that a subsidization regime may cause.

We infer from this model that the circumstances surrounding a pure merit goods industry means that it cannot be operated under a competitive regime. Competition is simply not feasible; and in fact, forcing competition upon a pure merit goods industry would just result in higher costs than necessary, and misallocation of resources; and may impair the (long-run) competitiveness of the economy. However, the issue of the resulting deadweight as well as economic losses involved in the industry is adequately compensated by the massive external social benefits (positive externalities) that the industry and its products confer to the society. This is easily verified from Figure A5.2.

Besides its massive social benefits, the society would derive a positive net monetary benefit by providing the level of the service Q_0. This is done by simply comparing the magnitudes of monetary benefits and costs. At this level, the total monetary benefit that society obtains from the service is given by the area under the demand curve: the area GDQ_00. However, the total monetary cost of providing Q_0 level of the service is the area FEQ_0, which is clearly less than the area GDQ_00. This shows that the total utility (benefits) that accrues to society far outweighs the total cost in providing a given level of the service. This provides economic justification for public-sector funding of services such as education or health care.

From this model, it can be proposed that, in order for society to obtain maximum social and economic benefits from pure merit goods, and for these goods to provide the maximum support toward relative competitiveness of the economy, pure merit goods industries (such as education and health care) must be operated under public sector subsidization, and provided to the market (general population) at relatively low prices (such as P_0 in Figure A5.2) which makes it generally affordable. The private-sector profit incentive setting would not yield the level of the product that is adequate for the achievement, promotion, and maintenance of the economy's competitiveness.

NOTES

1. "How Canadian Companies Have Been Restructuring Themselves." [June, 1998].
2. Economic structural reforms are often generally referred to as *structural adjustment programs*.
3. In a typical agrarian country, the vast majority of the population are self-employed,

family farming units of the subsistence type. The sector provides means of livelihood for about 65 percent to 70 percent of the labor force and over 70 percent of the population, although self-employment in nonagricultural sectors is also very prominent. Detailed accounts of these structural diversities across the world can be found in Ezeala-Harrison (1996a).

4. Although a reduced exchange rate of the currency may lead to greater demand for exports and lower demand for imports, and thus make the economy more (macro) competitive, greater capital flight and outflow of resources would exert far more devastating negative effects such as higher unemployment, lower productivity, and lower income.

5. See the *appendix* to this chapter for explanation of the *function coefficient* criteria for determining the existence of economies of scale in a firm or industry.

6. It is important to maintain a clear distinction between micro level and macro level parameters in our study of international competitiveness, on the one hand, and micro level and macro level policies in the study of macroeconomic matters, on the other. To stress the important (but related) distinction, we must point out that microeconomic policies are economic stabilization policies that are centered on specific and particular (micro) sectors of the economy. *Micro policies* are long-term policy frames that shape and expand the growth and development paths through their focus on specific sectors, for example, a human resource development policy or an agricultural productivity enhancement policy. Macroeconomic policies, however, are monetary and fiscal policies designed to have macro effects on macroeconomic indicators such as the GDP, inflation, or employment levels. *Macro policies* provide short-term "dressing" of the economy to cause it to progress along the desired direction.

7. Institutional reforms bear strong micro and macro dimensions because although such reform activities as, say, *privatization* or *deregulation* are national level actions, their primary effects fall directly upon firms and industries and shape their productivity and costs.

8. Inflation may be deliberately used as a means of "forced saving" in raising the needed finances for investment. (For in-depth analysis on this, see Ezeala-Harrison [1996a]). Rising inflation would raise relative prices in favor of producers and firms, increasing profits and subsequently encouraging more investment. Moreover, a higher inflation rate, especially where it is not immediately built into the going nominal interest rate, confers cheaper funding to borrowers, who then might borrow more for investment and consumption, boosting aggregate demand. In addition, rising inflation would cause resource transfers from nonsavers to savers, leading to greater investment capacity and growth.

9. These classes of goods differ from the other two classes: (1) the *pure private goods* category such as those that individuals consume without any externality dimensions because they are excludable, and whose production does not involve any economies of scale or natural monopoly characteristics; and (2) the *pure public goods* category such as defence (the military), public security or civic law and order enforcement (peace officers or security guards), environmental cleanup and quality maintenance, or, say, street lighting. The consumption of these services are totally non-excludable, involving *free-rider* problems.

10. These peculiar conditions surrounding the demand and supply sides of public (merit) goods mean that they cannot be produced and traded like any other product (pure private goods) in the economy. In a competitive free-market driven economy, the profit

incentive provides the impetus for entrepreneurs to provide goods and services for distribution, as long as the market does not *fail* as an effective mechanism for the transactions between producers and consumers. For public goods, however, a market failure is encountered in their production (supply) and demand.

11. This practice is very popular because of its political appeal. It allows governments to demonstrate evidence of genuine commitments to the well-being of their citizens by subsidizing the provision of essential services to them.

6

Communication and Information Technology in International Competitiveness

This chapter considers the emerging role of *communication and information technology* (CIT) in a country's international competitiveness and growth prospects. The later part of the twentieth century ushered in a new electronic world where technologies, especially CIT, combine to strengthen or even change the competitiveness of businesses and all other aspects of economic life. It is a world where such facilities as the *internet*, within the new technology infrastructure, are being used as instruments of change in the way firms conduct business with each other, interact with their clients and customers, and carry out their regular operational activities, even on a global scale. In such a world, one important fact has become clear: many of the traditional ways of business conduct, processes, and organization have simply become inadequate, and have become obstacles to competitiveness within a globally competitive market environment.

The CIT revolution and the new technology infrastructure is a topic of considerable significance in the economic performance of nations today. The knowledge-based economy has arisen and increasingly become dominant in the world during the last quarter of the twentieth century. The label of *knowledge-based economy* is used to refer to the economic era in which there has been an unprecedented growth in the number of workers involved in the discovery and application of new knowledge, as well as the widespread ability to develop, store, rapidly retrieve, and apply new knowledge in everyday economic tasks and activities, using the available CIT. Since the mid-1950s, the world has massively developed the silicon-based computer chip, and applied it in the storage and transmission of information in computers and related information technology devices. This is the factor that profoundly changed the way in which knowledge is used for production and organization of economic and business activities in the modern world. It has changed the ways of exchanging information and business transactions.

It is important to stress that the so-called new economy is so named not because of the advent of CIT in itself, but rather because of the massive development, transmission, and application of *knowledge*, which CIT enables. In itself, CIT simply amounts to the ability to create and manipulate digital and computerized facilities; it can neither drive an economy nor be capable of advancing productivity or enhancing economic growth *per se*. The new economy hinges on the rapid application of knowledge and the use of CIT in implementing the application of knowledge to economic activities. Knowledge, at the individual level, involves insight, critical thinking, deep understanding, creativity, and education. At the social level, knowledge includes teamwork, collaboration, time management, and communication. The role of CIT in the rapid and universal application of these attributes to economic and business activities in the modern world is what the new economy is about.

GLOBALIZATION AND THE CONVERGENCE PHENOMENON

One of the most remarkable developments in the world during the second half of the twentieth century has been the greater internationalization of many economic activities that used to be regarded as typical domestic ventures. Inevitably, this development would result in increasing integration of economies in terms of trade, investment, monetary unions, currency affiliations, and economic agreements. This is the phenomenon of *globalization*. Bryan (1994, p. 2) gives a precise definition of globalization as "the increasing integration of economies through trade and investment flows, and the creation of production in numerous countries through foreign direct investment in order to be internationally competitive." Globalization is also defined by Harris and Watson (1993) simply as the internationalization of production, distribution, and marketing of goods and services.

A world economic scene, no longer kept apart in the traditional way by limitations imposed by transportation and communication needs, has emerged to define the state of affairs in today's international transaction relationships. The globalization phenomenon now embraces almost all aspects of national and international economic activities. Production and consumption activities are now easily carried out multinationally without being restricted by national origins of the goods and services involved. For example, as Bryan (1994) explains, a car assembled in one country (such as Canada) may contain parts made in another country (such as the United States, or Japan, or Mexico, or South Korea). Despite the fact that this is not a new development, globalization has made such relationships routine, resulting in different cost, efficiency, and operational implications for domestic firms and industries.

Demand and supply of many varieties of goods and services can now be transacted transnationally without the traditional barriers that inhibit the movements of persons and products across national boundaries. Consumers in one country, driven by the desire for more competitive prices, are now able to reach out deep into the markets of other countries and patronize the demand for products in those countries, to the detriment of domestic firms engaged in the market for those products. In the same way, foreign firms are able to dominate the market supply of products within a country. One of the most significant forces behind the globalization phenomenon is the CIT revolution.

Globalization actually means greater interconnection between the various regions of the globe; modern CIT is the principal agent in the globalization phenomenon. As a result, the world has, in effect, shrunk, interaction wise. We now inhabit a *global village* in which individuals, communities, and nations alike easily communicate and relate to each other irrespective of the physical distances between them. Information is passed and processed almost instantly through the various channels of facsimile transmission, (computer facilitated) internet linkages, and the expanded cellular telephone networks. For example, the use of the internet has provided firms with the means of taking competition to almost any level without being handicapped by any proximity advantages of their competitors. New capabilities being developed in communications and knowledge transfer, through widespread applications of such CIT facilities as electronic mail (e-mail) and electronic data interchange, have transformed the ways of seeking and creating markets, delivering products, and serving customers.

The Convergence Phenomenon

The most immediate effect of CIT on international trade is the *convergence phenomenon*. Convergence is the term given to the increasing close links between the economies of the world, whereby firms and industries of different countries regularly transact businesses in a *world market* not demarcated by national boundaries and trade barriers. The fact is that, even where individual countries have imposed trade barriers, the use of CIT would override the effectiveness of such barriers. The result is convergence—a factor that has characterized today's world economic environment. Convergence is the greater interconnection between the various regions of the globe, which, in effect, has brought the world together in terms of communication and information dissemination.[1]

The emergence of CIT into the global economic scene has important implications for a country's international competitiveness. For a typical firm, for example, internet access and use allows it to expand its sales horizon, reach and buy resources cheaper, and interact with customers and suppliers in easier and more cost-effective ways, besides the impact on productivity. This aspect of CIT involves virtually the least expensive way of doing business as the cost of access remains fairly unchanged irrespective of the volume of electronic transactions that are effected. Through rapid electronic information dissemination, firms could reduce their operational costs through lower paper use, postage, inventory management, and above all, timeliness in production and supplies. Rapid use of CIT greatly minimizes the time spent sorting through paper files, finding documents, physically arranging, storing, revising, retrieving, and exchanging them whenever required. By massively reducing these processing costs, the firm raises its employee efficiency and productivity.

Moreover, CIT widens the scope of products that firms can engage in transacting on across the globe. In particular, companies can extend their international transactions and trades into services, rather than just tangible goods. With the internet as a means of carrying out *electronic commerce*, there would be greater globalization of services into such products as health and medical care services, financial accounting services, legal services, banking, insurance, shipping, education, retailing, courier, entertainment, advertising, and so on. This means that geographical boundaries, and for that matter, customs control of the entry and exit of products across national borders, no longer constitute impediments to international trade. The CIT phenomenon has, indeed, caused a convergence phenomenon, especially as it changes the nature of global transactions in nontraditional tradeable products, namely, services. This bears significant implications for relative international competitiveness among countries. We now consider these issues in more in-depth focus.

THE CIT REVOLUTION

The onset of CIT can be likened to the changes that occurred in the world during the industrial revolution. At that time, workers had to learn new skills to fit a labor market demand that was quickly turning from rural agriculture-based and becoming urban manufacturing-based. The global economy became dominated by industrial manufacturing, with iron and steel, electricity, and rapid rail, highways, air, and sea transportation providing the infrastructure for the industrial economy. The agricultural sector simply turned from a *leading sector* role to a *supportive sector* role.

At the present time, the switch is from a manufacturing resource-based economy to a service knowledge-based economy. The industrial manufacturing and resource sector is now turning from a leading sector role (a role that it has occupied from the industrial revolution period until the 1980s) to a supportive sector role. The leading sector, now, is the service knowledge-based sector, driven by CIT, which, in turn, is driven by high-level education, in-depth knowledge of computer technology, flexibility of usage of communications networks, and manipulation of sophisticated communications equipments. This is all based on state-of-the-art electronic infrastructure. Thus, the present era is, in effect, the era of *CIT revolution*.[2]

CIT does not just consist of the programming, networking, analyzing, and administration of computers and communications facilities. It also deeply involves knowledge of the usage of computers and related equipments to design, improve, and enhance products, and to speed up production activities, with an overall view to reducing production and marketing costs. It is in this respect that it holds significant implications for international competitiveness of nations. Examples include the use of computers to analyze the diagnosis of patients in the hospital, or to lay out passages in books or magazines, or using facsimile transmissions to conclude important business transactions instantly across the Atlantic. Thus, in most modern societies, almost any job task requires some level of CIT involvement; and almost any industry requires some personnel with expertise in CIT user-analysis.

The *new (global) economy* ushered in by CIT is a *digital economy* driven by information carried and transmitted rapidly through computer networks and systems. It renders most sectors of economic production information-sensitive and knowledge-based; and products themselves are being increasingly produced with high knowledge content. Tapscott (1996, p. 10), sees the new economy as one in which innovation rather than access to resources, plant, and capital, is what would count most (toward the relative competitiveness of firms). This has even affected who a firm's real potential competitors would be. In the CIT-based environment, competition comes from every source.

The key aspects of CIT that have revolutionized the conduct of business operations include the applications of *multimedia* and *call center* facilities. Simply defined, multimedia involves making traditional technology interactive through digitizing it. In this way, multimedia can be used in all manner of businesses, including manufacturing, marketing, finance, education, entertainment, health services, and administration. The call center is a special extension of multimedia. Call center application is used for such purposes as the creation and maintenance of business contacts, lead generation, and research and consultancy developments.

The CIT factor would greatly affect international competitiveness at both the micro and macro levels of competitiveness. At the micro level, the application of CIT would influence individual factor productivity as well as total factor productivity. It would influence production costs as it affects the efficiency of resource utilization. At the macro level of competitiveness, the application of CIT would affect the degree of economic liberalization within an economy; CIT usage has the ability to limit the effectiveness of such restrictive instruments as exchange rate controls and trade barriers.

These various issues demand consideration in greater detail as their potential impacts on economic growth appear to be significant. The CIT phenomenon is one of the most unique characteristics of the so-called new economy of the twenty-first century. What CIT means for firms and industries of any country in terms of productivity, competitiveness, growth, and expansion in today's new global economic and business scene are now examined in greater detail.

CIT, CONVERGENCE, AND COMPETITIVENESS

Some recent research has stressed that information technology has become one of the key determinants of competitiveness and growth of firms and industries (and economies). This is because the means of achieving competitiveness in the modern world has changed from the traditional comparative advantage acquired from natural resource endowment to the comparative advantage acquired through the application of knowledge and modern CIT (see Oshikoya and Hussain, 1998).

The convergence phenomenon has been an immediate outcome of the coming of the CIT era. Physical distance no longer poses major constraints on the ability of firms and industries to produce and market products across international boundaries. Through CIT, economies are now linked closer in terms of their day-to-day transactions. In fact, convergence extends to both production (supply) and distribution and marketing (demand) activities of firms and industries across countries.

On the supply side, convergence would tend to make the mobility of resources, especially labor and capital, almost limitless. Therefore, a country with a relatively high cost of labor, say, would experience a weaker position in global labor market transactions, and moreover, would have its products being produced at relatively higher costs. The country would thus be rendered less internationally competitive, and this would be as a direct result of the convergence phenomenon.

On the demand side, a firm could easily lose market shares to its international competitors simply because consumers are able to reach out and establish contacts with those competitors for better deals. As a result, countries are more open and vulnerable to greater import penetration by foreign competitors. In such a case, the survival of a country's firms and industries would depend on their relative competitiveness. This is a situation that has been created by the CIT revolution, and a nation's economic growth and development would largely depend on it.

CIT and Micro Level Competitiveness

The most important effect of CIT on competitiveness exist at the micro level competitiveness stage. At this level, the key parameters are those of productivity, and the application of modern CIT can only massively enhance productivity in any sector of the economy.

To enhance competitiveness, the need for greater efficiencies and improved service in a modern world requires that the firm's work force be empowered with knowledge. The success of firms and enterprises would depend on the degree to which their workers are able to access and effectively apply knowledge and information. The various ways in which this process would enhance productivity and cost efficiency of firms are as follows.

CIT and Competitiveness in Production Process

Prior to the onset of CIT, important aspects of daily production tasks within the firm, such as a purchase requisition, often involved the system of lengthy and time-consuming multiple handling and administrative stages. For example, a common intermediate input requisition order would have the request taken to a supervisor for approval, who would then take it to a district manager. It would then be sent to a director from where it might then be forwarded to the appropriate purchasing department. This process could take anywhere from six to ten levels of approval, and up to thirty days to go through before the order is placed. In such a system, employees waste time tracking requisitions and data, with detrimental effect on the quality and timeliness of work. However, with CIT, purchase requisitions could be initialed and authorized on-line and forwarded by electronic mail (e-mail) to the appropriate purchasing personnel, who would then issue the order and *fax* it to the supplier.

This process frees staff time, saves resource costs, and quickens production time. CIT would enable staff to quickly check on the status of any order and monitor their budget and cost data on-line. Clerical workers who previously spent much of their time manually processing paperwork can now achieve greater output by use of an on-line facility to effect major high-volume transactions and records, involving less time. Productivity is therefore much higher. This is more so as their clerical job activities are effectively changed to more like researching purchasing strategies and solutions.

Recent research indicates that the application of CIT has caused cycle times on purchase orders for a typical firm to reduce from as many as ten days to between one and three days.[3] Where for a typical firm it was necessary to match about 110,000 invoices manually during one cycle, the use of CIT has cut that number to about 5,000. And while 75 percent of requisitions were previously queried or returned because of insufficient information, the onset of CIT has reduced such to 10 percent. CIT has reduced the cycle times for producing cheques in large firms from 2 weeks to just one day; this particular outcome allows the firm to enjoy cost-saving discount purchase advantages, as well as other supplier discount offers.

With the deployment of integrated enterprise software, production-cycle times are reported to have been reduced by 30 percent, delivery times cut by 40 percent, and inventory turnover increased by 250 percent. All these have increased effective production capacity in the average firm, leading to the doubling of sales without any increase in management staffing and costs.

Streamlining the various processes involved in the firm's transactions would allow workers to shift their attention to other higher value-added activities for greater overall productivity. For example, a recent research study reveals that, of the excess of $250 billion (U.S.) spent by U.S. companies on the purchase of "indirect" (intermediate) products—presumably these include such items as regular office supplies, stationary, and furniture—an average of $150 is spent to process the purchase of each item regardless of its dollar value.[4] This source also reports that a 1996 survey of Canadian computer distributors by market researcher International Data Corporation (IDC) Canada, showed a very significant cost differential between manual orders (involving telephone or fax interfacing with a sales representative) and on-line orders (involving interfacing electronically using *World Wide Web* or dial-up services). For whereas the average cost for manually processed orders was $35 per transaction, that of on-line ordering was $7 per transaction. This kind of cost can be eliminated through the use of CIT: products could be located and requests submitted electronically; the firm could connect directly to the supplier and be able to receive real-time product availability and pricing, and ensure the buying of the right types and quantities of products as required. This offers significant cost-savings and overall superior purchasing system.

CIT and Competitiveness in Team Effectiveness

The ability for faster communications would not only quicken production processes but would also facilitate management and administrative procedures as it reduces constraining complexities of management. In this particular regard, Davenport (1997) states that information technology can facilitate organizational change by allowing new methods of sharing information, as well as leading to the growth of partly autonomous work teams that are accountable for their own projects and also for a knowledge of everyone else's. This fosters the ability to tightly integrate a firm's core processes and link departments, divisions, and operational units.

With modern CIT, decision-making and transmission of commands, as well as consultation and team-functions, are no longer hampered by spacial or absentee constraints. According to Davenport (1997), the information-based organization is able to coordinate the efforts of specialized knowledge workers whose knowledge of particular areas is far superior to that of senior management. The huge productivity potential of this situation had been recognized by Beck (1992, p. 144) who noted that the development of work teams where the roles of bosses and employees become blurred (apparently within a knowledge-based work setting), would eventually give rise to a management and accounting revolution. In these circumstances, it is clear that productivity would be enhanced, and production costs would be lower.

Efficient operation demands that the firm employs a system that would provide a single point of data (information) entry along with the ability to share the data universally across all its subsidiaries and units. This would reduce the amount of data being duplicated, and thus eliminate costly (and inefficient) wasteful duplication. In the absence of CIT, traditional methods had several co-workers in separate departments of the firm maintaining the same data worksheets because, for logistic reasons, they were unable to share their data worksheets. This led to costly duplication and storage.

CIT enables such a large enterprise to deploy software modules for such tasks as financial accounting, sales, distribution, materials management, production planning, quality management, and human resources. The firm could operate a single, unified, and automated software system that ensures the integrity, accuracy, and reliability of information throughout all its operating units, linking the production, supply, and delivery of all product chains. In financial accounting, say, CIT features may be used to notify the credit department if a customer order places such a customer beyond the limits imposed by an outstanding debt. In sales, CIT enables the marketing department to have the advantage of carrying out profitability calculations at any time and as often as necessary, rather than waiting for traditional weekly or forthnightly reports. Such advantages allow for more pricing flexibility and quicker pricing decisions necessary for procurement of larger market shares and greater competitiveness for the firm's products.

In a large-scale firm, often the size and complexities of coordination lead to impairment of certain critical factors that affect competitiveness, namely, timeliness and efficiency of implementation of operational decisions. CIT offers the ability to overcome such a constraint. By applying it, the firm could generate reports that can be easily broken down by, say, geographic area or customer base, in order to foster more speedy handling for meeting the challenges of an ongoing competitive and changing marketplace.

CIT and Competitiveness in Product Quality

Application of CIT within the knowledge-based production environment results in extraordinarily rapid changes in product quality and design, and thus leads to the frequent introduction of new products inevitably made possible through this new phenomenon. This would involve cost savings that mean lower product prices; it would improve service quality and market penetration.

For instance, to achieve and maintain relative competitiveness, a firm must meet the challenges of managing and delivering a product that has to reach the marketplace promptly (and, fresh, in many cases). The firm must also be able to track changing world (and regional) prices for various competing brands of its product. It must also be able to administer its processing and distribution facilities (which may be scattered across wide spatial jurisdictions or located abroad), and maintain regular monitoring of its staff.[5]

In the economics sub-discipline of industrial organization we learn that one of the means by which firms try to obtain and maintain market share leverages for their products is *brand naming*. Using brand-naming, firms differentiate their products from those of their competitors, and promote them as unique, superior, and outstanding. A brand is something that exists in the minds of consumers, which they may or may not translate into action in their demand and purchasing profiles.[6] Brands were established as a means of preserving monopoly power over the product; and as such, branding works effectively through mass communication using the one-way media of the preceding generation, namely, the broadcast media (radio and television) and the print media (newspapers, fliers, posters, and bill boards).[7] The one-way media allows the marketers to be able to convince consumers through sustained advertising urging them to simply patronize the brand, such as "Have you driven a Ford lately" (*informative advertising*), or "Oh, what a feeling, Toyota," or "Things go better with Coke" (*persuasive advertising*).

However, it now appears that this procedure and the entire concept of *brand* has come under pressure as a result of CIT. The rise of digital media has changed the older technologies that used publishing, television, and radio to communicate; it has changed the approach that marketers use by moving them away from focusing on brand image and brand thinking, toward thinking about establishing (interactive) relationships with customers. The internet offers new opportunities for firms to advance the true quality and worth of their products through the creation of more trustworthy ties between the firms and their customers. This is to say that the rise of CIT has diminished the power of the (one-way) mass media—the power and leverage of the firm—and replaced it with the power of interactive media: the power and leverage of the consumer. Therefore, brand-name loyalties will now be based on substantive worth rather than on mere imagery and/or expectations that may or may not be met.

For instance, in the past some detergent brand could use the one-way media to claim that it "washes whiter than all," and there would be no means to refute such a claim in case it turned out to be less than valid. With interactive media, however, a consumer could find out (through interacting with others) whether or not the claim is valid. A consumer could go on the internet to examine other evaluations of that detergent, or participate in discussion groups to determine which brand of detergent actually "washes whiter than all."

Firms have realized that the "Net Generation" of the twenty-first century constitute a somewhat different type of consumers, with greater disposable income than the preceding baby-boomers generation. The internet empowers the present generation with better access to comparative product information. They are accustomed to a highly flexible consumer market environment in which they are able to exercise wide range of options in product choices. The internet enables consumers to be able to "try out" products beforehand without any purchasing commitments, and to "change their minds" more often in reaching their purchasing and demand decisions. Firms will have to give products and services away for such "trial" purposes, and will need to meet up the cost of this in some way.

In this environment, the development of brand-loyalties, which has been a way of attaining relative competitiveness, can no longer guarantee any significant market share to any firm's product brand. Firms and consumers become each other's software agents; agents are able to select everything from cookies to cars on the internet through which business transactions could be initiated, contracted, and concluded, in a *brand blind* setting. Firms are able to market products, and consumers are able to make purchases, on-line. The internet has become a new medium for not only sales but also after-sales obligations such as maintenance support, servicing, and product warranties.

This business scenario raises competition to a different level—the high-tech or CIT level of marketing competition. Network-based information transmission enabled through CIT has succeeded in bringing value and real benefits to the forefront of business transactions in ways that were totally unknown during the past generations. Don Tapscott[8] cites an example where grocery shoppers using the Peapod Inc. Network, based in Evanston, Illinois, could ask for products in a certain category to be sorted by criteria such as calorie count or nutritional value; and where the most frequently used sorting criteria is cost, followed by fat content. In this way, determining the healthiest peanut butter, say, could take only seconds, and the mass marketing of Kraft may have little impact on the purchasing decisions of consumers. Good brands would correspond more closely to good products. This uncontrolled access to information allows for greater free market and greater competition albeit elevated to some different heights. For in this scene, products that could not "differentiate" themselves in value and benefits quickly become simply "commodities" that are not associated with some level of special attributes.

The pace of the CIT revolution indicates that the future has room for the emergence of more sophisticated, smarter, software on the horizon, which will extend the weakening of brand-naming and brand loyalties. Researchers believe that consumers may begin to trust their software "agents" rather than trusting the brand and its maker; the agents being a kind of software that gets to know its users, their tastes and preferences, and their styles and choices (Tapscott, 1996). For example, one can surf the internet searching for requested data such as finding the sharpest tasting chocolate bar, assessing the most exciting new movie based on preferences and trusted opinions, or trying on different sizes and types of blue jeans. In most of such cases, trusting one's agent would be similar to trusting one's own experience.

CIT and Competitiveness in Customer Service

Jerre Stead, the former head of AT&T Global Information Solutions is noted to have stated that the collection, dissemination, and processing of customer information has become an essential prerequisite of any modern retailing operation.[9] Thus, CIT does not only help to promote the retail strategy but also has become the very strategy itself. In order to operate a competitive customer service needed for the ongoing state of competitiveness, a firm must effectively monitor its product inventory, distribution, sales tracking, and order fulfillment. This is to ensure that customers receive rapid response times in product and service deliveries. Employees of the firm would need to be constantly seeking, exchanging, and reconciling information needed to effectively maintain a level of leverage on customer satisfaction. This is more so as firms recognize that customers have found themselves in extremely dynamic markets, necessitating the continuous rescheduling of production supplies by firms. Achieving a competitive advantage in a global industry means reacting quickly and accurately to marketplace demand variations.

On-line reporting capabilities would reduce the task of compiling marketing and sales information to a matter of minutes (rather than several days or weeks), thereby improving customer/client response time span. This increases the effectiveness of order fulfillment and enhanced decision making, important and crucial parameters upon which maintenance of the firm's competitiveness hinges.

Application of CIT enables the firm to be capable of launching new products with the needed information background that would be appropriate for monitoring the feasibility of the pre- and post-launch (market) demand conditions. Increasingly more and more companies appear to be adopting mobile and network communications as a central part of their competitiveness strategy. Apparently, this is because they have come to recognize that survival in the competitive marketplace requires that efficient and cost-effective customer service be made the leading strategic weapon. A firm could employ CIT for its consumers anywhere in the world to use their standard Web browser to access its system to reach the requisite information and transact real-time business. This reduces (or even eliminates) advertising costs, while having the capacity of reaching a greater audience.

Maintaining ongoing competitiveness compels the modern firm to follow a *demand-pull* production scheduling. That is, a firm would follow the production schedule of quickly manufacturing and delivering products on the basis of actual customer orders, rather than basing production scheduling on periodic forecasts (that may be right or wrong) and hoping that such forecasts match market demand. Demand-pull production scheduling saves on unnecessary inventory buildup and costly maintenance.

Through CIT, the growth of *on-line commerce* has allowed retailers of products ranging from stocks and cars to colognes, in many countries, to be able to entice customers over the internet and the World Wide Web (WWW). Companies that are capable of raising profits in this way would gain enormous competitive advantage. Projections by the market researcher International Data Corporation indicate that internet commerce will rise to about $223 billion (U.S.) by the year 2001 worldwide, with the United States being the primary market (accounting for more than two-thirds of the world market). The Asia-Pacific region (excluding Japan) is set to experience about 179 percent annual growth in internet commerce through the year 2001. These situations will exert phenomenal influence on the relative international competitiveness of the regions concerned. This is because the medium represents a cost effective channel of product marketing and sales. On-line commerce is slated to be an important means for firms to transact business among themselves, and to conduct trade within the market, much cheaper than before. Those that fail to keep up with this new means of competition could hardly maintain relative competitiveness in the present new age of CIT.

CIT and Macro Level Competitiveness

At the national level, CIT plays a major role in the process and speed of innovation and improvements that companies need in order to attain relative advantages among their global competitors. A country must provide and maintain a state-of-the-art electronic infrastructure to enable its firms and industries to succeed in the CIT based global market economy. Porter (1990a, p. 74) noted that where companies only carry out innovations that respond (solely) to the circumstances of the domestic market, the international competitiveness of such a country could actually be retarded, apparently because the attention of firms in that country would be diverted from potentially very attractive global markets. But a nation's companies must be capable of accessing pertinent information that may either not yet have been available to competitors or that competitors may not have realized that they needed and therefore have not sought. The extent to which such information is important to the realization of macro level competitiveness may be analyzed by examining the various parameters of macro level competitiveness.

Macro level competitiveness parameters include general economic liberalization, availability of infrastructure, and flexibility of supportive institutional structures in the country. For economic liberalization, CIT would be crucial for maintaining an appropriate level of the country's currency exchange rate. This is especially essential in today's volatile world securities and money markets whose outcomes largely dictate the pace of the flow of foreign investment across the various countries of the world. In international money and securities market activities, timing is crucial. The application of modern CIT would be apt to enable a country to detect and effect the proper and timely response required to manage its currency exchange rate. By so doing, the country would achieve competitiveness in the attraction of foreign investment—an area that is critical for economic growth, and which has become very competitive in the international market.

The availability of infrastructure in itself relates to the development of modern CIT in an economy. CIT is central to the growth of such major sectors as banking, insurance, transportation, and tourism. These sectors have wide-ranging effects upon the state of general economic activity within an economy. To the extent that they are directly impacted upon by the degree of application or lack of application of modern CIT, it is apparent that the level of CIT holds a key determining influence on a country's international competitiveness.

Other factors that affect macro level competitiveness include availability of pertinent market and trade information such as awareness of producers, exporters, and consumers of each other's products, inventory capacity, shipping and handling frequencies, and delivery patterns. These activities used to be carried out traditionally through Trade Fairs, exhibitions, trade promotions, and establishment of product display locations. However, the use of CIT facilitates these activities of trade promotion. Through the internet, on-line information about market conditions, customs and excise regulations, and distribution network conditions, could easily be reached. Computer transmission of contacts could be used to cut out delays in product delivery. All these mean that business transactions within the economy are carried out with less friction. Thus, the economy becomes more competitive at the macro level.

NOTES

1. It is important to note the clear distinction between the convergence phenomenon, as expounded here, and a paradigm that has been traditionally referred to as the "convergence hypothesis" (see Bryan, 1994, p. 208). The convergence hypothesis refers to the process whereby low income countries (with limited capital resources) tend to have relatively higher marginal productivity of capital (than richer countries that have abundant capital resources), such that any new investment in the capital-deficient country would therefore result in relatively higher increases in output. The process, over time, could enable the poorer country to be able to "catch up" or "converge" with the richer country.

2. The CIT age necessarily created a remarkable demand for highly educated workers, not only to advance and manage the technologies themselves, but also to serve as experts in the design, financing, production, and marketing of the new products (goods and services) that the technologies make available (Davenport, 1997; Drucker, 1988).

3. Report on: Ericsson Communications Canada, *Globe and Mail*, July 17, 1997.

4. Research study by Cambridge research firm, Giga Information Group, reported under the caption: "Evolving Information Highway Bracing for Business Boom," *Globe and Mail*, July 17, 1997, p. D7.

5. A good example of such a firm is the Canadian conglomerate, George Weston Ltd., which has subsidiaries operating domestically and internationally, selling their products worldwide. Some of their operations include fish-canning plants in Canada, operations in Australia and the Solomon Islands, a share of a fishing fleet and cannery in the Philippines, and tuna-processing facilities in Ecuador.

6. It is important to note that whereas the brand refers to product differentiation from the consumer's point of view (the demand side), the trademark refers to product differentiation from the producer's (firm's) point of view (the supply side). A trademark is the legal "right" owned by the firm for purposes of pursuing monopoly power over the particular differentiated product.

7. We refer to the broadcast and print media as one-way media because, unlike the CIT media, they do not involve any interactive contacts. Consumers simply remain at the receiving end of whatever the firm dishes out to them through these media, without the means of reacting to such "messages."

8. *Globe and Mail*: Toronto, February 20, 1998.

9. Tapscott (1996, p. 25).

7

International Competitiveness and National Trade Policies

This chapter deals with the adoption of various systems of *national trade policies* by countries, and its implications for international competitiveness. Most countries now devise and implement certain *strategic* trade policies as a means of improving their economies' trade performances and enhancing their economic growths. However, the successful operation of any particular trade policy in an economy may be one thing, but the feasibility of such a policy in enabling the country to achieve and maintain international competitiveness may be another. In this chapter we analyze the strategic trade theory and examine its implications for the adoption of inner- and outer-orientation trade strategies, and consider how a country's international competitiveness may be affected by these strategies.

As world international trade expanded over the decades, countries realized that free trade brought with it certain dangers and problems. Traditionally, such problems have been identified to include dumping, infant-industry survival, unequal factor prices, varieties of product qualities and standards across countries, health and environmental concerns, and the like. Upon recognition of these problems, most countries tend to adopt certain trade policies aimed at controlling the effects of these situations within their economies. Ordinarily, a country would tend to adopt what is referred to as an *industrial trade policy*, aimed at managing the composition and direction of its international trade to the benefit if its national economy. Under a nation's industrial trade policy, its government implements certain rules and regulations, or even laws, designed to help domestic firms operate at lower costs. Export-producing firms are helped and encouraged through a range of measures such as subsidy grants, tax concessions, price supports, or free-interest loans.

The adoption of national trade policies arises not only because of the need to counter some of the adverse effects of free trade. They are adopted also for strategic, ideological, and political reasons. For example, the (structuralist) perception that there is a perpetual terms of trade imbalance maintained against the developing countries in a dualistic (center-periphery) world economic (dis)order has led to the adoption of import substitution policies across the developing countries. Likewise, most developed countries of the OECD group tend to adopt protectionist measures as a means to preserve their domestic markets for their home industries.

In light of these policies, one may argue that free trade policies (driven by comparative and competitive advantage motivations) are still superior to alternative (presumably interventionist) trade policies. The role of international competitiveness within alternative policies of inner orientation (import substitution), outer orientation (export promotion), and inner-outer orientation (trade-bloc regional integration) are examined. We discuss the potentials of these policies with a view, especially, to showing whether or not they are consistent with the pursuit of international competitiveness.

STRATEGIC TRADE POLICY AND INTERNATIONAL COMPETITIVENESS

Strategic trade policy implies how a country could engineer its economy to achieve international competitiveness with a view to emerging, and remaining, as a "dominant firm" in the world market environment.[1] Ordinarily, it often involves government intervention with a view to improving the competitiveness and overall productive conditions for domestic firms—conditions that would confer significant market leverages to the country's domestic producers. The policy is mostly applicable in markets in which *economies of scale* are present and significant. Possible and common strategic trade policy initiatives include granting of direct or indirect **subsidies** to a country's domestic firms (which enables them to produce and market their output at lower operational costs), or attracting more high-tech firms through, say, relaxation of environmental standards (see chapter 8); the high-tech firms confer high levels of technological (knowledge) spill-overs to others in the economy (see Krugman, 1986), enabling the economy to experience higher productivity.

Strategic trade policy appears to have become the driving force behind much of the international trade orientations that are increasingly taken by nations in the new world economic (dis)order of the twenty-first century. As a means of sustaining their gains from trade in the competitive scenario of the strategic trade relationship, a country must achieve and maintain relative international competitiveness. Porter (1987, 1990a, 1990b), raised the issue of international competitiveness far beyond the mere acquisition of relative favorable trade performance in the balance of national trade and payments positions. He pointed to the growing tendency among governments of countries to respond to the pressures being put upon them by their domestic companies to take steps to support some particular firms and industries within them. This has led to the adoption of various policies such as exchange rate management, trade treaties, antitrust relaxations, environmental compromises, and the like, all designed to promote national competitiveness. Porter emphasized the need for a country to achieve a strong relative position in playing the "strategic" trade game, and the need to succeed in being able to exact high levels of "gains from trade" by so doing, relative to its trading partners in the global market scene.[2]

In effect, strategic trade policy derives from application of the so-called New Trade Theory (see chapter 1) and is increasingly being adopted as a seemingly fanciful trade policy objective among countries, in the so-called new world economic order. Strategic trade initiatives are advanced through manipulation of a nation's productivity, designed to establish a strong international competitiveness position relative to its trading partners. Through its creation and maintenance of greater competitiveness, the country would capture and maintain higher market shares for its products in the world market, and thence achieve the benefits of economic growth within itself.

Apparently, the strategic trade policy is sustained through specialization in the production of those goods and services in which the country's industries are more productive relative to international competitors. This enables the country's industries to gain international *competitive advantage* relative to its competitors; the gains of which would sustain competitiveness. The increasingly wide adoption of this policy is attributed to the wide acceptance accorded to its preceding New Growth Theory, which, apparently, legitimized this New Trade Theory. The New Growth Theory stresses the role of technological progress and its determinants, plus the externalities that the development and application of new knowledge confers, as explicit variables that determine the pace of economic growth of a country.

Based on the New Growth Theory, strategic trade policy calls for more investment in human capital (knowledge) and technology, as well as in other capital resources, as a way of achieving higher competitiveness. It sees the world market as an oligopolistic one in which a country's export represents just a small proportion within a differentiated market where countries (firms) specialize in marketing their most productive goods and services. Thus, there are apt to be economies of scale, or massive technological leadership advantages, for firms in any country, which could result in those firms emerging as world monopolists in the world market.

The overriding objective in strategic trade policy would be to give domestic firms the option of technologies to be able to copy the leading firms and emerge as competitive rivals in the world market. The scenario amounts to the standard case of oligopolistic rivals engaged in strategic game settings in the world market stage, in which case the relative gains from trade accruing to a country would depend more on the successes of the trade "strategies" adopted, rather than comparative advantage (which depends on competitiveness). In this world market setting, the number of competitors is relatively small, and each competitor realizes that any significant move that it makes is likely to elicit countering moves by its rivals.

The question is: how competitive are strategic trade policies? It appears that only long-term strategic trade policies—those designed to enhance knowledge and technology—are clearly competitive. But short-term strategic trade policies such as those mentioned above (regarding granting subsidies to domestic firms or overlooking environmental degradation) defeat the very essence of competitiveness. They impair an economy's macro level competitiveness because they restrict trade, and are apt to provoke retaliation from trading partners.

Moreover, studies by Baldwin (1992) indicate that often the gains from strategic trade policies are relatively small compared to the potential gains from trade carried under the traditional banner. Therefore, it is clear that, although it may seem attractive as a way of expanding a country's potential gains from international trade, especially in the short run, strategic trade policy would tend to result in uncompetitive outcomes. It does not seem to be an effective means of promoting international competitiveness of a nation.

COMPETITIVENESS AND INNER-ORIENTATION TRADE POLICY

The inner-orientation trade policy refers to the policy of promoting and expanding industrialization and trade through the inward channels of the domestic economy. This policy is not new. Traditionally, it derives from the trade and development policy of import-substitution industrialization (ISI). The ISI strategy involves the establishment of industries that produce consumer goods in substitution of imports whose *demand threshold* would have been created earlier through the importation of such finished goods. The rationale is simply to promote the domestic production of import-competing products as a means of achieving rapid industrialization.[3]

After the country opens its doors through importation (after having thereby created a sufficient level of domestic demand threshold for the products), it then establishes the import-substituting (producing) industries, and places tariffs on the imported products. The case for protection of the domestic industries is then supported by the traditional infant-industry argument.[4]

Experiences with the ISI strategy have been marked by failures and disappointments, especially in most developing countries where they had been vigorously pursued. The main factors that work against the ISI include foreign exchange constraints, excessive dependence on foreign sources for resources (raw materials, management expertise, skilled labor, finance, etc.), and economic and technical inefficiencies in operation of the ISI industries. Generally, the tradition of protecting ISI industries by the use of tariffs results in the emergence of inefficient monopoly industries, burdening the economy with massive misallocation of resources and restricted market capacity growth.

The achievement of international competitiveness at the micro level—enhanced productivity and quality and optimal efficiency resource utilization—would clearly be at odds with an inner-orientation trade policy. This is because the country's products would have greater import-competing ability with foreign products in the domestic market. But at the same time, increased output that results from greater efficiency would need to be supported by export markets where they would again have high export-competing ability. Therefore, adoption of inner-orientation policies that would almost certainly attract retaliation from trading partners would not be helpful to the economy.

At the macro level, an inner-oriented trade policy defeats the very idea of trade liberalization. First, as tariffs are imposed and import prices rise, import-competing domestic industries slacken their drive toward greater efficiency of operation. Second, following an adoption of a fixed exchange rate regime, terms of trade distortions occur and exports/imports volumes become erratic. Hence, an inner-oriented trade policy works against a country's international competitiveness endeavors and would retard industrialization and economic growth.

In effect, the ISI policy is tantamount to disguised protectionism and represents an impediment to competitiveness. A domestic firm must be exposed to import competition to enable it to develop the necessary comparative advantage required for it to be able to catch up with the rest of the world. Protected industries inherently operate inefficiently, although they might make short-term profits because of the artificially high price. Therefore, the economy suffers massively, not only in terms of long-term competitiveness but also as potential gains from trade are lost to it. That is, the economy would be engaging in a line of production in which it is *relatively too expensive* for it to be producing goods. The (import-substituting)industries would be operating at great expense to the country. For example, Canada, say, would be producing coffee or bananas at very great expense relative to wheat, if it moves to construct hot-houses for growing bananas or coffee. Similarly, Brazil could create large acreages of fields by clearing rain forests and flattening hills, in order to grow wheat, but that would be at great expense. And the outcome of such moves would be that the unit prices of bananas or coffee in Canada, and wheat in Brazil, would be prohibitively high; it would be cheaper and economically wise for Canada to buy (import) bananas and coffee (from Brazil) than to produce them in Canada; and it would be more economical for Brazil to import wheat from Canada. In a free-market competitive world, coffee-producing firms in Canada or wheat-producing firms in Brazil cannot compete with imports of these products in their domestic markets or in the world market. Their countries' states of competitiveness are thus severely damaged.

The examples of coffee and wheat used here relate to cases where the regions are naturally suited to the production of these goods (wheat in temperate flat lands and coffee or bananas in tropical rain forests). However, for trading in manufactured goods or services for which the products could be produced anywhere, it may seem that the adoption of ISI would not impair competitiveness. The question, though, is whether or not the country has comparative advantage in the production of the good or service. And included in the requirements for comparative advantage are the availability of investment, capital resources, technical skill, managerial capacity, the labor force, as well as the raw material needs. Apparently, many countries (especially developing countries) lack the requirements for comparative advantage in manufactured goods and traded services. But because of the need to "achieve self-reliance and maintain national pride," they, nevertheless, tend to adopt the ISI policy. Unfortunately, such a move only defeats its prospects for competitiveness and ultimately the overall purpose of economic growth.

It appears that the best national trade policy for a country, especially during the current high communication and information technology period of the twenty-first century (see chapter 6), is the policy of open and unrestricted international trade based on the achievement and maintenance of national competitiveness. And this is irrespective of whether it is a developing country or a developed country. For in either case, this policy must be carried by the country's ability to increase its productive resource base and potential such as capital availability, the availability of the appropriate mix of labor force and technical skill, entrepreneurial and managerial know-how, and technological application. An inner-orientation trade policy is self-defeating if not self-destructive, on both technical and strategic grounds.

COMPETITIVENESS AND OUTER-ORIENTATION TRADE POLICY

The outer-orientation trade policy emphasizes a slant toward "export substitution," involving the dual approaches of export promotion and export-led growth. This is a policy of pushing the economy toward more international trade specialization, whereby economic activity is more concentrated toward the export sector. It includes a strategy of emphasizing exportation of nontraditional products involving processed semi-finished and finished manufactured goods. This would be in addition to the economy's traditional export products.

Export orientation would expose domestic firms to market competition in the international (world) market. This fits them better for greater efficiency of operation and sustainability. Firms are given greater incentives for expansion of their capacities, and realization of economies of scale. Increased specialization results in improved technology and expanded resources because the export sector receives much greater incentive and opportunity to expand greatly.

Greater competitiveness at the micro level stands as the most critical basis for an outer-oriented approach. Relatively lower priced and higher quality products would ensure greater market shares for the country's firms. In this connection, it must be stressed that a country's outer-oriented trade policy need not be pursued in the spirit of traditional strategic trade policy based on mercantilist principles.[5] But as we make this point, it is important to remember that export-led growth could hurt a country, especially if that country has a large market share in the world export market—for example Chile (copper exports), Saudi Arabia (crude petroleum oil exports), South Africa (diamond exports), or Colombia (coffee exports). As the country achieves greater export growth, the expanding supply of the product in the world market results in lowering the price of the export product, amounting to falling terms of trade for the country. The country then faces a worse-off situation from the export growth and trade. Such an outcome is termed *immiserizing growth*.

However, the problem of immiserizing growth is not actually a drawback to a competitiveness policy sought through export-led growth. Potentially falling terms of trade would hurt an economy only if the exporting firms fail to operate at *minimum unit costs* of production. This means that the firms fail to achieve micro level competitiveness. For if exporting firms are able to produce and market their products at minimum unit costs, then falling prices cannot hurt their profitability (for prices cannot possibly fall below minimum unit production cost in a competitive market). Therefore, still, export-led growth policy based on the efficient operation of firms would enhance competitiveness despite the potential problem of the *immiserizing growth syndrome*.

Surely, international competition in world export markets would be fierce and would almost certainly give rise to commercial rivalries. However, such rivalries would prove to be healthy or even desirable toward fostering greater competitiveness at the micro level for each trading country. This is because each country would realize that the survival of its exports in such circumstances would depend solely on its products price/quality mix relative to others'. And it should be noted that macro level parameters should be constant in this regard to avoid actions that would result in "trade wars."

COMPETITIVENESS AND INNER-OUTER ORIENTATION

By *inner-outer orientation* is meant the combination of measures to promote international trade mixed with efforts at economic integration. The search for a larger export market led to formations of the so-called free-trade areas and regional trading blocs among trading nations. Countries did awaken to the need to form free-trade alliances with their neighbors so as to take full advantage of what free trade could offer.

Economic integration enables countries to reduce or abolish all trade barriers among them. This could range from the loosest form of integration (such as a mere preferential trade agreement), to a deeper form (such as a completely free-trade area), or a customs union, a common market, an economic union, and a much complete form of total economic and monetary union.

The formation of regional economic blocs is widely regarded as a potential threat to further expansion and development of multilateral and liberalized world trade. This is more so as the global economy increasingly polarizes around regional economic interests built mainly around the European Union (EU), the United States, and Japan. Regional integrationism is on the rise worldwide, especially among the developed countries, and it is fueled by the rise of concentrated (narrow) interests of groups who perceive that they would lose out if free trade were allowed to run its course. Such groups include owners and workers of various industries such as textiles, steel mills, automobiles, chemicals, or even agricultural produce. These *pressure groups* lobby their political leaders to enact strict protectionist laws to guard their respective industries against foreign competition.

Competitiveness within Regional Trade Blocs

Several forms of trade blocs among nations exist. While some involve very mild trading arrangements, others extend to wider economic and even political cooperation. The various forms of trading blocs (already discussed in chapter 1) are as follows.

1. Preferential Trade Agreement (PTA): The PTA is an arrangement among countries, whereby members adopt reduced tariff rates and extend preferential treatments to the imports of each other. This seems to be the loosest form of integration.
2. Free-Trade Area (FTA): This is the form of agreement that removes trade protectionist barriers among the member countries, while allowing each country to retain these barriers against nonmembers.
3. Customs Union: In addition to all the provisions of the FTA, the Customs Union stipulates that member countries retain common trade barriers against nonmembers.
4. Common Market: A Common Market provides for a much more involved form of integration. In addition to the provisions of the Customs Union, a Common Market involves the free movement of productive resources (such as capital and labor) between each other's economies.
5. Economic Union: The Economic Union is a much more complete and extensive form of economic integration. It not only provides for all the above conditions but also goes further in integrating the monetary systems of member countries. The Economic Union, basically, unites member countries toward the formation of a political union.

One of the most effective and modern regional integrations is the European Union (EU). It began in 1957 as the European Economic Community (EEC), a Customs Union. It then converted to a Common Market in 1970, and now is becoming a complete Economic and Monetary Union. Among the developing countries, Latin America entered a Free Trade Association in 1960, while the Caribbean countries formed their Free Trade Area (CARIFTA) in 1968. In Africa, the East African Community (EAC) was formed in 1967, while the Economic Community of West African States (ECOWAS) was formed in 1975. A Preferential Trade Area (PTA) agreement was reached in 1984 among some

Eastern and Southern African countries. In Asia, the Association of South-East Asian Nations (ASEAN) was formed since 1967.

Generally, despite the widely recognized common interest in it, the history of regional economic integration among the developing countries is marked by failure. Since the 1950s, a number of regional agreements have been concluded. Many of these achieved successes initially; but many have failed to operate successfully, for reasons ranging from internal squabbles and hostilities (for example, the Central American Common Market), to lack of sufficient drive needed to sustain the agreement (for example, the East African Community), or outright internal opposition among member states (for example, ECOWAS).

As a result of these experiences, regional integration has neither helped to promote rapid growth in intraregional trade nor led to rapid economic growth and development in most regions in the ways expected. Currently, most developed countries have renewed their interests in regional integration, and many have pursued it vigorously and concluded major agreements. A major example is the North American Free Trade Agreement (NAFTA) between the two developed economies of North America, United States and Canada, and their developing neighbor, Mexico.

The renewed efforts at regional integration since the 1980s is not unconnected to the relative successes of the NICs of Asia and Latin America, as well as the Japanese export dynamism, especially as these deeply penetrate and threaten to overwhelm the markets of the other trading partners. This happens as the developed countries increasingly encounter the decline of their aging industries whose productivities now face aggressive competition in world markets.

This then raises the prospects of enhanced competitiveness. It could only enable a country to benefit the most from being in a trade bloc, in the following important ways:

1. At the micro level, enhanced productivity and quality would enable the country to achieve greater import penetration within the markets of its trading partners, and also compete more successfully with imports within its own domestic market.

2. At the macro level, trade liberalization would improve the terms of trade and yield greater economies of scale as deregulation and privatization give rise to more competition across the economy.

Integration leads to virtually unparalleled attainments in trade policy as the exchange of goods and services are completely liberalized. In the case of the European Union (EU), for example, a country's citizens can make their purchases in any member country and freely transport goods across international borders. And in border districts, purchases could be made and paid for in the currencies of either neighbouring country, and borders are crossed without immigration checks and controls. This is also liberalization in labor and employment transactions enabling any citizen of the EU member countries to freely engage in employment within each other's country. In the case of the EU, these liberalization measures are reported to have resulted in international cross-border transaction of goods in excess of 1.2 billion U.S. dollars in 1995 alone. And this is besides the steady growth in foreign trade for member states, for whom intra-community trade now dominates trade relations.[6]

Role of Regional Integration in International Competitiveness

Two major developments have come to characterize the trend of world trade in the present age: (1) international product flow is expanding steadily, with the rate of growth generally surpassing that of total world output; and (2) global trading relations have become closer with significant trade liberalization between countries in various regional blocs. Some new regional blocs have been formed since the forty years that the Treaty of Rome laid the foundation for the European Union (EU), and the thirty years of the Association of South-East Asian Nations (ASEAN). Some of the new blocs include the North American Free Trade Agreement (NAFTA), South America's Mercado Commun del Cono Sur (MERCOSUR), and the Southern African Development Community (SADC).

With cooperation extending well beyond the establishment of a free-trade area and elimination of tariffs, numerous political arrangements have been harnessed between the various regional member countries. And there is much to be said for regional trading associations when it comes to fostering global trade. Since the various regions of the world would be represented by single delegations, it removes the apparent problems (often presented by a large number of participants at the negotiating table) that would otherwise inhibit progress in liberalizing world trade.

Of course, on behalf of each member country, it is highly benefical for regional blocs to enter global negotiations with a common position. This is what the EU often does; the EU trading policy is formulated in Brussels and then taken to enter negotiations at the World Trade Organization (WTO) with a uniform position representing all members of the EU. Furthermore, certain projects can be executed only on a joint basis. A prominent example of this, revealing more vividly the type of competitiveness advantages that membership of a regional bloc offers a country, is Airbus Industrie, a European consortium that has enjoyed great international success as a worldwide supplier of large-capacity passenger aircraft. These factors have led to a steady increase in the volume of EU trade with other nations, to the advantage of individual EU countries who would otherwise have not enjoyed such benefits.

Another example that indicates the immense advantages of regional integration to the international competitiveness of nations is the massive expansion of trade between the EU and ASEAN that not only has been disproportionately strong but also has produced impressive growth rates of about 20 percent per year in recent years. These are evidenced by the dynamic growth of South-East Asian economies coupled with increasing globalization of the world economy. It is important to note that all ASEAN member countries are benefiting from this strong export performance, represented in a sustained increase in the outbound flow of goods to Europe, with Singapore and Malaysia maintaining the lead positions. Thus, regional competition within ASEAN has definitely helped prepare individual member countries for the rigors of the (immensely competitive) global environment.

Despite the immense mutual advantages that integration could confer, many countries (especially rich countries) worry that free trade with poorer countries would threaten their jobs and economic prosperity. For example, the North American Free Trade Agreement (NAFTA), covering the United States, Canada, and Mexico, has been viewed by many in the United States and Canada as more to their losses and more to Mexico's gain. The general view is that firms in the rich (high wage) countries would move to relocate in the low wage countries (thereby causing unemployment in the rich countries), and then only use the rich countries as markets for the final output. The various expositions of the theory and evidence so far presented in this book suggest that this fear is unfounded. A country that is committed to the pursuit of long-term efficiency and ultimate competitiveness by ensuring the existence of micro and macro level parameters of these attributes, need not entertain this inward-looking fear of economic integration and globalization.

Perhaps the most important question about regional trade blocs would be why countries would desire to enter into special agreements designed to promote greater trade with their closest neighbors in an increasingly globalizing world? Afterall, regionalism impedes global trade liberalization—and are therefore "stumbling blocks" rather than "building blocks" in the freeing of worldwide trade. Also, existence of trading blocs result in *trade diversion* whereby preferential trade concessions (such as preferential tariff) encourage countries to import from member countries on a tariff-free basis rather than importing from those countries that have greater comparative advantage in the goods concerned.

The answer to this question is that countries have realised that their engagement in regional trade blocs may, indeed, promote the international competitiveness of their firms/industries. One possible means of such a promotion is geography: as trade blocs give rise to low tariff barriers, transportation costs become relatively more important in production and marketing of goods. Thus, countries whose firms have access to nearer markets gain advantage of lower marketing costs.

Competitiveness and Trade Agreements: The GATT

As discussed in chapter 1, the tide against global free trade led the world's leaders to seek to negotiate and safeguard mutual interests in world trade. As the wave of protectionism raged during the 1930s, international trade simply collapsed. The post-depression era, therefore, brought increasing efforts in the developed countries to seek for ways to forestall any such trade slumps in the future. Through a series of meetings and conferences arranged to discuss the need to lessen trade restrictionist policies among countries, the GATT evolved.

The negotiations (after World War II) took place under the auspices of the newly formed United Nations Organization, aimed at forging new international cooperation in world trade. The General Agreement on Tariffs and Trade (GATT) was established in 1947 as a multilateral treaty made up of a set of agreements governing global trade relations. GATT rules were enacted to govern tariffs and act as a supervisory mechanism among the world's trading partners. A very prominent GATT provision is the *most favored nation* (MFN) status that is accorded to a GATT member. MFN grants that every member of GATT automatically receive tariff reductions as long as such reductions have been extended to any member. Also, under the auspices of GATT, various global trade negotiations aimed at promoting more global trade liberalization are frequently pursued. One such attempt is referred to as the Uruguay Round of trade agreements, in which various countries sought to reach agreement toward simultaneous tariff reductions and the lowering of other forms of trade barriers.

From its inception, GATT has generally resulted in significant tariff reductions through multilateral agreements. Under this first multilateral accord to lower international trade barriers since Napoleonic times, 23 countries cut tariffs on each other's exports in 1948 (*The Economist*, 1998, p.21). It is agreed that the level of tariffs facing member countries of GATT are much lower today than they have ever been. Today, average tariffs stand at about one-tenth of their pre-GATT levels. In this respect, the GATT has tended to promote competitiveness among nations. Through its elaborate mechanism of settling disputes, there have been several "Rounds" of tariff negotiations, aimed at lowering trade barriers. The evidence indicates that the results of tariff reductions under GATT are remarkably high. For example, Bryan (1994, p. 302) reports that, for the United States, the average tariff on dutiable imports was reduced from about 32 percent, the level it was during the pre- and post-World War II period, to 12 percent between 1950 and 1965, and further to 6 percent by 1980.

The GATT also succeeded in reducing nontariff trade barriers across the world. As most countries tended to impose other trade barriers that circumvent the GATT rules, world trade was faced with this new problem of the *new protectionism*.[7] GATT's added objective is to remove tariffs and nontariff trade restrictionist measures, and also to have other forms of protectionist arrangements covered under the GATT regulations. As a framework aimed at streamlining and promoting world trade, GATT's policy objectives enhance competitiveness. Unlike the formation and operation of trading blocs, a country's participation in GATT would contribute to both short- and long-run macro level competitiveness for the country.

Each of the total number of eight rounds of global trade talks organized under the GATT since its implementation in 1948 had involved more countries, and each round had resulted in further advancing, from the preceding round, the cause of global trade liberalization. For example, the Uruguay round of negotiations of 1993 gave rise to further cuts in industrial tariffs, export subsidies, licensing, and customs valuation, as well as the first agreements governing trade in services and protecting intellectual property (such as patents, copyrights, and computer software). These were items that had always been difficult to cover under the GATT. Then in 1997 there were agreements passed on telecommunications services, information technology, and financial services. Such extensive provisions within the GATT have given countries greater confidence to invest more in research and development without fear of having their products compromised through unauthorized copying by foreign potential competitors.

One of GATT's greatest impacts on global international competitiveness lies in its creation of the World Trade Organization (WTO) in 1995, with power to settle disputes between member countries. The WTO is an even more firmly organized permanent body, set up with far more greater powers to arbitrate international trade disputes, than the GATT. Unlike the provisions of the GATT, the WTO does not allow for the exercise of veto powers that an offending member country could use to block any ruling against itself. The WTO rules requires that offending countries refrain from any actions that violate the agreements, compensate for their violations of the rules, or face punitive sanctions. As a result, many countries have tended to bring their bilateral trade disputes to the WTO's dispute panels rather than resorting to retaliatory actions. In this way, global free trade and competitiveness are greatly enhanced.[8]

The WTO's successes have attracted over 30 countries (including China and Russia, which had not previously joined the organization) that are currently seeking to join the GATT, which currently has 132 member countries. The result has been a remarkable growth in world trade. In 1997 the volume of global merchandise trade grew by 9.5 percent, over three times higher than the growth rate of global output. However, the tendencies for countries to adopt protectionist measures are ever alive and present. In agriculture, for example, tariffs and other barriers on farm products are reported to average 40 percent worldwide, creating significant distortions that impair productivity, deter competitiveness, and limit trade. Again in textiles, trade barriers still exist in form of high tariffs (the United States still maintains a 14.6 percent tariff on imported clothing—five times higher than the country's average tariff rate). And in both agriculture and textiles, import quotas still exist.[9]

Many countries (including those of the European Union and the United States, which lead the clamor for global open markets), citing the fear of hurting domestic workers, still show reluctance in opening up their economies. However, under the new GATT negotiations scheduled for the early years of the dawning century (a set of global farm talks planned for 1999, and trade in service talks due for 2000), there is bright outlook for progress, especially toward the easing of the European Union's Common Agricultural Policy.

Many more issues of crucial importance to international competitiveness that need to be included in GATT and WTO coverages are foreign investment restrictions, antitrust rules, labor and human resource movements, and environmental protection. Most countries consider these issues as domestic policy matters, which makes it difficult to bring them into GATT/WTO deliberations without having countries feel that their national sovereignties are being infringed. But these issues are central to trade restrictions and anticompetitive practices in many countries. It is important that the need to strike a balance be recognized across the world.

One of the greatest impacts that the WTO could have on promoting competitiveness is through forcing all its members to implement competition laws, thereby acting in that capacity as a protector of global competition rules. It would also oversee the contentious issue of the links between global trade and investment with a view to formulating global investment rules. However, it must be noted that the ability of the WTO to succeed in promoting and overseeing smooth and harmonious global trade and investment relationships and transactions lies in the willingness of participating countries to abide by the "fair trade" rules imposed by the WTO. Often, in the desire to protect their own individual interests, trading countries tend to violate the rules, and deliberately so. It is important that the WTO be given greater "regulatory powers" to contain such issues that may arise.

The Multilateral Agreement on Investment (MAI)

The world's developed countries that belong to the Organization for Economic Cooperation and Development (OECD) have moved to conclude an investment agreement among themselves, whereby there would be free movement of investment resources and capital between them. This is the Multilateral Agreement on Investment (MAI), which amounts to extending the policy of "free trade" to cover investment.

With the MAI in effect, the need for a country to achieve international competitiveness becomes even more tremendous. As controls are removed on capital movements, countries that do not have efficient institutions (financial markets, labor markets, banks, legal systems, and particularly infrastructure) would suffer net loss of investment flows. This is because investors would take their capital to the most profitable markets where returns are highest. And returns and profitability on investment depend on how efficiently these institutions function. Thus, countries that operate, say, stringent labor laws or environmental quality controls, would lose net investment flows.

Inclusion of certain "strategic" industries (such as broadcasting and other culture-sensitive industries such as motion pictures, books, or art), has raised contentions within the MAI. But the Agreement itself is a worthwhile exercise toward greater competitiveness and expansion of global productivity. However, serious questions arise over the fact that the MAI excludes developing countries, and fails to address the issues surrounding labor standards and environmental concerns.

Labor Standards

Maintenance of labor standards refers to the need to ensure that firms pay their workers adequate level of wages that are sufficient to give an acceptable standard of living. There is also the requirement to protect workers' rights, and, especially, to eradicate the use of "child labor." Declarations on these issues were made at the WTO's first summit in 1996.

It turns out that the so-called "standards" are being set and pushed by rich (developed) countries, to be forced upon, and implemented within, developing countries. Apparently, the rich countries do not generally understand the actual circumstances and conditions under which "child labor" is used in developing countries. The rich countries fail to understand the vast cultural differences between their societies and those of most developing countries. In many of the developing countries, contributions of children are integrated early in the lives of their families. Children are employed as domestic workers, cleaners, messengers, and even cooks. The incomes that they earn in these capacities are used to supplement the income levels and upkeep of their families (which are often subsistence family units).

Unfortunately, there seems to be a lack of understanding in the rich countries regarding these cultural differences that affect economic outcomes. "Standards" in North America need not be equal to "standards" in Asia or Africa, just as the levels of "development" are not equal for these societies. For example, although a daily wage of $2 (U.S.) sounds ridiculously low to anyone in North America, it does represent a (relatively) substantial earnings level (although not a terribly high one) to someone in Indonesia (equivalent to about 30,000 Rupiah in 1998), or Nigeria (equivalent to about 160 Naira in 1998).

Therefore, campaigning that firms be prevented from hiring fourteen-year-old children in Indonesia or Nigeria at daily wage rates equivalent to $2 (U.S.) is tantamount to campaigning that these children and their families be abandoned to lives of unemployment. It may make sense to people in North America to not allow child labor at wages below $4 (U.S.) per hour (average earnings of child labor engaged in the fast-food industry in North America), but in South Asia or sub-Saharan Africa, such a policy would simply create greater hardships and exacerbate poverty levels. What is regarded as child labor in North America is indeed perfectly legitimate labor in most developing countries.

The "labor standards" policy has very significant implications for international competitiveness. Developing countries suspect that the real motive behind the push for labor standards (by developed countries) is to bring wage costs in developing countries upward in order to reduce the labor-cost advantage that developing countries have over the rich (high-labor-cost) countries. For if producers in poorer countries are forced to bring their wages up to the "standards" of the rich countries, the exports of the poorer countries would lose competitive advantage, and the poorer countries would lose international competitiveness. Moreover, citing "poor labor standards" as an excuse, the rich countries could seek ways to discriminate against exports of the poor countries. (Already there are calls in North America to that effect).

NOTES

1. The concept of the dominant firm has been explained in chapter 3, as a term that qualifies a leading firm in an oligopoly industry. It faces a competitive fringe of rivals who together constitute the "followers" of the dominant firm in sharing the market.

2. Porter's position on the role of national strategic trade policy in the attainment of international competitiveness (for the country concerned) is that such policies are flawed. He believes that strategic trade policies could only generally confer very short-term benefits, and fail to accurately perceive the true sources of competitive advantage. Porter clamored for (micro level) approaches to competitiveness that are based on learning from well-established and successful internationally competitive industries. This position may be well founded. The adoption of strategic trade policies by trading partners would amount to a zero-sum game situation; it is clear that such a universal adoption of strategic policies by all trading nations cannot yield a real sustainable competitive advantage to any one country or to all trading countries simultaneously.

3. More detailed treatment of the import substitution strategy of economic development can be found in Ezeala-Harrison (1996a).

4. The infant-industry argument for protection of domestic industries holds that newly established industries, having not yet reached the stage where they can reap scale economies, need to be protected from foreign competition with mature foreign companies who may already be enjoying economies of scale of production. However, it is important to ensure that the products of the "infant industries" be marketed at prices comparable to the pre-ISI imports.

5. See Irwin (1992) for an interesting account of the standard (aggressive) mercantilist export-promotion trade policies, which are often promoted by use of export subsidies.

6. It is believed that in 1995, nearly 80 percent of all exports of the Netherlands, 70 percent in the case of Ireland, and 60 percent in the cases of Italy, Britain, and Germany, were within the EU region. A similar trend exists for other regional trade blocs. It reveals a pattern of expansion of volume of trade due to regional liberalization.

7. Some of the nontariff barriers in the new protectionism are the use of voluntary export restraints (for example, as used by the United States in the 1980s to make Japan to reduce its exports of automobiles to U.S. markets), and local content requirements (requiring that export goods be made to contain some portion of inputs procured from the importing markets).

8. Recent reports (*The Economist*, May 16, 1998) indicate that within three years the WTO has arbitrated 132 cases, as against the total of 300 complaints that the GATT dealt with since its 50-year history. The WTO's attractiveness lies in its being an effective body in which even the smaller countries could have their complaints against bigger

countries heard on an equal platform. Unlike the GATT, the WTO is not perceived as a mechanism used by big countries to trample upon small countries. Costa Rica was able to have the WTO rule against the United States for imposing trade barriers against Cost Rican exports of men's underwear. The U.S. was forced to comply and alter its practices.

9. *The Economist*, May 16, 1998, pp. 21-23.

8

Impact of Environmental Issues on International Competitiveness

The subject of a nation's environment and how it might impact upon its international competitiveness is dealt with in this chapter. All countries, the world over, have awakened to a deeper understanding and appreciation of the close links between their economic prospects and the states of their natural environments. Often, however, in making the link between environmental issues and economic growth, we tend to jump over the role that competitiveness plays in it, namely, the link between environmental issues and international competitiveness, and then subsequently economic growth. The aim of this chapter is to explore this link and thereby highlight the central importance of environmental factors in the state of a nation's competitive advantage and international competitiveness.

The relationship between trade and the environment has become a very thorny issue. Since the benefits of trade depend on the assumption that relative prices in different countries reflect differences in factor endowment and productivity, then countries that allow their firms to operate with lax environmental standards (say, by allowing them to pollute freely) would, in effect, be subsidizing the operations of their firms. This is because relative costs would no longer reflect the differences in factor endowment and productivity if firms in some countries are allowed to pollute freely while firms in other countries are made to bear the cost of pollution cleanups. By not forcing its firms to bear the costs of maintaining environmental quality standards (through cleaning up their own pollution or installing their own costly emission reduction facilities), relative costs of production would be lower for these firms.

That a nation's environmental situation has significant bearing on its economic growth and development has become well recognized by economists and policy makers. In a recent article on the subject, Sachs (1997a) offered some enlightening quantitative measures of how much shortfalls (in terms of percentage national output) countries in certain regions of the world suffer as a result of their peculiar natural and geographical (that is, environmental) factors.[1]

Just as environmental sustainability has become a central issue in the economic performance of nations today, so have modern communication and information technology given rise to greater interconnection between the many regions of the globe. Therefore, the prospects for the twenty-first century are for the world to increasingly shrink (interaction wise), allowing nations to easily relate to each other in ways that were not previously apparent. This development has been termed the *convergence phenomenon* (see chapter 6).

Convergence would mean, also, that the environmental conditions of the various regions of the world would tend to have important implications for the other regions. As economies are linked more closely by trade, a region's environmental circumstances may easily affect other regions both economically and socially. National and regional environmental issues easily become global issues today. The 1986 Chernobyl nuclear plant accident in the former Soviet Union, the 1988 Exxon-Valdez oil spill off the Alaskan coast of North America, the threatened extinction of the Amazon rain forest and some of its rare species, and the general problems of global environmental degradation, all represent significant environmental issues that have global (rather than merely regional) implications.

The need for international cooperation to address the issues of sustainable development prompted the Earth Summit of 1992 in Brazil, during which nations sought to determine and adopt more environmentally benign policy approaches. Among the summit's key proposals that are currently driving the environmental policies of various countries are:

1. The world should recognize that there is a crucial link between economic growth and development, and the environment.

2. Negligent or inadequate environmental policies tend to be very costly (in terms of both social and monetary costs), nationally, as well as globally.

3. To effectively address environmental problems, poverty must be reduced.

4. Economic production, distribution, and consumption must be made to involve prices and quantities that incorporate environmental values.

5. There should be regional and global concerted efforts in tackling environmental problems since such problems cannot be confined to national or regional borders.

In a recent contribution, Thomas and Belt (1997) considered the potential impacts of economic growth on environmental quality. They observed that the achievement of high growth and poverty reduction in the Newly Industrializing Countries (NICs) of East Asia and China have been at the expense of severe environmental losses. The writers cited several environmental facts as the evidence of the severe environmental threat that growth has brought to the East Asia region.[2] For example, it was noted that nine of the world's fifteen cities having the highest levels of *particulate air pollution* are in this region. Also, close to 20 percent of vegetation-covered land in the region suffered from soil degradation through erosion, water-logging, and over-grazing beyond world averages. Furthermore, the region had undergone some of the highest rates of deforestation in the world, and about 50 percent to 75 percent of its coastlines and marine protected areas were classified as areas of highly threatened biodiversity. The study suggested that the challenges of growth and the environment must be addressed simultaneously as a matter of high priority.[3]

As far as it concerns international competitiveness and trade among nations, environmental problems and ways to effectively address them are quite crucial. A country's (potential) state of international competitiveness is apt to have some close correlation with its environmental circumstances. Environmental factors do have important effects on the performance of national and international economies. Therefore, we must consider the crucial questions of:

1. What exactly is meant by the environment?
2. In what specific way(s) could a society's environmental matters and related issues influence its ability to achieve or not achieve international competitiveness?
3. What appropriate environmental policy postures are required in a country that would minimize the impairment of the country's relative international competitiveness?

As international competitiveness is always a *relative* attribute between different countries and different regions, it is affected in a major way by the environmental policy situations that exist between different countries and regions. For example, consider two countries: country A and country B. If, all things being equal, country A implements a stringent environmental policy rule while country B implements a weak environmental policy rule (or fails to implement any environmental policies whatsoever—as many developing countries often do), this is bound to cause significant differences in the relative states of international competitiveness between countries A and B. The differences arise from the fact that while production costs in country A will be higher due to the internalized environmental externalities, production costs in country B will involve no environmental costs (as environmental externalities are not internalized). The rest of this chapter is devoted to analyzing these issues and addressing the above pertinent questions.

THE STATE OF A NATION'S ENVIRONMENT

A country is almost exclusively dependent on its environment and natural resources for all its ongoing social and economic well-being. A nation's environment consists of its natural and material resources as well as human resources. The size and capacity of endowment of these resources determine the society's environmental *generative capacity* and *assimilative capacity*. The generative capacity is the extent of the volume of material and human resources that can be derived from the society's environment, with regard to their ability to generate and support life. The assimilative capacity is the ability of the environment to absorb and contain the byproducts of human and animal life without manifesting *negative environmental impacts* (NEIs)—the deterioration of environmental quality (indicated by the NEI indicators such as the absolute per capita level of sulphus dioxide, ground-level ozone, nitrogen oxide, and other suspended particulates).

The main aspects of a society's environment may be categorized as: the level of population, the habitats, and the sizes of renewable and nonrenewable resources. Each of these is described in greater detail as follows.

Population

The population is the number of people living in a country at any time. Population growth is often referred to as *natural increase* and is the single most important factor with serious implications for the environment. People must demand the natural needs and wants of life, not only at a particular time of life but also over time. Therefore, a given level of population must have an adequate level of living resources, and the extent to which this requirement is or is not met determines the degree to which the environment is exploited. As far as it concerns a nation's competitiveness, the level of population has implications from both an over-population and under-population concern. This point is discussed further below.

Habitats

The habitats include the land surface, earth, forests, waters, atmosphere, and the space. Different countries have different levels of acquisition of habitats. While some countries have superabundant natural resources, others have very scanty amounts of these. The differences in national habitat acquisitions are responsible for the different environmental circumstances that various countries face.

Renewable Natural Resources

Renewable environmental (natural) resources include the wildlife and livestock, the fisheries, trees and plants, and water resources. They are thought to be indefinitely replenishable, although some (for example, land) are location-specific. It is easy for the rate of exploitation of these physical and biological resources to exceed their natural regenerative abilities. Therefore, many renewable resources (for example, fresh water, fertile soil, or clean air) are increasingly scarce, and more damage is being done to the underlying systems that sustain and renew them. It is possible to increase generative capacity of the environment's renewable resources through the process of *recycling*. Recycling, however, has its limits as a ratio of the recycled material tends to be lost during the process.

Nonrenewable Natural Resources

The nonrenewable environmental resources include various material deposits in the earth (such as oil deposits, gas deposits, and mineral contents. Being nonreplenishable, these are finite and are depletable through high levels of consumption. Although there is currently no evidence that the world is facing the danger of immediate depletion of nonrenewable resources, it is still prudent that conservatory measures be practised.

ENVIRONMENTAL ISSUES AND INTERNATIONAL COMPETITIVENESS

Following the application of a more complete definition of international competitiveness in this study, it should be reckoned that both the micro level and macro level aspects of competitiveness must be in view during every application of the concept. In this regard, it should be asserted that environmental matters need not affect international competitiveness at the macro level, by definition. Environmental issues would be a micro level parameter of international competitiveness, especially relating to productivity and relative costs. In this section, therefore, we would posit competitiveness strictly in its micro level sense, namely, higher total factor productivity and lower unit production costs.

The level of a country's competitiveness would have increased if and when its total factor productivity (TFP) increases (see chapter 2), which is consistent with lower unit cost of output within the representative industry in that country, over a given time period, say, one year. A country would be losing competitiveness whenever its TFP falls (consistent with its representative industry's unit cost of output increasing) over a given time period.

The economic activities of production and consumption tend to place heavy physical demands on the environment. Construction of industries, agricultural development, housing, construction and operation of machinery, mining, forestry, and construction and use of infrastructure, all bring about environmental deterioration. For example, industrialization processes bring with them air and water pollution, as well as pollution of the earth surface in areas where industrial solid wastes were discarded. These are problems that are often taken lightly until their effects begin to manifest themselves in severe negative impacts on human health, production costs, and resource availability.

The heavy use of chemicals in the industrial production processes of Europe,

North America, and Japan has given rise to the formation of massive industrial byproducts that pollute the atmosphere around these regions, resulting in such environmental hazards as acid rain, ozone layer depletion, and unclean breathing air. Major examples of these areas that are under serious environmental pollution threats include the northeast U.S. corridor, the Windsor-Quebec corridor and the Vancouver-Fraser Valley, in Canada, the Ruhr Valley in Germany, and the Tokyo-Osaka corridor in Japan. Existing evidence indicates that countries in these regions incur significant costs in combating the health and material hazards associated with these environmental conditions. There can be no doubt that these factors affect the international competitiveness of these regions.

The level of environmental quality of a given location could be measured by the level of concentration of *particulate air pollution* and other pollutants in the atmosphere within and around that location. The average level of *ambient sulphur dioxide* in the atmosphere across a country would be a very close indicator of the concentration of particulate air pollution. The higher the level of concentration of ambient sulphur dioxide, the lower would be the level of environmental quality, and *vice versa*.

The impact of negative environmental conditions on a country's competitiveness relates to both the direct and indirect costs that these conditions impose, as well as the costs involved in environmental quality control (usually to combat their effects or eliminate or reduce their sources). These include such measures as air quality control, water quality control, hazardous waste disposal, solid waste management, and management of toxic substances from industrial production.

Some examples are the imposition of emission standards on industries and automobiles, installing water purification facilities, and imposing vigorous conservation measures on natural resources use (such as fish stocks, minerals, and trees). There is no question that these environmental enhancement measures would likely result in higher short-run production costs in firms and industries within the country. But this would not reduce the country's international competitiveness. In fact, these measures would pave the way for greater competitiveness in the long run. This is because of the lower production costs that would result in the absence of the negative environmental impacts of a poor environmental condition.

Before we examine the various ways in which negative environmental impacts on competitiveness could manifest, it will be illuminating to analyze the possible links and relationships between environmental factors (such as the pursuit of environmental quality) and international competitiveness. In this, we recap the formulations of competitiveness and environmental quality outlined earlier: the level of a country's competitiveness is given by the level of its TFP (which is closely correlated with the negative of unit cost of output). The level of a country's environmental quality is indicated by the negative of the average level of ambient sulphur dioxide in its atmosphere. Applying these formulations, we now study the potential relationships between a country's environmental quality and its state of international competitiveness.

The Environmental Quality-Competitiveness Tradeoff

A country must exploit its resources for economic growth and development. The necessary production and consumption processes of life do threaten the sustainability of the environment and thereby jeopardize the country's competitiveness. These processes give rise to discharges of solid, liquid, and gaseous byproducts into the environment. The accumulation of these byproducts again threaten the sustainability of the environment, further negating the prospects for greater competitiveness.

Society's economic and social life involves the processes of production and consumption. Production, for example, involves the use of natural resources in industrialization, construction, and infrastructural development. These result in depletion or possible extinction of natural resources. As a result, the country's resource base is reduced, and its prospects for competitiveness is curtailed.

Both processes of production and consumption would give rise to byproducts in the environment, including toxic contamination of the air, atmosphere, the earth and the waters, desertification, deforestation, endangered animal species, acid rain, global warming, ozone layer thinning, and solid waste disposal. There is also the "eye sore" effect of environmental use—some members of society are denied their "psychic" benefits from an *unspoiled* environment.[4]

Under these circumstances, it is easy to see how a country's competitiveness and its environmental quality would be negatively correlated. Wastes that are discharged into the environment are often harmful to the environment and its occupants. This, in turn, impairs the human activities of production and consumption, resulting in lesser international competitiveness for a society.

However, a country would try to initiate *environmental control* measures designed to reduce the negative environmental impacts—measures such as industrial emission regulations to ensure clean air, uncontaminated water, nonhazardous living space, and unpolluted food supply. Firms and industries that discharge pollutants into the atmosphere would be made to incorporate such *social costs* in the determination of their output levels and pricing. Environmental quality measures such as these are apt to raise production costs of firms and industries, and thus render their products less competitive internationally. Environmental policy measures designed to make firms and industries to bear the environmental cleanup costs of their activities would result in higher prices for the country's products relative to other countries that do not implement environmental measures. As a result, the country would lose relative competitiveness.

Many countries are able to invest in rapid environmental cleanups and promotion of environmental quality. Emission standards are imposed on industries and automobiles. Facilities are installed for water purification, and vigorous conservation measures are imposed on natural resources (such as fish stocks, minerals, and trees). These environmental enhancement measures are carried out in many countries (especially developed ones) with minimal economic and social costs.

Figure 8.1 illustrates the *environmental quality-competitiveness* tradeoff phenomenon. The figure depicts production possibility curves that link levels of competitiveness and levels of environmental quality for a country. A country's level of international competitiveness, measured by the level of TFP, is depicted on the vertical axis. The level of environmental quality, measured by the negative of the average level of ambient sulphur dioxide (SO_2)—concentration of ambient sulphur dioxide across the country, is depicted on the horizontal axis. The level of environmental quality is depicted by the negative of the average level of ambient sulphur dioxide across the country.

It is clear from the discussions so far that a country's international competitiveness would tend to suffer in the short run as it pursues policies to enhance its environmental quality. For example, as all other things remain constant, imposing environmental quality control measures such as moratorium on natural resource use (for instance, fish stock harvesting quotas, conservation of mineral deposits, and logging quotas), emission standards on industries, environmental cleanup rules on firms, and the like, are apt to raise operating costs and lower TFP.

Figure 8.1
Environmental Quality-Competitiveness Tradeoff

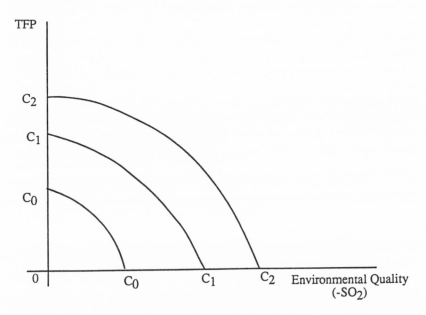

Other potential environmental costs include regulatory controls on automobile operations (such as mandatory catalytic converter requirements) and the installation of water purification facilities. As production costs rise as a result of these measures, the country loses international competitiveness. However, competitiveness would improve (in the short run) if and when environmental quality control measures are neglected and their cost-increasing effects are averted.

Thus, a country's level of TFP and level of environmental quality are negatively correlated. This is illustrated by the negative slopes of the tradeoff curves such as C_1C_1 or C_2C_2 in Figure 8.1. The curves indicate that the higher the level of competitiveness (higher TFP), the lower the level of environmental quality (lower $-SO_2$, in absolute value).

Clearly, a country could operate on different levels of environment-competitiveness tradeoffs. For example, a country could move from the curve C_0C_0 to the curve C_1C_1, say. This would represent a rightward shift of the tradeoff curve, indicating the country's ability to attain higher international competitiveness and greater environmental quality at the same time. Many developed countries are able to achieve this fit by investing significant resources in environmental control and protection while maintaining or even increasing their competitiveness through the various measures analyzed in chapter 2.[5]

Given their different levels of economic development, some countries may have to be content with a tradeoff such as from point B (relatively low competitiveness with high environmental quality) to point A (higher competitiveness at the expense of lower environmental quality). To achieve greater competitiveness without deterioration of environmental quality (that is, to cause a tradeoff curve such as C_0C_0 either to tilt rightward at the horizontal axis or totally to shift horizontally rightward), a country must invest substantial amount of resources in environmental preservation measures whenever it initiates steps to enhance its competitiveness.

The most crucial point surrounding the environment-competitiveness tradeoff is that, where a country chooses to operate on its tradeoff curve, it would greatly affect its long-term prospects of economic growth and international competitiveness. For example, assume that a country chooses to operate at a point such as A, that is, a choice of relatively high competitiveness with low environmental quality. Over time, the deteriorated environment would give rise to higher production costs and lessening TFP as natural resources become extinct and environmental pollution bring to bear on human and animal welfare. The long-run outcome would be a significant loss of international competitiveness.

It appears, therefore, that the important policy implication of the tradeoff model is that a country must endeavor to shift its tradeoff curve rightward, over time. Environmental protection may not be sacrificed for the convenience of short-term competitiveness. A country must pursue environmental control, while seeking to promote its international competitiveness toward the pursuit of growth. In this regard, it must be pointed out that the importance of the macro level parameters of competitiveness come into focus. This is because most measures designed to maintain or enhance environmental quality would likely impact negatively on the micro parameters of competitiveness, namely, production costs and TFP. Such measures would result in a (tradeoff) movement along the tradeoff curve.

Therefore, only policy measures that could shift the tradeoff curve (outward) would be effective in enhancing competitiveness and maintaining (or at least not negating) environmental quality. And under prevailing economic and political circumstances in most countries, it appear that it is the macro parameters of competitiveness such as economic liberalization, trade liberalization, and exchange rate flexibility, that could shift the tradeoff curve outward.

Negative Environmental Constraints on Competitiveness

As seen in the preceding section, environmental factors and related aspects do present significant negative impacts on a country seeking to achieve greater competitiveness. We now examine more closely the sources of these negative environmental impacts, and the various problems they pose for international competitiveness. This can be analyzed under the categories of: (1) problem of sustainability, (2) byproducts of society's economic and social life, and (3) constraints of natural environmental conditions. These three categories of environmental issues virtually encompass the most direct means whereby a country's state of international competitiveness may be impacted by the environment. We examine each of these in turn, with a view to determining relevant policy directions for their containment.

Sustainable Development and International Competitiveness

One of the most pressing environmental issues of international competitiveness is that of the *sustainability* of the society's environmental (including human and material) resources. This implies the problem of how (at what rate) society should use its environmental resources not only to ensure prolonged support of human economic activity for the ongoing generation, but also to ensure that these resources are not made extinct through overuse, thereby jeopardizing the economic growth and well-being of the society's future generations.

Regarding human resources, the problem center mainly on the population issue. A situation of either over-population or under-population would negatively affect productivity of resources. Over-population would likely result in undue pressure and over-use of the environment, thus jeopardizing productivity of resources. Under-population would result in the relative scarcity of labor, higher labor costs, and overall relatively higher production costs in the country.

Of course, there is a need to avoid the extinction of natural resources. The country must devise ways to adopt the most efficient rate of harvesting (utilization) of, say, the fishes, or trees, or even crude petroleum, to ensure that: (1) while the rate of utilization sufficiently meets the economic developmental goals of the current generation, the stock does not get depleted; and (2) the resource use and the processes involved in its harvesting and utilization neither harm the environment nor pose major health risks to present and future generations.

There is currently a great fascination with the principle of *sustainable development* in most societies. Sustainable development is a rule of maintaining an *optimal* rate of resource and environmental exploitation that would neither result in making future generations worse off nor leave the needs of the present generation unsatisfied. Thus, environmental resource allocation rates that either enrich the current generation but (might) impoverish future generations, or impoverishes the current generation in order to enrich future ones, defeat the sustainable development objective. Ordinarily, by definition, the sustainable development objective could hardly be met insofar as depletable environmental resources are concerned. This is because every unit of depletable resource used by the current generation is a unit that is unavailable for the use of future generations, indicating that the future generation will probably be worse off than the current generation in this regard.

A country would normally have its broad economic policy goals which would include that a *sustainable yield* policy of natural resource use must be maintained. The sustainable yield in the harvesting of (replenishable) natural resources is the harvesting rate that equals the natural rate of growth of the resource biomass. At this rate of resource use, the resource stockpile would remain undiminished from period to period, thereby safeguarding the society from the ever present fear of extinction of the resource. Of course, the question of whether or not this rate is consistent with the country's target goals of economic growth and full employment is ever present.

To achieve and sustain the long-term international competitiveness objective, the economy must adopt corrective measures to address its inevitable violation of sustainable development conditions. The most important and most effective of such corrective measures would include:

1. *Promotion of greater recycling initiatives among the population*, based on a 3-Rs policy framework.[6] This would enable the country's firms and industries to obtain resources at relatively lower costs for greater competitiveness. This could be achieved through an active national (solid, liquid, and gaseous) waste reduction drive.

2. *Greater emphasis on resource management*. This is an active ongoing program of natural resource conservation, allowing for replenishment of reserves. The potential problems of, say, deforestation, overfishing, overgrazing, soil degradation, or waterlogging would be averted.

3. *An optimal population and human resource policy*. This calls for a population program aimed at ensuring a rate of population growth that is commensurate with the rate of economic growth. Adequate levels of public-sector investment in education and

training would yield a steady source of productive labor.

4. *Public-sector investment in construction and maintenance of physical infrastructure and social-overhead capital.* The infrastructure may be passed on to the use and benefit of the future generation to compensate for the current generation's use that may have violated the sustainability principle. Moreover, availability of ample infrastructure would yield lower production costs and attract foreign investment.

Impact of Economic Byproducts on Competitiveness

The necessary social and economic activities of life in a country involve byproducts that result from such activities. All of these activities involve the processes of either production or consumption—the two main activities that could highly affect the state of national competitiveness. The environmental byproducts of human life on earth generally include the toxic contamination of the air, the atmosphere, the earth, and the waters; desertification, deforestation, endangered animal species, acid rain, global warming, ozone layer thinning, and solid waste disposal. There is also the "eye sore" effect of environmental use—some members of society are denied their "psychic" benefits from an *unspoiled* environment.

The production (supply side) and consumption (demand side) economic activities of society each have their necessary byproducts, namely, gaseous, liquid, and solid wastes generated in the course of these economic activities. These wastes that are discharged into the environment are often harmful to the environment and its occupants. This then, in turn, impair the human activities of production and consumption, resulting in lesser international competitiveness for a society.

To achieve greater competitiveness, a country must implement appropriate short-term and long-term measures to minimize the inevitable adverse environmental effects of its social and economic activities. The measures would not only help to avoid the direct and immediate consequences for the present generation but also promote the preservation of the environment toward greater competitiveness for future generations.

The byproducts of production, the supply side of economic activities, affect the availability of clean air, clean and uncontaminated water, nonhazardous living space, and unpolluted food supply. The economy should be able to ensure that industries or firms that discharge pollutants into the atmosphere are made to incorporate such *social costs* in the determination of their output levels and pricing, so that their consumers would properly bear such costs.

It may be that environmental policy measures designed to make firms and industries to bear the environmental cleanup costs of their activities would result in higher prices for the country's products relative to other countries that do not implement environmental measures. As a result, the country would then lose competitiveness. This situation could, however, be addressed by a policy whereby the government would bear the costs of the environmental cleanups, in order to safeguard the international competitiveness of its firms and industries. Such a policy amounts to a quasi-subsidy program.

On the other hand, if all trading countries uniformly and genuinely implement environmental measures, there would be no need for government assistance to firms. Relative states of international competitiveness would then be maintained by individual countries with environmental preservation measures intact.

The byproducts resulting from consumption activities, the demand side of the economy, are closely associated with the population level of the country. Often, a high population level would bring about high waves of rural-urban migration and their attendant explosive growth of urban communities. Urban slums erupt, where the often poor living conditions give rise to congestion, squalor, and unsanitary conditions, with their resulting social problems such as crime and insecurity. Such an environment becomes prone to the spread of diseases and epidemics, all of which are detrimental to economic growth and international competitiveness.

In many countries with significant levels of industrial expansion as well as large-scale applications of chemicals to agricultural production and mining, rivers and lakes have often been used as a means of disposing toxic waste products and heavy metals. These rivers and other groundwater have been largely contaminated by seepage of hazardous materials from industrial sites and solid waste dumps. This presents serious environmental hazards to the society.

Poor environmental situations such as pollution would impair human health, and would also impair the productivity of labor. This would reduce total factor productivity. Higher medical costs would often result in higher production costs as firms pay higher health-care expenses to their labor force.

Many countries face increasing environmental problems of deforestation, global warming, and species extinction. The rapid depletion of the forests that absorb atmospheric carbon dioxide, means that the increased concentration of carbon dioxide gas in the atmosphere results in elevated temperatures on the earth's atmosphere. This is the so-called global greenhouse effect, which worsens the already unsuitable high temperature problems in many countries. These problems impair competitiveness. A country must effectively address its environmental problems to achieve and maintain competitiveness in the long run.

Natural Environmental Constraints to Competitiveness

Many countries (especially in the continents of Africa, Asia, and Latin America) must deal with very serious natural environmental problems. Then they face the dilemma of having to pursue the achievements of international competitiveness and economic development while maintaining environmental quality. To such countries, the necessary tradeoff between a country's competitiveness and the quality of its environment as analyzed in the above section, can be very costly. These countries lack the resources required to be able to shift the environmental quality-competitiveness tradeoff curve outward (thereby simultaneously achieving international competitiveness while promoting environmental quality through effective abatement of environmental pollution and improvement of natural resource conservation).

That many countries in the less developed regions of the world are those occupying the least environmentally favorable parts of the universe, is not merely coincidental. In effect, the environment is a major force to reckon with regarding whether or not a country attains or fails to attain sustained economic growth and development.[7] It then impacts heavily on the country's ability to achieve and maintain international competitiveness.

Indeed, environmental issues in the context of economic development and competitiveness do present themselves very differently to the developed countries and the less developed countries. For one, in developed countries the most serious environmental problems are mainly human-made. This is to say that they result from the pattern of choices of lifestyles of the people in the society. In less developed countries, however, much of the environmental problems are natural. They are imposed by nature. Apart from those arising from the problems of high rates of urbanization and congestion in unhygienic "ghetto" dwellings, as well as some problems of industrial pollution in certain areas of Latin America, most of the less developed countries' environmental problems arise from natural causes. In water pollution, for example, parts of Africa and South Asia suffer from water contamination due to pollution from natural sources rather than by industrial waste products.

Another example may be seen in climatic conditions. The regions of Africa, Asia, and Latin America and the Caribbean are all tropical and semi-tropical, with unconducive weather and climatic conditions for human, animal, and plant growth and development. Most of these areas have arid or semi-arid climates, associated with very harsh environmental living conditions. The climates of these tropical areas range in extreme temperatures from lows of 15°C to highs of 42°C all year round, with very infertile soils and little or no rainfall.

Geographically, the bulk of the areas occupied by the underdeveloped continents lie within a span of about 2,500 kilometers on either side of the equator, with their tropical effects extending much wider than this range. The *wet equatorial tropical climate*, characterized by high humidity and constant (equatorial) rains of about 190 to 300 centimeters per year; *the monsoon tropical climate*, characterized by a mix of alternate wet and dry seasons; and *the arid tropics*, characterized by little or no rainfall, are the three types of tropical climates found in these regions.[8]

The environmental adversities presented by the tropical conditions of many countries have tended to grossly impede not only their international competitiveness but also their overall economic production and general developmental activities. The natural environmental constraints impede education and human resource development, agriculture, infrastructural construction, and industrialization. The severe dehydrating effects of the tropical heat are restrictive of the application of human mental and physical efforts in production.

It necessitates the constant need for food and nourishment during the course of every production activity involving labor, thereby tending not only to raise the labor costs of production but also to render labor relatively less productive than capital (resulting in the desire for employers to prefer capital to labor, that is, relative unemployment of the labor force). Where such a country is a labor-surplus economy (as most less developed countries tend to be), it is effectively deprived of the productive-efficiency benefits of its cheap labor and rendered less competitive at the micro level.

The tropical environment, with its attendant extreme heat, high humidity, and absence of frost, are conducive to the growth of destructive bacteria, parasites, insects, pests, and several species of tropical diseases that constantly inhibit plant and nt and can be extremely destructive. The unpredictable torrential rains simply wash away the soil with its ferocious erosions, often sweeping away agricultural crops and leaving behind lands that are largely unsuitable for habitation.

Arguably, some potentially fertile areas exist in the tropics. Much has been written of the volcanic soil of the East African highlands and parts of Asia and the Pacific regions, as well as the clay soil of the alluvial plains of Africa and South America. These are all areas of the tropical zones that may be particularly suitable for agricultural development. Other than these, however, the bulk of the soils found in much of the tropics are formed from old acid parent rock, poor in calcium and other plant nutrients. Most parts of West and Central Africa, South Asia, and South America, are rain forest regions. Agricultural land tenure in these areas must involve the removal of the forest, and as this is done, the proportion of iron and aluminium hydroxides in the soil tends to increase, resulting in the formation of laterite soil which becomes intractably hard and uncultivable. Agricultural output is, therefore, always very limited relative to the amount of investment made; this is a major constraining factor in competitiveness and economic growth.

The harsh and unsuitable environmental conditions that many developing countries must deal with have tended to have devastating effects on their prospects for international competitiveness. The environmental hazards substantially impair human as well as animal health. They cause rapid deterioration of physical structures such as buildings, machines, and infrastructure, and they impair human productivity in almost all spheres of economic activity. The problem is now widely recognized as central in the perpetually dismal economic and social development of many developing countries.

What is clear from this discussion is that the most promising way to pursue international competitiveness for countries with severe natural constraints is to vigorously pursue steps to raise the overall pace of economic growth and development. This will, in turn, enable the developing country to be capable of tackling the natural environmental hazards. The country's development agenda must involve programs designed to improve environmental conditions.

Of central importance, for instance, would be the need to encourage wider choices of rural dwelling among the population, through aggressive programs of rural development and agricultural development. These programs would be combined with programs of education, urban planning, and infrastructural construction. With the improved level of development that these policy actions would give, the country could easily be capable of shifting its competitiveness-environmental quality tradeoff curve outward.

The environment is often concerned with the issues of externalities and property rights. Much of the forests and lands are not owned by individuals or groups; rather, they are essentially open-access or common-property resources. Therefore, users of these resources, basing their economic decisions on the cost-benefit outcomes to themselves, are likely to disregard the (negative) externalities their actions inflict upon the environment, often resulting in the over-exploitation of the (environment) resources. Thus, inappropriate property-rights allocation is recognized as the major problem that results in the uneconomic use of the environment. Hence, an important environmental preservation policy would be the creation and effective functioning of property-rights institutions.

Instituting a system of individual or group property rights over forests and lands would create incentives for the owners to invest in environmental rehabilitation (such as fighting erosion and constructing irrigation facilities for farming), conservation (through appropriately priced and guarded exploitation of natural resources), and preservation (such as enforcement of environmental standards). This system could be accompanied by governmentally legislated standards for industrial emissions.

Poverty in developing countries most affects the degree of use and abuse of the environment. Conservation measures, or sustainability measures, designed to promote environmental preservation would have little importance in a society where there are, say, food shortages. Increasing wealth and economic well-being is the ultimate solution to this environmental problem, for, as people get better off economically, there is a reduced tendency to exploit natural resources more ruthlessly. But people are not getting better off in many countries today. Thus, the forests are depleted by slash-and-burn farmers, and the trees are depleted by loggers who ignore environmental costs as they pursue their immediate means of sustenance. Therefore, income redistributive policies designed to reduce mass poverty should be the starting point for any long-term environment-competitiveness enhancement drive for a country.

INTERNATIONAL COMPETITIVENESS AND POLLUTION HAVENS

The *pollution-haven hypothesis* (Field and Olewiler, 1994) asserts that some countries (especially developing countries) act as "pollution havens." Pollution havens are countries where industries are allowed to operate without being compelled to comply with stringent environmental standards and regulations that may obtain in other countries. Countries may act as pollution havens due to at least two underlying premises:

1. Tough environmental control measures in some countries (especially developed countries) tend to cause firms and industries in them to seek to relocate in developing countries where such controls are either lax or nonexistent.
2. Many developing countries, in their desperate bids to attract industries for the creation of jobs and income needed for growth and development, have encouraged, or even tended to lure, such firms and industries from developed countries with promises of minimal, or outright waiver of any, environmental standards and controls.

Evidence in support of the pollution-haven hypothesis and its underlying axioms is generally based on opinions formed from observations of the environmental conduct of many multinational corporations (MNCs) that operate in developing countries. A well-known incident is India's Bhopal pollution disaster in 1985.

Following the overwhelming negative long-run impacts of environmental deterioration on competitiveness, it is clear that acting as a pollution haven would seriously jeopardize a country's chances of achieving and maintaining competitiveness. Although there may be some short-term gains, the country would be worse off in the long run. Therefore, a country must not neglect to implement environmental control measures in order to promote and maintain environmental standards for long-term competitiveness.

ENVIRONMENTAL POLICIES FOR INTERNATIONAL COMPETITIVENESS

The bulk of the policy prescriptions derived from our discussions so far have been presented within the various sections in which they have applied. This final section of the chapter presents some general policy framework and overview regarding the important link we have seen between international competitiveness and the state of a country's environmental situation.

Although the competitiveness-environmental quality tradeoff model suggests that short-term international competitiveness would tend to be accompanied by negative environmental outcomes, it should also be understood that there are clear long-term positive links between competitiveness and environmental quality. These links reflect cause and effect relationships. On the one hand, the maintenance of high environmental quality would ensure more sustained international competitiveness. On the other hand, the achievement of greater international competitiveness could help alleviate environmental problems as the country could afford to invest in environmental enhancement programs. However, these cause and effect relationships are far from automatic; appropriate policy directions are required to initiate and attain them.

As mentioned earlier, environmental protection may not need to be sacrificed for the convenience of short-term competitiveness. This is to say that the so-called policy of "grow first and clean up later" which many countries seem to choose to adopt in their bids for quick achievement of growth, would prove to be a very costly and unwise strategy both economically, socially, and ecologically. A country must pursue environmental control, while seeking to promote its international competitiveness toward the pursuit of growth and development.

A country must always promote environmental preservation by maintaining strict but reasonable environmental controls and standards. It must not yield itself as a pollution haven. As it is, the benefits of environmental preservation extend not only to the country implementing it but also to the entire world. For example, rain forests (in developing countries) support much of the world's species which possess overwhelming ecological, biological, and medicinal values. Rain forests also absorb the carbon dioxide that is released as a byproduct in human and animal respiration, production, and consumption processes, the buildup of which is responsible for global warming. As such, these forests are global *public goods*: they extend significant benefits to every society in this world.

This means that poorer countries ought not be expected to solely bear the costs of preserving these environmental resources, although they exist within their jurisdictions. A developing country should be compensated and given greater incentive to promote conservation of these resources. The rest of the world has an important stake in this preservation. The rich countries, in particular, should extend much greater compensation to the poor countries in this regard.

NOTES

1. In his report based on a study carried out at the Harvard Institute for International Development, Sachs found that Africa, for example, suffered a shortfall in growth due to "poor geography" and natural health hazards of an estimated 2.3 percentage points per year. The author emphasized, among other things, that "... bad climates, poor soils, physical isolation, infectious tropical diseases (and the consequent poor human and animal health) are likely to hinder growth whatever happens to policy." Apparently, this observation echoes an earlier emphasis in Ezeala-Harrison (1996a) on the pervasive adverse effects of unsuitable environmental factors in the growth and development of less developed countries.

2. The study specifically covered the southeast Asian countries of Malaysia, Singapore, Indonesia, and Thailand. Apparently, similar situations have occurred in other Asian countries of Japan, South Korea, Hong Kong, and Taiwan where rapid economic growth and development have taken place during the twentieth century.

3. It must be pointed out that these environmental problems are not caused solely by rapid economic growth and development. In fact, they could equally be the results of growing poverty and underdevelopment. Experiences of many countries in Africa, South and Central America, and parts of East Asia indicate that slow-growing or negative-growing economies could equally suffer from severe environmental deterioration brought on by the fact of their economic deprivation and underdevelopment. Pressures of over-

population and mass poverty cause severe deforestation, overgrazing, and the growth of urban slums and squalor in the bid to eke out basic existence.

4. This involves the issue of *existence value* or *nonuse value* of environmental resources. Existence value is the measure of the satisfaction (utility) that people derive from knowing that some good exists in its unspoiled or natural state. The existence value is found by asking people how much they would wish to pay or contribute to ensure that some natural scene or *common property* resource, such as a game reserve, natures park, rare scenery, and the like, is preserved.

5. The need to maintain global competitiveness while effectively controlling environmental quality, presents a major bottleneck to many developing countries. Most developed countries can afford to impose stringent environmental standards on their firms and industries without necessarily jeopardizing the prospects of further growth and development as firms (especially multinational companies) shy away from tough, cost-increasing, environmental standards. A lower tradeoff curve such as the curve $C_0 C_0$ would represent the situation of a typical developing country, indicating that such a country has low (weak) international competitiveness and environmental quality.

6. The 3-Rs principle—*reuse, reduce, recycle*—refers to a recycling program driven by the practical policies of reusing, reducing, and recycling of material resources in the acts of production and consumption.

7. For an extended analytical treatment of this issue, see Ezeala-Harrison (1996a), which also is the source of the major portion of the remainder of this sub-section.

8. In recent years, the effects of the severe drought characteristic of these areas have been seen through the famines of Ethiopia (1985 and beyond), Somalia (1993 and beyond), Mozambique, and Sudan, in Africa. These effects have also been evident in the Philippines and Bangladesh, in Asia. In 1998, large areas of Central America (especially Nicaragua and Honduras) were devastated by the hurricane Mitch which brought sweeping land-slides and flood that caused massive and irreparable damages to lives and resources.

PART III

STRATEGIES OF GLOBAL COMPETITION AND COMPETITIVENESS

9

Concepts in Global Market Competition and Analysis

It is important to understand the microeconomics of firms and industries, and the nature of their operation within the competitive environment. These are what ultimately determine the state of competitiveness of firms and industries; these factors shape the competitiveness abilities of firms and industries. This chapter and the ones that follow it present the background exposition of the necessary analytical concepts in industrial organization required to enable us to appreciate the analyses and discussions presented in the earlier chapters.

THE GLOBAL FREE MARKET

The central aim of the industrial market organization is to enable the free-market system to organize its economic processes of production and consumption. In order to perform these functions effectively, the concern is that the system needs to be competitive, which is the subject of this book. The "organization" of the system deals with the issues of:

1. How the free-market system works, and how it could malfunction. This involves the necessary adjustments that are needed in the system whenever it fails to self-adjust sufficiently to avoid failure in achieving its goals.
2. Which firms and industries in the economy should be private sector businesses (privatized), which should be entirely operated as public enterprises, and which should be operated under regulatory controls. Involved in this is also the issue of regulation or deregulation of public utility industries.
3. How to appropriately act to promote competition through such measures as granting patent rights, subsidies, tax levies, tax exemptions, antitrust laws, or trade liberalization policies. This also concerns the question of protection of domestic producers, tariffs, and sanctions.

Systems of Organization

Depending on the political and ideological system of its choice, a society would operate a particular type of market organization. The various systems of economic organization are:

1. *Free-Enterprise Market System*. This is the system based on the principle of *laissez faire* ("Let it alone"), based on individual freedom of choice, property ownership, entrepreneurship, and profit incentive. In this system, the free market is the medium for most economic activity. Producers (supply) and consumers (demand) are allowed to freely interact to determine the volume of transaction and its rate of exchange (price). The *price mechanism* is the means of allocation and distribution of resources; pricing provides the incentive through which the "invisible hand" allocates goods and services to those who need them. The free enterprise system is the system operated in most Western societies and developing countries.

2. *Planned Economy*. The planned economy is a system based on *central planning*. The state becomes the agent of resource allocation and distribution. Ownership of property, wealth, and means of production are regulated by the government. The government determines the what, how, where, and when of production. This is the system of *socialism*, which has existed in Eastern European countries, many of which are currently undergoing major reforms toward the system of free enterprise.

3. *Communist Economic System*. Communism is the extreme form of central planning. The state owns all means (factors) of production; it allocates production and consumption through the process of rationing to all members of society. All production outlets, firms and industries, are nationalized; and private ownership of property is disallowed. This is the system operated in the former U.S.S.R., and still operational today in China (albeit under significant reforms), North Korea, and Cuba.

4. *Mixed Economy*. This is a system that operates a mixture of free enterprise and central planning. Usually, certain "strategic" industries (such as education, health care services, public utilities, and infrastructure) are operated under close regulatory control, under which the firm's production level, pricing, profit, employment level, and investment activities are controlled by the government, while the product is distributed through the free market. The economy therefore operates a "mixed" system of free enterprise and regulatory control. The mixed economy does not indicate a mixture of free enterprise and central planning *per se*. The control is exercised by the government in an attempt to minimize the economic impacts of *market failure* in such *merit goods* sectors (see chapter 5). Examples exist in most Western European countries, Canada, and most developing countries.

Goals of the Economic System

The overriding economic goals of any society are the two broad goals of promoting, achieving, maintaining, and sustaining economic *efficiency* and *equity*. These two goals summarize the ultimate objectives of all systems of organization, although with different levels of emphasis. For example, the communist system may be thought of as a system that emphasizes the goal of equity, while the free enterprise system may suffer from equity for greater efficiency. Usually, however, there is a tradeoff relationship between the two goals.

Goal of Economic Efficiency

Efficiency is the need for the economy to operate optimally. The criteria for the goal of economic efficiency in an economy may be categorized as:

1. Maximum employment of the society's resources (labor, capital, and natural resources).
2. Maintenance of full capacity utilization in businesses, and avoidance of idle capacity of productive enterprises (firms and industries).
3. Ensuring *minimum costs* of production in firms; that is, firms/industries should produce output at minimum unit costs (least average cost of output).
4. Goods and services should be marketed (distributed to reach consumers) at some *competitive leverage* (see chapter 3). This is the only way to ensure competitive product prices and maintain *competitiveness* for firms and the economy.
5. There should be macroeconomic stability in the economy. This means that high inflation and unemployment rates must not exist. To avoid cost-push inflation as well as unemployment, flexibility in the labor market is necessary; to prevent demand-pull inflation, the economy should be flexible enough to allow for the appropriate self-adjustment mechanisms of supply and demand.
6. Economic liberalization: firms and industries should be operated under private enterprise and profit incentives (wherever possible) to ensure management efficiency and competition. This means that entry barriers and central regulatory control should be dismantled. In addition to operating a regime of privatization and deregulation, the economy must maintain *trade liberalization* as well as currency *exchange rate* flexibility.

If the above conditions exist in an economy, there is economic efficiency; if they do not exist, there is economic inefficiency in the economy. The degree of an economy's efficiency varies according to the extent to which the above conditions exist. The existence or otherwise of the above conditions is what really makes one economy different from another in terms of economic efficiency, which further determines the relative state of competitiveness of different economies. The various factors that determine economic efficiency act on both the micro and macro level parameters of competitiveness.

Goal of Economic Equity

Equity is the need to maintain fairness in income distribution. It involves a normative assessment of relative well-being among the members of the society. Optimal equity requires that social welfare not only be maximized but also be spread equitably among the members of society. This needs not mean that there be equality in earnings and wealth; rather, it means that there be no vast differences in earnings and wealth within the population. The criteria for determining the existence of equity within the society are:

1. Minimum income inequality among the members of the population.[1]
2. Minimum level of absolute poverty across the population.

These criteria are closely related to each other (and are related to the level of unemployment in the economy). The state of equity within a society is a very crucial determinant of social and political stability—important factors in a society's state of efficiency and competitiveness. Inequity would cause social dissatisfaction and civil problems such as crime, civil disobedience, mob-action, and political instability. These threaten the society's well-being and impose high costs upon economic activities, thereby jeopardizing competitiveness.

MARKET FAILURE

Market failure occurs because the free-enterprise market system, on its own, is unable to sufficiently self-adjust in order to sustain the society's economic goals of efficiency and equity. The market organization on which the society bases its allocation and distribution of resources, is beset with major problems, which may cause it to *fail*.[2] That is, the free-market system fails in enabling society to achieve its overriding economic goals based on the criteria outlined above. Evidence of market failure exists in the form of abundant idle capacity in businesses, massive unemployment, inflation, recessions, poor quality products, massive poverty, and severe inequalities in income and wealth distribution. Thus, the free market has failed in achieving efficiency and equity.

Causes of Market Failure

Four main causes or sources of market failure can be identified within the free-market system. These are: (1) market imperfection inherent in the free market; (2) existence of public goods; (3) existence of externalities; and (4) existence of information impactedness. Due to the crucial importance of these factors in determining the economy's efficiency and competitiveness, we analyze each in greater depth.

Market Imperfection

The *perfect market* is the ideal competitive market (see chapter 10). It is the (ideal) *market structure* that would enable the economy to achieve its goal of maximum efficiency. Ordinarily, however, the free market falls far short of being a *perfect market* in this sense, because several of the conditions that give rise to a perfect market do not exist in a free market. A perfect market is one with *ideal competition*. It is a market that is governed by the market structure of *perfect competition*.

Perfect competition is analyzed in the next chapter. It is the market structure characterized by the conditions of large number of participants (buyers and sellers), homogeneous products (perfect substitutes of each other), freedom of mobility of resources and participants, and complete free flow of information and awareness. These conditions would guarantee that it is not possible for any participant to change the price level of the product in this market, meaning that the product price would always be constant in the market. Thus, any participating firm in the market would have to take the product's market price as given, for it could not unilaterally alter this price. So would any participating consumer. Therefore, the market price is determined only by the interaction of the demand and supply of the product.

With market imperfection, however, there could be monopoly (single firm), oligopoly (few firms), or monopsony (single buyer), whereby there would be entry barriers. The barriers could lower the employment level, capacity utilization, and output level, and give rise to higher cost of production and higher market prices of the output.

Generally, market imperfection results in the following economic outcomes in the free-market system.

1. *Technical inefficiency*. A firm (or firms) within an industry is said to be technically inefficient if and when it operates to produce and market its output at higher unit cost than necessary. This would be because (as an uncompetitive firm) it would not be operating at the minimum point of its average cost curve. (Chapter 10 contains the detailed analysis of this subject).

2. *Allocative inefficiency*. There would be allocative inefficiency in a firm or industry if it produces and markets its goods/services at a price that is greater than the marginal cost of output. This indicates that the consumer's real valuation of the product (given by the product's price) exceeds the cost of producing the product—resulting in the imposition of *deadweight loss* (of welfare or wellbeing) upon society. Moreover, the market does not operate in equilibrium as the market price does not equate the supply to the demand of the product.

3. *Distributive inefficiency*. Uncompetitive firms/industries tend to reap super-normal profits—returns that are over and above the *normal profit* level which is the payment necessary to retain the entrepreneur's services. Super-normal profit represents an economic *rent*, and thus represents a payment (accruing to the firm) which is not a reward to any factor (for its productive services) but rather a return over and above what is necessary.

Thus, the free market fails in the face of the technical, allocative, and distributive inefficiencies that beset uncompetitive firms that operate in it. And as long as a free-market economy is not completely governed by (perfectly) competitive markets, the society's economic goals of efficiency and equity would not be achieved.

Public Goods

Public goods (and services) are those having the characteristics that their use by one person does not interfere with (or reduce) their use by another person. They differ from *private goods* whose use by one person make them unavailable to other persons. Public goods are subject to the *free-rider* problem because of their non-excludability characteristic. That is, for some public goods, it is not possible to prevent someone (who does not buy the good or service) from using it.[3] Therefore, due to its free-rider property, no one would be willing to produce a public good, because it would not be possible for it to be marketed effectively (to charge a price for it and have people actually pay to use it). Common examples of (pure) public goods include street lights, national defense, neighborhood security service, policing, or environmental cleanup.

Because of the nature and character of pure public goods, it would be inefficient (insufficient amounts would be produced at very high costs) and inequitable (free-ridership) for it to be marketed and allocated through the workings of the free-market system. It would not be possible to properly price and distribute efficient quantities due to non-excludability. Therefore, since the private sector could not effectively be driven by self-interest incentives to produce and market a public good within a free-enterprise market system, it is said that there is market failure involving the free-market system.

Externalities

Closely related to the existence of public goods is the phenomenon of *externalities*. Externalities are spill-overs or social costs/benefits. They are positive or negative side effects that an activity imposes upon others.

An externality is a certain event or outcome (X) which is not part of another activity (Y), but benefits (positive externality) or harms (negative externality) that activity (Y). The effect of the externality (X) is not usually included in the activity (Y); thus, externalities are spill-overs. A positive externality is spill-over benefit or social benefit; a negative externality is spill-over cost or social cost. The externality is not included or *internalized* in determining the pricing and output level of the activity.

An example of a negative externality could be cited in the case of, say, a textile firm located upstream along the bank of a river, using the river as a waste disposal for its byproducts. This firm is causing a negative externality. A corn farmer, say, who is located downstream along the banks of this river, and who uses the river as a source of water for irrigation, will suffer reduced productivity of corn, because of pollutants discharged into the river by the textile firm.[4] The farmer and society bear the externality in form of higher production costs, lower employment, and lower output level and quality, and higher prices of corn. Hence, as the free market could not compel the textile firm to incorporate the emission costs into its output and pricing decisions and outcome, the cost of textiles would be lower than it should be, greater level of output would be produced than should be, the consumers of textiles would be paying lower prices than they should, and textile producers would be making higher profits than they should. These outcomes defeat the society's economic goals of efficiency and equity—market failure.[5]

Information Impactedness

Information impactedness refers to the lack of free flow of information and the phenomenon of *information asymmetry*. Information asymmetry is the situation that information acquisition is not symmetric—the existence of information for someone at the exclusion of another person. This refers to the fact that information that is acquired by one party would not necessarily be available to someone else. For example, asymmetric information exists when one party in a business transaction (say, the producer or the seller) knows more information about the product (such as the exact contents, quality, performance, age, cost of production, etc.) than the buyer knows. This is vital information about the product that is not available to the buyer.

As a result of the lack of free flow of information in the society, the free market would fail to sustain efficiency in resource allocation because, among other things:

1. Product contents and product quality could fail to truly measure up to the standard that were expected by the consumer.

2. Advertisement could be misleading and misrepresenting.

3. An employer may not know fully the employee's skills and other unobservable traits that could affect productivity positively or negatively.

4. There could be *moral hazard* problems in business transactions (such as when a buyer of a life insurance or fire insurance is a heavy smoker although the insurance company does not know about it).

PATTERN OF FREE MARKET ORGANIZATION

The free market involves the interaction of business firms and industries, on the one hand (supply), and private individuals and consumer groups, on the other (demand), in production and consumption economic activities and transactions. Analysis of the composition of a market system can be carried out in the traditional approach of industrial organization. The market is composed of its structure, the conduct of its agents, and the performance outcomes that result.

By the *structure* of the free market is meant the general state of being of the market. The market's structure refers to the nature, components, and factors that the market is shaped by. The market structure is constituted of: the size of the market—the number of producers and consumers involved in any particular industry; the degree of economic liberalization in the market—the nature of entry condition in it, existence or otherwise of entry barriers; degree of product homogeneity or product differentiation; the degree of information impactedness and asymmetry; and the nature of elasticity of demand and supply of the product. The structure of the market largely determines the state of efficiency and competitiveness of firms in it.

The *conduct* of the free market refers to the strategic behaviors, actions, and reactions of all actors in the market. The actors include firms and industries, the government, and individual consumers and consumer groups that operate in that market. The market's conduct refers to the behaviors, actions, and reactions of firms, such as the nature of advertising, rivalry behavior, retaliatory measures, aggressive pricing, collusion and mergers behavior. Conduct also includes the actions of government, such as taxation, tariff protection, regulatory and deregulatory control, and the manipulation of macroeconomic instruments (such as money supply, interest rate, exchange rate, and the national budget). The market's conduct is a key factor influencing the state of efficiency and competitiveness of firms in it.

The *performance* of a free market refers to its achievements in terms of efficiency and competitiveness. These are determined in terms of: production efficiency, level of employment, profitability levels, international competitiveness, and economic growth. Performance is the criterion by which the success or otherwise of a market system (and its organization) is measured. The following chapters consider the intricacies of the structure and conduct of the market system with a view to their implications for competitiveness and performance.

NOTES

1. This means that the *Gini Coefficient* statistic should be near to zero. The degree of equity in income distribution is usually analyzed and measured by application of the *Lorenz Curve*—a graphical model showing the percentage of total GDP received by any given cumulative percentage of the country's population. The Gini Coefficient is the ratio of the inequality gap to total GDP. For in-depth analysis on this, see Ezeala-Harrison (1996a).

2. Any system of economic organization, whether it is a planned economy, communism, or free enterprise system, could fail. Communism failed in the former U.S.S.R. after being in operation for 70 years. Evidence of failure in central planning exists in Eastern Europe; and market failure in free-market economies is the subject of focus in our present study.

3. In fact, even if exclusion could be enforced and the free-rider problem is prevented, it may be inefficient (and uneconomical) to exclude someone from using the public good, because the marginal cost of "providing" (producing) it to that person is zero, while the marginal benefit to society in allowing that person to use it, is positive.

4. A good example of self-corrective (mutually) positive externality is that of a flower

merchant that is located near a honey producer. As the flowers bloom, bees feed on the abundant nectar in the flowers, to produce more honey, benefiting the honey producer with greater productivity and higher output. Then, in turn, the bees and other insects pollinate more flowers, resulting in greater productivity for the flower merchant.

5. This negative externality can be corrected, although the measures that could correct it are bound to impair efficiency and competitiveness. The appropriate combination of the following measures could be applied: (i) emission fees could be imposed on the textile firm, and the proceeds used to grant subsidies to the corn firm; (ii) a higher excise tax could be levied on the textile firm (to include the social cost of the discharges into the river), and tax reduction granted to the corn firm; (iii) an exclusive property right could be given to a third party, who would then charge appropriate fees.

10

Global Market Structure and Competitive Interaction

This chapter presents an in-depth analysis of the nature of industries and their interaction within the global competitive market setting. An economy's ability to sustain a healthy state of competitiveness depends on the ability of its firms and industries to compete. However, this ability to compete depends largely on the *structure* of the free market, especially regarding the way it affects a firm's *competitive leverage*.

The market structure of free enterprise is composed of perfect (competitive) and imperfect (uncompetitive) markets. The perfect markets are those that have ideal competition—referred to as *contestable markets*—and are characterized by perfect competition. The imperfect markets may exist in any of five forms: monopoly (which could be pure monopoly or natural monopoly), duopoly, oligopoly (which involves monopolistic competition), and monopsony—which usually exists in the labor market when a single employer is the only "buyer" of labor from several (or a large number of) potential employees. The market structures of perfect competition, pure monopoly, and duopoly are analyzed in greater detail in this chapter with a view to determining their implications for competitiveness. Natural monopoly has been treated fully in chapter 8, while oligopoly is the subject of chapter 11.

It is important to stress that a competitive market structure does not necessarily confer competitiveness to its firms, and an uncompetitive market structure does not necessarily impose uncompetitiveness to its firms. The firms' (or industries') market structure simply indicates the nature of the market system in which the firms operate; the firms' ability to achieve *competitive leverage* (which determines their competitive advantage and hence competitiveness) depends of the micro and macro parameters analyzed in chapter 3. Firms in competitive market structures may end up being uncompetitive while firms in uncompetitive market structures may end up being competitive, according to their ability to achieve *competitive leverage*. We now turn to some detailed study of these important issues of global market competition and competitiveness.

GLOBAL PERFECT COMPETITION

Perfect competition is the market structure characterized by the conditions of:

1. Large numbers: There are a large number of participants—large number of buyers (consumers) and sellers (firms)—in such a way that none of these could unilaterally influence the market supply or market price.
2. Homogeneous products: All units of the product being transacted in the market are exactly alike; all units of the product are perfect substitutes of each other.
3. Freedom of mobility: There are no entry or exit barriers to and from the market for any participant. There is absolute freedom of entry and exit (for any firm and any consumer) in and out of the market at all times.
4. Complete information: All participants are always aware of information concerning conditions in the market, especially regarding price level and output variations, product quality, and profit levels.

Given the existence of these conditions in the market, it is not possible for any participant to change the price level of the product. This means that the product price would always be constant. Thus, any participating firm would have to take the product's market price as given, for it could not unilaterally alter the price. The firm is therefore a *price taker* in a perfectly competitive market. The market price is determined by the interaction of the market demand and market supply of the product. A perfectly elastic demand curve faces the firm at the constant market price that is, by definition, equal to the firm's marginal revenue.

The efficiency and competitiveness of firms in a perfectly competitive industry can be illustrated with the application of a simplified linear demand model. Assuming the demand curve is of the linear (inverse) form:

$$p = a + bQ \qquad\qquad (10.1)$$

where

   p = price of the product
   a = the intercept term representing the parameters of demand, such that
       $a > 0$
   $b = dp/dQ$ = the slope of the demand curve (determining the price-
       elasticity of demand), such that $b < 0$
   Q = quantity of the product bought and sold in the market

On the supply (production) side, assume there are n number of firms in the industry, each facing similar cost conditions as they face the same input markets.

The cost of production is given by:

$$C = cq_i \qquad (10.2)$$

where

C = total cost of production
$c = dC/dq_i$ = the marginal cost (MC) of production
$i = 1, 2,...n$

The total industry (market) output is $Q = \Sigma q_i$. The *market share* of each firm is the amount of output each firm produces and supplies in the market. Assuming that the firm's overriding objective is to maximize its profits, then, with the market price of the product constant, the typical firm's profit is given by:

$$z_i = p.q_i - cq_i$$

To maximize profit,

$$dz_i/dq_i = p - c = 0$$

Hence

$$p = c$$

that is

$$a + bQ = c$$

or

$$Q^* = (c-a)/b \qquad (10.3)$$

Equation (10.3) is the equilibrium market output level (produced by all firms) in a perfectly competitive industry. Assuming each firm produces identical level of output, then each firm's equilibrium output level would be:

$$q_i^* = (c-a)/nb \qquad (10.4)$$

Thus, we see that each firm's output level is a function of industry size, n, technological conditions (proxied by marginal production cost, c), market forces, a, and the elasticity of demand parameter, b.

The market price of the product is:

$$p^* = a + bQ$$
$$= a + b[(c-a)/b]$$
$$= a + c-a$$
$$= c$$

This confirms that in the perfectly competitive industry, the price of the product equals the marginal cost of the product—marginal cost pricing. This means that the consumer pays exactly a price equal to the marginal cost of production of the good: *consumer valuation* of the product (the value the consumer places on the product, signified by the price) exactly equals (matches) the marginal cost of producing the product.[1]

The profit level of a typical firm i is

$$z_i = pq_i{}^* - cq_i{}^*$$

$$= q_i{}^*(p-c)$$

$$= 0, \text{ since } p=c$$

The firm makes no *supernormal* profit (profit over and above cost). As we learned in chapter 3, the magnitude $p-c$, represents the firm's *competitive leverage*. This magnitude equals zero in perfect competition, indicating that the firm has no competitive leverage whatsoever in a perfectly competitive market. However, the firm is able to remain in business since it covers its operating costs.

Clearly, under the perfectly competitive market structure, firms engage in cutthroat competition. Every firm must continually find ways to avoid losing its hold and market share. Such ways may involve constant efforts at research and development initiatives and innovations. This means the introduction of new and higher quality products in the market over time, and therefore, that at any time the product will be of the highest quality.

MONOPOLY IN THE GLOBAL ENVIRONMENT

Monopoly is the market structure in which a single firm constitutes the industry as the only producer and supplier of the product. The monopoly power is increased if the product has no close substitutes and has inelastic demand. Since the monopolist is the only firm in the market, it alone constitutes the industry; the industry (market) demand curve is the demand curve facing the firm.

Again, applying our linear model under the firm's assumed profit-maximization objective, the firm's profit is:

$$z = pQ - cQ$$
$$= (a+bQ)Q - cQ$$
$$= (aQ+bQ^2 - cQ$$

To maximize profit,

$$dz/dQ = a + 2bQ - c = 0$$

from which the market output level is determined as

$$Q^* = (c-a)/2b$$
$$= \tfrac{1}{2}[(c-a)/b] \tag{10.5}$$

This result indicates that production level in a monopoly market is affected only by technological factors and market forces of demand, and not affected by market size, unlike the case under competition. Further, equation (10.5) reveals that total industry output in a monopolist market is simply half of its level in a perfectly competitive industry. This outcome shows that the monopoly firm operates below the capacity utilization of its plant—a situation of *excess capacity*. This means that the industry's output level is produced under *technical inefficiency*: the output is produced and marketed at unit cost (average cost of production) that is unnecessarily higher than the **minimum** average cost at which the firm could produce. Moreover, at this higher unit cost, the output level would be unnecessarily lower than the optimal capacity level.[2]

What this outcome indicates is that the monopoly industry is economically inefficient. However, although the monopoly market is uncompetitive, this fact, and the fact that it is economically inefficient, need not mean that it would lack international competitiveness. It must be emphasized that economic inefficiency has mainly domestic consequences. This is because it may or may not affect the competitive leverage of firms. If a firm operates under economic inefficiency (by being technically and allocatively inefficient), and if this condition affects its competitive leverage (by reducing it), then it would impair its international competitiveness. But if this firm's inefficiency does not jeopardize its competitive leverage, its competitiveness may not suffer. In fact, this condition may help it to sustain global competitiveness since it could apply its profit to reinforce its competitive leverage and competitive advantage.

Monopoly market price is:

$$p^* = a+bQ^*$$
$$= a + b[(c-a)/2b]$$
$$= a + \tfrac{1}{2}c - \tfrac{1}{2}a = \tfrac{1}{2}a + \tfrac{1}{2}c$$
$$= \tfrac{1}{2}(a+c) > 0 \tag{10.6}$$

Monopoly profit is:

$$z^* = pQ^* - cQ^*$$
$$= Q^*(p-c)$$
$$= (c-a)/2b\{\tfrac{1}{2}(a+c) - c\}$$
$$= (c-a)/2b \cdot \tfrac{1}{2}(a-c)$$
$$= (c-a)(a-c)/4b > 0 \tag{10.7}$$

A monopoly firm is able to operate with a significant profit margin that is over and above its total cost. But, again, what does this mean for its efficiency and competitiveness? We verify by assessing the firm's competitive leverage. Competitive leverage is given by:

$$p - c = \frac{1}{2}(a+c) - c$$
$$= \frac{1}{2}a - \frac{1}{2}c$$
$$= \frac{1}{2}(a-c) > 0 \tag{10.8}$$

as $a > c$.

This indicates that the monopoly firm/industry has positive competitive leverage. The existence of competitive leverage indicates that the firm could have competitive advantage and would therefore be apt to achieve and sustain a state of international competitiveness (subject to the suitability of the macro level parameters of international competitiveness—the sufficiency conditions). This observation, however, does not mean that the monopoly industry does not impose other types of inefficiencies on the economy. The possible use of the firm's competitive leverage to enhance the state of international competitiveness is one thing; the level of *deadweight loss* that the monopoly firm imposes on the economy is another.

DUOPOLY IN GLOBAL COMPETITION

Duopoly is the industry that has only two competing firms in the market. Examples of duopoly in most countries can be found in the airline industry, the railways, and sometimes the media (newspapers, radio, and television) industries. The two rival firms have to operate by adopting the strategies of either collusion (cooperation) or competition (rivalry). In the collusion case, the two duopoly firms, say, Firm 1 and Firm 2, decide to pool together in order to operate jointly to produce (supply) a monopoly output and charge a monopoly price in the market. In this way they reap monopoly-type supernormal profits and then share it accordingly. The overall market outcome of this setting is similar to the case of monopoly discussed above.

Usually, however, either or both of the two duopoly firms might believe that it could do better (earn higher profit) by operating under a state of competition, by trying to out-compete its rival. Moreover, it might be illegal, under antitrust laws, to operate collusive mergers (in setting prices and output in the market). Hence, often the two firms that are involved in a duopoly market tend to engage in a competitive, rather than a collusive, relationship. And this affects the efficiency and competitiveness of the industry.

Competitive Interaction of Duopoly

Economists normally apply the *Cournot model* in the study of competitive duopoly. A thorough presentation and application of the Cournot model is given in the *appendix* to chapter 11. We outline the approach here to illustrate how competitive duopoly markets operate.

Assume that Firms 1 and 2 are the two firms in the duopoly market, producing and marketing output levels q_1 and q_2, respectively. Each firm knows of its rival's influence on the market. The market price depends on the total market output Q of the two firms. We continue to apply our supply and demand conditions as above; that is, with the market demand curve $p = a + bQ$, and cost condition $C = cq_i$.

Total market output is

$$Q = q_1 + q_2 \tag{10.9a}$$

so that the demand curve is actually

$$p = a + b(q_1 + q_2) \tag{10.9b}$$

We assume that each firm competes by altering its output level. This is a simplifying assumption because firms could, and often do, compete through manipulating their prices rather than output levels. This simplifying assumption, however, is justified on grounds that the market price would always be constant for both duopolists (as each of them would not allow itself to be undercut by its rival). Therefore, the output level (and the various attributes that may be associated with it, such as, quality or packaging) is likely to be the medium of the competition.

Each firm must decide its own output level while taking its rival's output level as a given (constant). That is, each duopolist can only *conjecture* (guess) about how its rival would react to its own unilateral action regarding its own output. The term *conjectural variation (cv_i)* refers to the belief (conjecture) that each competitor has regarding how its rivals would react (vary) to its own unilateral actions and initiatives. Thus, each firm's conjectural variation is the presumption of each firm regarding how its rival would react to its actions. That is,

$$cv_1 = dq_2/dq_1$$
$$cv_2 = dq_1/dq_2$$

To simplify the presentation, we invoke the standard Cournot assumption that $cv_1 = cv_2 = 0$. That is, we assume that each firm believes that its rival would not alter its behavior in response to its own unilateral actions.[3] Each firm operates to maximize its profit by producing and marketing the corresponding output level.

For Firm 1, profit is

$$z_1 = pq_1 - cq_1$$
$$= (a+bQ)q_1 - cq_1$$
$$= [a+b(q_1+q_2)]q_1] - cq_1$$
$$= aq_1 + bq_1^2 + bq_1q_2 - cq_1$$

Profit maximization for Firm 1 requires that

$$\partial z_1/\partial q_1 = a + 2bq_1 + bq_2 - c = 0 \tag{10.10}$$

Similarly, for Firm 2, profit is

$$z_2 = pq_2 - cq_2$$
$$= (a+bQ)q_2 - cq_2$$
$$= [a+b(q_1+q_2)]q_2] - cq_2$$
$$= aq_2 + bq_2^2 + bq_2q_1 - cq_2$$

and profit maximization for Firm 2 requires that

$$\partial z_2/\partial q_2 = a + 2bq_2 + bq_1 - c = 0 \tag{10.11}$$

Equations (10.10) and (10.11) are solved simultaneously to determine the individual output levels of each of the two duopolists.[4] First, subtracting equation (10.11) from (10.10), and rearranging, we obtain:

$$q_1^* = q_2^* \tag{10.12}$$

This indicates that two duopolists would always produce equal levels of output. Adding equations (10.10) and (10.11), and rearranging, we have:

$$(q_1+q_2) = Q^* = 2/3[(c-a)/b] \tag{10.13}$$

This result indicates that the total duopoly market output is simply two-thirds of what the total output level would be under perfect competition. And, as each duopolist produces an equal amount of output, each producer's output level would be given by

$$q_1^* = q_2^* = \tfrac{1}{2}\{2/3[(c-a)/b)]\}$$
$$= 1/3[(c-a)/b] \tag{10.14}$$

Like the case of a monopoly market, we see that production level in a duopoly market is also just influenced by technological factors and market forces of demand. Again, as equation (10.13) reveals that total market output in a duopoly market is only two-thirds of the total level in a perfectly competitive industry, it means that each duopoly firm operates below its plant's capacity utilization (at excess capacity). It means technical inefficiency. Each firm's output is produced and marketed at average cost of production that is unnecessarily higher than the minimum average cost at which the firm could produce. And at this higher unit cost, the output level would be unnecessarily lower than the optimal capacity level.

In the case of monopoly, we noted that this inefficient and hence uneconomical outcome in an uncompetitive market may not mean that the firms and industries concerned would lack international competitiveness. In the case of duopoly, however, the competitive situation facing each firm does present a different scenario. This is because each firm faces a competitive environment in its domestic market. The degree of the competition would determine the level of competitive leverage that each firm could have, which would determine whether or not it would have competitive advantage.

To verify the situation, duopoly market price is found by substituting equation (10.13) into equation (10.9b):

$$p^* = a+b[2(c-a)/3b] = 1/3.(a+2c) > 0 \qquad (10.15)$$

Each firm's competitive leverage is given by:

$$p\text{-}c = 1/3.(a+2c) - c = 1/3.(a\text{-}c) > 0 \qquad (10.16)$$

since $a>c$.

This indicates an existence of competitive leverage for each duopoly firm. The firm could achieve and sustain international competitiveness (again, subject to availability of sufficiency conditions).

Each duopoly firm's profit is:

$$z_i^* = pq_i\text{-}cq_i = q_i^*(p\text{-}c)$$

which, upon substituting the values of q_i^* (equation 10.14), and $(p\text{-}c)$ (equation 10.16), becomes

$$z_i^* = \{1/3[(c-a)/b]\}.\{1/3.(a\text{-}c)\}$$
$$= 1/9b.[(c-a)(a\text{-}c)] \qquad (10.17)$$

and given that $a>c$ and $b<0$, then $(c\text{-}a) < 0$ and $(a\text{-}c) > 0$, so that equation (10.17) is positive, that is, $z_i^* > 0$. This indicates that the duopoly firm makes (supernormal) profit. The firm is well placed to have competitive advantage. It could achieve and sustain international competitiveness.

NOTES

1. This condition, the equality of marginal cost and price, is called the *allocative efficiency* condition. It means that the market is allocatively efficient because the cost to society of having the product produced (marginal cost) is matched by the value (utility) that the product yields to society (price).

2. As we shall see later in the chapter, the monopoly market price is greater than the marginal cost of the product. This means that the market does not satisfy allocative efficiency—the output is produced and marketed under allocative inefficiency because the value that the society places on the product (its price) is greater than its marginal cost (actual worth of the product).

3. This assumption is a myopic (and even unrealistic) one. Conjectural variations of firms are often not zero. Managers do exercise clever judgments, and often adopt sophisticated strategies in their competitive moves and actions against their rivals. In such case, a firm's conjectural variation would be a parameter that could vary with market conditions (see Note 4 and also *appendix* to chapter 11).

4. See the *appendix* to chapter 11. The assumption of zero-conjectural enabled us to treat dq_1/dq_2 as if it is identical with $\partial q_1/\partial q_2$ (or dq_2/dq_1 as if it is identical with $\partial q_2/\partial q_1$). Relaxing this assumption and recognizing the fact that $\partial q_1/\partial q_2 \neq dq_2/dq_1 \neq 0$, and then maximizing Firm 1's profit, would give: $dz_1/dq_1 = a+2bq_1+b(q_1.dq_2/dq_1+q_2)-c = 0$. Similarly, maximizing Firm 2's profit gives $dz_2/dq_2 = a+2bq_2+b(q_2.dq_1/dq_2+q_1)-c = 0$. Then, denoting each firm's conjectural variation as $dq_1/dq_2 = v_1$ and $dq_2/dq_1 = v_2$, these maximum profit conditions become $a+2bq_1+b(q_1v_1+q_2)-c = 0$ and $a+2bq_2 + b(q_2v_2+q_1)-c = 0$. The model becomes more realistic albeit more complicated, involving strategic games and manoeuvres. This is analyzed and discussed more in-depth in the *appendix* to chapter 11.

11

Strategic Behavior in Global Competitive Markets

In this chapter, we examine the type of behaviors that govern strategic competition among companies, with a view to determining the impact of such moves on international competitiveness. The phenomenon of globalization has opened all markets to competition. The kind of interaction among firms within the global market environment is akin to that of an oligopoly market structure in which firms compete on an almost equal footing. We apply the oligopoly model to analyze the competitive environment in the global market. For in such a setting, the firm's ability to achieve and sustain international competitiveness would be the crucial factor that determines whether or not such a firm survives.

Oligopoly is the market structure in which a few firms exist as rival competitors in the production and marketing of products that are close substitutes. The number of firms could be two (duopoly) or more (monopolistic competition), but often not enough for the market to be a perfectly competitive one. Each of the firms in oligopoly have some *market share*, measured by the percentage of the total (global) output level it supplies. The competitive scenario of the oligopoly structure is referred to as *monopolistic competition*—monopolist firms engaged in competition. This is because each firm's product is a *differentiated* product, often produced and marketed under a *brand name*; therefore the producer of the product would be a monopolist of that brand. However, each firm's product would be a very close or even perfect substitute of the products of the other firms. Thus, there is a continuous state of competition among these various brands (of the same product)—monopolistic competition.

MARKET COMPETITION IN GLOBAL OLIGOPOLY

The global market is likened to the classic case of oligopolistic market competition where a few firms interact with each other in production and marketing of their differentiated products. The standard oligopoly analysis is given here while a more complicated (albeit more realistic) version is presented in the *appendix*; we continue to apply the linear model of the previous chapter.

On the demand side we assume linear demand curve of the form

$$p = a + bQ \tag{11.1}$$

The total market output, Q, is the global market quantity bought and sold. It is defined as

$$Q = \Sigma q_i, \ i = 1, 2,...n$$

n is the number of companies competing in the global marketplace.

The critical distinguishing factor among oligopoly firms engaged in the global marketplace exists on the supply side. Since competing firms are located in different countries, the firms would not have identical cost conditions. Each firm's cost condition depends on the circumstances existing in its country, such as labor market circumstances (wage levels, labor unions, payroll taxes), tax circumstances (high tax regime or low tax regime), technological conditions, existence of supporting infrastructure, and the like. These are the factors that determine the firm's productivity and cost efficiency (micro level competitiveness). Therefore, each firm's cost function would be

$$C_i = c_i q_i \tag{11.2}$$

By definition (actually, assumption) of the linear cost function, c_i represents the *average cost* (AC)—the cost per unit of total output. It must be stressed that c_i is not constant, and since it is not constant it is not equal to the *marginal cost* (m_i). The firm's marginal cost is given by

$$m_i = \partial C_i / \partial q_i = c_i + q_i \cdot \partial c_i / \partial q_i \tag{11.3}$$

The nature of this marginal cost indicates that it is greater than the average cost (cost per unit of output); from equation (11.3) it can be seen that the average cost is

$$c_i = m_i - q_i \cdot \partial c_i / \partial q_i \tag{11.4}$$

The term $\partial c_i / \partial q_i$ represents the *cost-effectiveness parameter* of the firm's operations; it indicates how the firm's unit cost is affected as the firm conducts business. The magnitude of $\partial c_i/\partial q_i$ is critical for the firm's survival in the global market competitive environment. Equation (11.4) simply states that the firm's average cost is equal to marginal cost minus the amount by which cost is reduced (cost-efficiency) for producing the given amount of output. For example, for two firms, say, Firm i and Firm j that are competing in the global market, if $\partial c_i/\partial q_i > \partial c_j/\partial q_j$, it implies that Firm j would be more competitive than Firm i. The magnitude of the *cost-effectiveness* parameter depends on the firm's efficiency of operation; it would be the key factor that determines the firm's ability to sustain competitiveness.[1]

The typical firm wishes to maximize its profit, with profit function given as

$$z_i = p.q_i - c_iq_i$$
$$= (a+b\Sigma q_i)q_i - c_iq_i$$
$$= aq_i + b\Sigma q_i^2 - c_iq_i$$

Profit is maximized where

$$dz_i/dq_i = a + 2b\Sigma q_i - (c_i + q_i.\partial c_i/\partial q_i) = 0$$

that is,

$$a + 2b\Sigma q_i - m_i = 0$$

This yields the individual firm's optimal output as

$$q_i^* = (m_i-a)/2b - \Sigma_2^n q_i^* \tag{11.5}$$

Equation (11.5) gives the minimum market share that a company must have in the global market scene in order to remain in business. It indicates that each firm's output level is a negative function of its global rivals' collective output level ($\Sigma_2^n q_i^*$), as well as the regular domestic technological factors (reflected in m_i), and market forces (reflected in a and b) that influence a firm's output level.

Competitiveness of the Global Oligopolist

As the global marketplace is likened to an oligopoly market in which firms from different countries compete, the oligopolist competitor in the global market scene must achieve and sustain an ongoing state of competitiveness in order to remain in business. This would depend on the extent to which the firm is able to retain competitive leverage within its market. The global market price is

$$p^* = a + bQ$$
$$= a + b(m_i-a)/2b$$

$$= a + \tfrac{1}{2}m_i - \tfrac{1}{2}a$$
$$= \tfrac{1}{2}(a+m_i) > 0 \tag{11.6}$$

This suggests that the market price is a function of the individual firm's costs. Thus, a firm that is able to achieve lower costs could sell at a lower price and retain greater market share.

The firm's competitive leverage is given by

$$p-c_i = \tfrac{1}{2}(a+m_i) - (m_i - q_i.\partial c_i/\partial q_i)$$
$$= \tfrac{1}{2}a + \tfrac{1}{2}m_i - m_i + q_i.\partial c_i/\partial q_i$$
$$= \tfrac{1}{2}a - \tfrac{1}{2}m_i + q_i.\partial c_i/\partial q_i$$
$$= \tfrac{1}{2}(a-m_i) + q_i.\partial c_i/\partial q_i$$

Substituting $m_i = c_i + q_i.\partial c_i/\partial q_i$, we have

$$p-c_i = \tfrac{1}{2}a - \tfrac{1}{2}(c_i + q_i.\partial c_i/\partial q_i) + q_i.\partial c_i/\partial q_i$$
$$= \tfrac{1}{2}a - \tfrac{1}{2}c_i - \tfrac{1}{2}q_i.\partial c_i/\partial q_i) + q_i.\partial c_i/\partial q_i$$
$$= \tfrac{1}{2}q_i.\partial c_i/\partial q_i - \tfrac{1}{2}(a-c_i)$$
$$= \tfrac{1}{2}\{a-c_i + q_i.\partial c_i/\partial q_i\} > 0 \tag{11.7}$$

This result indicates that competitive leverage exists, but its magnitude is sensitive to the firm's cost-effectiveness parameter. Equation (11.7) reveals an interesting relationship concerning competitive leverage: a comparison of this equation and equation (10.8) reveals a relationship between the firm's competitive leverage in the global market $[\tfrac{1}{2}(a-c_i)+\tfrac{1}{2}q_i.\partial c_i/\partial q_i]$, and its competitive leverage in the domestic market (where the firm would be a monopoly), $\tfrac{1}{2}(a-c)$. The difference is the term $\tfrac{1}{2}q_i.\partial c_i/\partial q_i$ in the global market case. It shows that the firm must maintain ongoing cost-effectiveness in order to succeed in the global market. For if $\partial c_i/\partial q_i = 0$ (zero cost-effectiveness), it implies a domestic case, in which case the firm could retain competitive leverage without being cost-effective.

This model is able to completely explain both the micro level (necessary conditions) and macro level (sufficiency conditions) of global competitiveness, together. The two aspects are represented in the expression of the firm's competitive leverage within a global market: the term $(a-c_i)$ captures the productivity and cost (technological) parameters, while the cost-effectiveness parameter $\partial c_i/\partial q_i$ captures the effect of macro level factors—how macro level parameters affect cost and hence competitiveness.

Strategic Interaction in Global Oligopoly Market

We model how global oligopolist competitors actually operate in their business interactions with each other. Given the rivalry condition in which they operate, oligopolists are very sensitive to the strategic actions of their rivals—mainly because their business actions are not independent of each other's.

Apparently, each firm is conscious of the competitive global market conditions, especially that the market price would be constant irrespective of its own actions. At any given time period, let the going market price, the normal price, be denoted by p*, a price level that represents a *critical price* in the industry. At this price, should any firm unilaterally deviate and charge a higher price than p* for its products (*price hike*), its rival firms would *ignore* this action (as this firm would lose sales and market shares to competitors). As a result, the demand for the firm's products would become elastic (as there would be a greater percentage decrease in demand for its products relative to its percentage price increase). On the other hand, at the price p*, should any firm unilaterally deviate and charge a lower price than p* for its products (*price cut*), its rival firms would *match* this action (as they would lose sales and market shares to this rival if they fail to follow suit with a price cut). As a result, the demand for the firm's products would be inelastic (as there would be no significant change in demand for its products relative to its percentage price cut). Thus, demand is elastic for all prices above p*, and inelastic for all prices below p*. This describes the phenomenon of *kinked demand*, which faces an oligopolist competitor in the global market, and has important implications for each firm's competitiveness.

Each firm operates at the price p* and markets the output level (market share) q*. The market price (p*) is stable and rigid, because minor changes in individual competitor's cost situations would not likely be passed on to price increases. This is because the competing firms are located in different countries with different factor and productivity circumstances. Any firm that is unable to achieve and maintain sufficient competitive leverage at the global market price p* would not succeed in the global competition.[2] The *kinked model* explains price rigidity and uniformity (under given cost and technological conditions) in global market competition.

Collusion and Cartels in Global Competitive Strategies

This is a competitiveness strategy whereby international firms explicitly agree to set output (quotas) with a view to setting (fixing) the global market price. A typical example is the Organization of Petroleum Exporting Countries (OPEC) cartel. Cartels are collusive bodies formed by oligopoly firms for this purpose.[3] They simply set output levels (supply) for each firm, and set the corresponding price (according to the demand curve) at levels where they would not otherwise have been under competitive oligopoly.

The cartel would either set the market output level and allow the market demand/supply conditions to determine the market price, or set the market price and allow the market to determine its output level. Cartels succeed much more easily if the demand for their product is inelastic. But international cartels often face major problems that threaten their ability to sustain their goals. Their main problems are:

1. Different cost conditions cause some countries not to join the cartel.
2. Cheating by members tends to threaten the breakdown of the cartel.
3. Consumers may find substitutes for the product, and this weakens the cartel's power.

These problems cause weaknesses in the competitiveness of international cartels. Rarely do all producing countries of any particular product join a cartel. Therefore an international cartel usually accounts for only a portion of the total global market output. As such, the cartel must take into account the supply responses of its competitors (nonmember producers) when setting its output and price levels.

A cartel simply acts like a pure monopolist in the global market. It seeks to maximize its (joint) profits by setting the marginal revenue in the global market to the representative (aggregate) marginal cost of the cartel producers. The total global market supply (S) would be the sum of the individual cartel members' supply (s):

$$S = \Sigma s_i$$

where $s_i = m_i$ represents each individual cartel member's supply. The global market price p^* and output bought and sold Q^* would obtain at some equilibrium where the supply S equals the demand.

The inherent instability of a typical international cartel is the main factor that impairs its global competitiveness. Though each individual member country of the cartel (Firm i) could be making supernormal profits at the cartel price, it would not be maximizing its profits. This is because its marginal cost m_i would not be equal to its (global) marginal revenue at its profit-maximizing output q_i^*. In fact, at p^* a cartel member's m_i would be lower than the marginal revenue because the marginal revenue would be constant (equal to p^*) since a member could sell only a given quota at the going price.

Therefore, Firm i would have the *selfish incentive* and tendency to seek to optimize (maximize profit) by producing a larger output toward the level where the fixed marginal revenue equals its m_i. Thus, cartels are inherently unstable because although it is in the cartel's best interest for every member to restrict output in order to conform to the organization's optimal global market level, it is in Firm i's best interest to raise its own output as long as all others, except itself, restrict theirs. This explains the incessant tendencies of cartel members to engage in cheating, which, in turn, jeopardizes the cartel's ability to attain its objectives.

APPENDIX

In this appendix we present a generalized model of global oligopoly that applies fundamental assumptions to analyze how the global market works in an ongoing competitive setting. The main underlying assumptions are that the oligopoly market involves several firms competing with each other and resolved to maximizing their individual (rather than joint) profits. Each firm is a rational business unit that applies consistent cojectures about rival moves and actions to formulate its own moves and actions. Therefore, the conjectural variation of the global market competitor is non-zero—a positive parameter.

Parametric Conjectural Variation in Global Oligopoly

Parametric conjectural variation means that the conjectural variations of competing firms are positive parameters.[4] We consider a model that applies this reality in determining strategic interaction among oligopolistic competitors.

The traditional Cournot-Nash assumption of zero (inconsistent) conjectural variation among oligopolist competitors cannot adequately explain the nature and outcome of the competitive global oligopoly market. This is because the assumption of zero conjectural variation on the part of a competitor implies that competitors are not only naive but also behave unrealistically. That is, each firm believes that its rival would not alter its behavior in response to its own unilateral actions. This assumption is unrealistic because conjectural variations of firms are not zero: conjectures should be realistic and therefore consistent.

Firms do exercise realistic judgments, and often apply preemptive and sophisticated strategies in their competitive moves and actions against their rivals. Therefore, a firm's conjectural variation would be a positive parameter that could vary with market conditions. Therefore, the model of oligopoly market interaction under consistent strategic conjectures is one in which firms react to their rivals' actions more realistically.[5]

Oligopoly Conjectures

The global market satisfies the characteristic oligopoly interdependence among participating firms in which rival parties act out their respective strategies. The various strategies are formulated as firms act and react to each other's actions and reactions, which, in turn, depend on conjectural variations adopted. We examine the traditional Cournot model as the background against which the oligopoly parametric conjectural variation model is explored.

The Cournot-Nash Model of Inconsistent Conjectural Variation

The traditional Cournot zero-conjectural variation moves are strategic moves within the broad definition of the concept (Bresnahan, 1981). Assuming a general case where the output of each firm depends on the (market) output of the other firms involved in the global market, the basic Cournot presumption is that each competitor maintains conjectures (about strategic reactions of its rivals to its own) that are inconsistent. That is, each competitor takes it that its rivals' output decisions would always remain unchanged irrespective of its own. This means that an individual competitor reckons that its rivals will always tend to either ignore its own strategic moves or react in a certain predictable fashion.

The strategic model named after its formulator—French mathematician Augustine Cournot—known as the *Cournot model* is usually applied in the study of competitive oligopoly because of the practical appeal of the approach in modeling how competitive oligopolist markets function. As already explained in chapter 10, the standard Cournot model assumes two firms competing in the (duopoly) oligopoly market: Firm 1 producing and marketing output q_1, and Firm 2 producing and marketing output q_2. Each firm knows of its rival's influence on the market as the market price depends on the total market output of the two firms. The market demand curve is $p = a + bQ$, and production cost is $C = cq_i$. Total market output is $Q = q_1 + q_2$, so that the demand curve is actually

$$p = a + b(q_1 + q_2)$$

We assume that each firm competes by altering its output level. This is a simplifying assumption because firms could, and often do, compete through manipulating their prices rather than output levels. This simplifying assumption, however, is justified on grounds that the market price would always be constant for both duopolists (as each of them would not allow itself to be undercut by its rival). Therefore, the output level (and the various attributes that may be associated with it, such as, quality or packaging), is likely to be the medium of the competition.

Each firm must decide its own output level while taking its rival's output level as given (constant). That is, each duopolist can only *conjecture* (guess) about how its rival would react to its own unilateral action regarding its own output. The standard Cournot assumption is that conjectural variations of Firms 1 and 2, cv_1 and cv_2, respectively, are zero and equal:

$$cv_1 = dq_2/dq_1 = cv_2 = dq_1/dq_2 = 0$$

Applied to a global oligopoly setting, we assume that n firms compete in the global market, with inverse demand function $p = p(Q)$, where p is market price, and Q is total market output defined as $Q = \Sigma_1^n q_i$, where q_i is firm i's market output, $i = 1, 2,...n$. We assume further that firms face similar cost conditions:

$c = c(q_i)$, with the overriding objectives to maximizes their respective profits:[6]

$$Max \; \pi_i = q_i p(Q) - c(q_i) \qquad (A11.1)$$
$$(q_i)$$

The first-order conditions for optimal operation (profit maximization) give the reaction functions:

$$q_1 dp/dQ(1+q_{21}+q_{31}+..+q_{n1})+p-\partial c/\partial q_i = 0$$
$$q_2 dp/dQ(q_{21}+1+q_{23}+..+q_{2n})+p-\partial c/\partial q_i = 0$$
$$q_3 dp/dQ(q_{31}+q_{32}+1+..+q_{3n})+p-\partial c/\partial q_i = 0$$
$$.$$
$$.$$
$$q_n dp/dQ(q_{n1}+q_{n2}+1+..+q_{nn})+p-\partial c/\partial q_i = 0$$

where
$$q_{ij} = \partial q_i/\partial q_j$$

The terms q_{ij} (equal to $\partial q_i/\partial q_j$) are the conjectural variation parameters. Solving the model under the standard Cournot "myopic" assumption of zero conjectural variation, that is, substituting $q_{ij} = 0$, we obtain

$$q_1 dp/dQ + p - \partial c/\partial q_1 = 0$$
$$q_2 dp/dQ + p - \partial c/\partial q_2 = 0$$
$$q_3 dp/dQ + p - \partial c/\partial q_3 = 0$$
$$.$$
$$.$$
$$q_n dp/dQ + p - \partial c/\partial q_i = 0$$

Then, each firm's *reaction function* (the equilibrium market output of each firm) is obtained as

$$q_1^* = (\partial c/\partial q_1 - p)/dp/dQ$$
$$q_2^* = (\partial c/\partial q_2 - p)/dp/dQ$$
$$q_3^* = (\partial c/\partial q_3 - p)/dp/dQ$$
$$.$$
$$.$$
$$q_n^* = (\partial c/\partial q_n - p)/dp/dQ$$

This shows that the reaction function of each firm is independent of the conjectural variation. This is clearly unrealistic because, by definition, a firm's reaction function must be a function of its conjectural variation. That is, a firm's profit maximizing output must be a function of the total output levels of its rivals as well as the firm's belief about the reactions of those rivals to its own actions.

Anything short of this would be inconsistent (Bresnahan, 1981); and for this reason the standard Cournot assumptions cannot adequately model the oligopolistic conditions of the global marketplace. We need assumptions that not only reflect that in equilibrium each firm exercises beliefs about the others' responses which are justified in the interim, but also that capture the essential aspects of consistency in a firm's perception of, and beliefs about, its rivals.

Consistent (Parametric) Conjectural Variation

Each firm sets out to maximize its own profit as indicated by equation (A11.1).[7] As conjectures and reactions ought to be correct and consistent, what an individual firm conjectures affects (determines) how it reacts to the moves of its rival(s). It is under this setting that each firm realizes the inherent interdependence between them, in that the profits of any one firm depend on the actions of the other firms.

The first-order condition of optimizing operation for firm i is given by

$$q_i \frac{dp}{dQ}(q_{1i}+q_{2i}+q_{3i}+1+...+q_{ni})+p-\frac{\partial c}{\partial q_i} = 0$$

from which the reaction function for a typical firm with consistent conjectures is obtained as

$$q_i = \frac{\partial c/\partial q_i - p}{(dp/dQ)[1+\Sigma_2^n q_{ji}]}$$

This equation of the firm's reaction function expresses the firm's market output which is seen to be a function of technology ($\partial c/\partial q_i$), market price (p), market forces (dp/dQ), and the conjectural variations of its rivals ($\Sigma_2^n q_{ij}$).

The slope of the firm's reaction curve (obtained by differentiating the equation of the reaction function with respect to q_j), given by $\psi_i = \partial q_i/\partial q_j$, is a strategic parameter known as the *strategic manoeuvre* of a competing firm. It precisely measures firm i's behavior in responding to its rivals' output changes (a firm's disposition to react to rivals' actions). As we shall see later, the firm's strategic manoeuvre is an important factor that determines its ability to compete successfully in the (global) market, and hence its competitiveness.

Thus, differentiating the equation of the reaction function with respect to q_j yields,

$$\partial q_i/\partial q_j = [dp/dQ\{\partial^2 c/\partial q_i^2 . \partial q_i/\partial q_j - dp/dQ . \partial Q/\partial q_j\}$$
$$- d^2p/dQ^2 . \partial Q/\partial q_j(\partial c/\partial q_i - p)]/[(1+\Sigma_2^n q_{ji})(dp/dQ)^2]$$

The parameter $\partial Q/\partial q_j$ is known as the *rivalry effect* (on firm i), which denotes the market effects of rival actions and reactions whenever those rivals respond to firm i's own initiatives. The rivalry effect must be positive; it gives an indication of the risks a firm takes in eliciting rivals' retaliatory (or otherwise) actions through its own actions at any time. Denoting the rivalry effect as

$$\lambda = \partial Q/\partial q_j$$

the foregoing expression simplifies to

$$\psi_i = \{-\lambda(dp/dQ)^2 - d^2p/dQ^2\lambda(\partial c/\partial q_i - p)\}/[(dp/dQ)^2(1 + \Sigma_2^n q_{ji})]$$

which, upon substituting $d^2p/dQ^2 = 0$, yields

$$\psi_i = \frac{-\lambda(dp/dQ)^2}{(dp/dQ)^2[1 + \Sigma_2^n q_{ji}]}$$

This equation expresses firm i's strategic manoeuvre. It shows that the firm's strategic manoeuvre is a function of two key parameters that are central to oligopolistic interaction. One of these is related to the individual firm, namely, the firm's conjectural variation, $\Sigma_2^n q_{ji}$. The other relates to the global market as a whole, namely, the market's *rivalry effect*, λ. Besides these, the strategic manoeuvre equation also indicates firm i's preconceived beliefs about its rivals' actions in response to its own strategies.

Important global market strategic dispositions (from the firm's standpoint) can be derived from these results. It can be shown that:

$$\frac{\partial \psi_i}{\partial \lambda} = -\frac{(dp/dQ)^2}{(dp/dQ)^2[1 + \Sigma_2^n q_{ji}]} < 0$$

This explores how a competitor's strategic manoeuvre (ψ_i) may be affected whenever a change occurs in the market's rivalry effect (λ). That the sign of this equation is negative suggests that under a given conjectural variation, a firm will scale down its strategic manoeuvre (that is, the firm will switch its strategic mode disposition) if rivals adopt more aggressive strategies (and *vice versa*). Further,

$$\frac{\partial \psi_i}{\partial \Sigma_2^n q_{ji}} = \frac{\lambda[(dp/dQ)^2]^2}{(dp/dQ)^2[1 + \Sigma_2^n q_{ji}]} > 0$$

This equation also explores how a competing firm adjusts its own strategic disposition to align with its beliefs about rival strategies (its conjectural variation). That is, it shows how a firm's strategic manoeuvre—which really is the competing firm's disposition to react to rivals' actions—will be affected if and when the firm alters its conjectural variation. That the sign of this equation is positive suggests that altering beliefs about rivals' strategies (due to, say, not taking their threats as credible or believing that their decisions would be less than rational), would lead the firm to revise its strategic manoeuvre in the same direction. In this way, the global market (oligopolistic) competitor is able to remain active as an effective and potentially successful player in the competitive global market scene.

NOTES

1. It is possible that $\partial c_i/\partial q_i < 0$. This implies that the firm's unit cost would decrease as output increases—a condition describing *economies of scale*. This condition often characterizes the public utilities (public goods) industries, and is rare in other industries.

2. If, however, a universal *supply shock* (such as an oil crisis) occurs, which negatively affects most countries and substantial raises cost of production globally, output and price would alter accordingly (and a new "normal" price and output would obtain at that level).

3. Cartels are mainly international organizations only, because usually antitrust laws are passed domestically to prevent collusive business strategies (to protect consumers and the economy from high-price shocks).

4. As explained in chapter 10, the term *conjectural variation* refers to the belief (conjecture) that each competitor has regarding how its rivals would react (vary) to its own unilateral actions and initiatives.

5. As a positive parameter that is subject to change in accordance with market and strategic conditions, a firm's conjectural variation may be correct or incorrect. In other words, the nature of the ongoing competitive interaction among oligopolistic competitors requires that oligopoly market rivalry be that in which a competitor's conjectural variation about rival moves has a probability of being either correct or incorrect. For a recent contribution addressing this situation, see Ezeala-Harrison (1996c).

6. This section is based on Ezeala-Harrison (1996c).

7. The global market demand curve is assumed to be linear: $dp/dQ < 0$, $d^2p/dQ^2 = 0$. Linear cost functions are also assumed: $\partial c/\partial q_i > 0$, $\partial^2 c/\partial q_i^2 = 0$. The assumption of linear cost functions is made here to simplify the analysis, although relaxing this assumption (and assuming that firms operate a usual technology of rising marginal costs as analyzed earlier in this chapter) may not significantly alter our purported results beyond complicating the solution of the model.

Selected Bibliography

Arndt, H. W. 1993. "Competitiveness." *Discussion Paper*, No. 20, Center for Economic Policy Research, Australian National University.

Balassa, B. 1976. "The Changing Pattern of Comparative Advantage in Manufacturing Goods." *Review of Economics and Statistics*, 58: 259-266.

Baldwin, R. E. 1992. "Are Economists' Traditional Trade Policy Views Still Valid?" *Journal of Economic Literature*, 30: 804-830.

Beck, N. 1992. *Shifting Gears: Thriving in the New Economy*. Toronto: HarperCollins.

Bhagwati, J. N. (ed.). 1977. *The New International Economic Order: The North-South Debate*. Cambridge: Cambridge University Press.

Bhagwati, J. N. 1985. "Trade in Services and the Multilateral Trade Negotiations." *The World Bank Economic Review*, 1 (4): 549-569.

Bhagwati, J. N. 1987. "GATT and Trade-In Services: How Can We Resolve the North-South Debate." *Financial Times* (November 27).

Blanchard, O., Commander, S., and Coricelli, F. (1994). "Unemployment in Eastern Europe." *Finance and Development*, 31 (4): 6-9.

Bliss, C. 1989. "Trade and Development." In H. Chenery and T. N. Srinivasan (eds.), *Handbook of Development Economics, Volume 2*. Amsterdam: North Holland Elsevier Science Publishers.

Boltho, A. 1988. "Is There a Future for Resource Transfers to the LDCs?" *World Development*, 16 (10): 1159-1166.

Boyer, M. and Moreaux, M. 1983. "Consistent versus Non-consistent Conjectures in Duopoly Theory: Some Examples." *Journal of Industrial Economics*, 32: 97-100.

Bresnahan, T. F. 1981. "Duopoly Models with Consistent Conjectures." *American Economic Review*, 71: 934-943.

Brue, S. L. 1994. *The Evolution of Economic Thought*. New York: Dryden Press.

Bruton, H. 1970. "The Import Substitution Industrialization Strategy for Economic Developmet: A Survey." *The Pakistan Development Review*, 10 (2): 123-146.

Bruton, H. 1989. "Import Substitution." In H. Chenery and T. N. Srinivasan (eds.), *Handbook of Development Economics, Volume 2*. Amsterdam: North Holland Elsevier Science Publishers.

Bryan, I. A. 1994. *Canada in the New Global Economy: Problems and Policies*. Toronto: John Wiley and Sons.

Carter, C. 1992. "Determining Industry Policy." *Australian Journal of Management*, 17 (1): 121-152.

Cas, A. 1988. "Productivity Growth and Changes in the Terms of Trade in Canada." In R. Feenstra (ed.), *Empirical Methods for International Economics*. Cambridge: MIT Press.

Chenery, H., Robinson, S. and Syrquin, M. 1986. *Industrialization and Growth*. Oxford: Oxford University Press.

Chichilnisky, G. 1981. "Terms of Trade and Domestic Distribution: Export-led Growth with Abundant Labour." *Journal of Development Economics*, 8 (2).

Cline, W. R. 1982. "Can the Asian Experience Be Generalized." *World Development*, 10: 81-90.

Cuddington, J. T. and Urzua, C. M. 1989. "Trends and Cycles and the Net Barter Terms of Trade: A New Approach." *Economic Journal*, 99 (396): 426-442.

Davenport, P. 1997. "The Productivity Paradox and the Management of Information Technology." Paper Presented at the Conference of the Centre for the Study of Living Standards. Ottawa, Canada (April).

Deardoff, A. V. 1984. "Testing Trade Theories and Predicting Trade Flows." In R. W. Jones and P. B. Kenen (eds.), *Handbook of International Economics*. New York: North Holland Press.

Dollar, D. 1993. "Technological Differences as a Source of Comparative Advantage." *American Economic Review Papers and Proceedings*, 83 (2): 431-435.

Dollar, D. and Wolf, E. N. 1993. *Competitiveness, Convergence, and International Specialization*. Cambridge: MIT Press.

Dornbusch, R. 1993. *Stabilization, Debt, and Reform: Policy Analysis for Developing Countries*. Englewood Cliffs, N. J.: Prentice Hall: chap. 5.

Drucker, P. F. 1988. "The Coming of the New Organization." *Harvard Business Review*, July/August.

Economic Council of Canada. 1992. "Competitiveness and the Public Sector." *Au Courant*, 13 (1): 17.

Ellsworth, P. T. 1961. "The Terms of Trade Between Primary-Producing and Industrial Countries." *Inter-American Economic Affairs*, 10 (1).

Enoch, A. C. 1978. "Measures of Competitiveness in International Trade." *Bank of England Quarterly*, 18 (2): 181-195.

Ezeala-Harrison, F. 1995. "Canada's Global Competitiveness Challenge: Trade Performance Versus Total Factor Productivity Measures." *American Journal of Economics and Sociology*, 54 (1): 57-78.

Ezeala-Harrison, F. 1996a. *Economic Development: Theory and Policy Applications*. Westport, Conn.: Praeger.

Ezeala-Harrison, F. 1996b. *Canada's Competitiveness: Should We Judge Trade Performance or Total Factor Productivity?* Ottawa: Department of Foreign Affairs and International Trade (Research Paper).

Ezeala-Harrison, F. 1996c. "New Brunswick Gasoline Industry: An Oligopoly Tacit Collusion Under Consistent Conjectures?" *Canadian Journal of Regional Science*, 19 (2): 225-243.

Ezeala-Harrison, F. 1997. "Prospects for Growth in LDCs through International Competitiveness." Paper presented at the Department of Economics Seminars, University of Newcastle, Australia (October).

Ezeala-Harrison, F. 1998. "Conceptions and Misconceptions of International Competitiveness." *Briefing Notes in Economics*, 37 (November).

Fagerberg, J. 1988. "International Competitiveness." *Economic Journal* (June): 355-374.

Field, B. C. and Olewiler, N. D. 1994. *Environmental Economics*. Toronto: McGraw-Hill Ryerson.

Flanders, M. J. 1964. "Prebisch on Protectionism: An Evaluation." *Economic Journal*, 74.

Frank, A. G. 1992. "The Development of Underdevelopment." Reprinted in C. K. Wilber and K. P. Jameson (eds.), *The Political Economy of Development and Underdevelopment*. New York: McGraw-Hill.

Gillis, M., Perkins, D. H., Roemer, M., and Snodgrass, D. R. 1992. *Economics of Development*. New York: W. W. Norton.

Goulder, L. H. and B. Eichengreen. 1989. "Savings Promotion, Investment Promotion, and International Competitiveness." In R. C. Feenstra (ed.), *Trade Policies for International Competitiveness*. Chicago: University of Chicago Press.

Grossman, G. M. and Helpman, E. 1994. "Endogenous Innovations in the Theory of Growth." *Journal of Economic Perspectives*, 8: 23-45.

Harris, R. G. 1985. *Trade, Industrial Policy and International Competition*. Ottawa: Royal Commission on the Economic Union and Development Prospects for Canada and the Canadian Government: 9.

Harris, R. G. 1992. *Exchange Rates and International Competitiveness of the Canadian Economy*. Ottawa: Economic Council of Canada.

Harris, R. G. and Cox, D. 1988. "The Service Sector and Trade in the Canadian Economy: An Input-Output Analysis." *Discussion Paper*, The Fraser Institute, (Vancouver).

Harris, R. G. and Watson, W. J. 1993. "Three Visions of Competitiveness: Porter, Reich and Thurow on Economic Growth and Policy." In T. J. Courchene and D. Purvis (eds.), *Productivity Growth and Canada's International Competitiveness*. Kingston, Ontario: John Deutsch Institute, Queen's University.

Harrison, A. 1991. "Openness and Growth: A Time-Series, Cross-Country Analysis of Developing Countries." *Mimeo*, World Bank.

Helliwell, J. 1984. "Stagflation and Productivity Decline in Canada, 1974-1982." *Canadian Journal of Economics*, 17 (2).

Helliwell, J. 1986. "International Comparisons of the Sources of the Productivity Slowdown 1973-1982." *European Economic Review*, 28: 1-2.

Hirsch, S. 1974. "Capital or Technology? Confronting the New-factor Proportions and Neo-Technology Accounts of International Trade." *Weltwirtschaftliches Archiv*: 535-563.

Hirschman, A. O. 1958. *The Strategy of Economic Development*. New Haven, Conn.: Yale University Press.

Hirschman, A. O. (ed.). 1961. *Latin American Issues: Essays and Comments*. New York: Twentieth Century Fund.

Hirschman, A. O. 1987. "The Political Economy of Latin American Development: Seven Exercises in Retrospection." *Latin American Research Review*, 22 (3).

Irwin, D. A. 1992. "Strategic Trade Policy and Mercantilist Trade Rivalries." *American Economic Review Papers and Proceedings*, 82 (2): 134-139.

Johnson, H. G. 1967. "Analysis of Prebisch's Views on the Terms of Trade." In H. G. Johnson (ed.), *Economic Policies Towards Less Developed Countries*. London: Allen and Unwin.

Jones, C. and Kiguel, M. A. 1994. "Africa's Quest for Prosperity: Has Adjustment Helped?" *Finance and Development*, 31 (2):2-5.

Khan, M. H. and Khan, M. S. 1995. "Agricultural Growth in Sub-Saharan African Countries and China." *IMF Papers of Policy Analysis and Assessment No. 95/7*, (Washington, D.C.).

Krueger, A. O. 1997. "Trade Policy and Economic Development: How We Learn." *American Economic Review*, 87 (1): 1-22.

Krugman, P. (ed.). 1986. *Strategic Trade Policy and the New International Economics*. Cambridge, Mass.: MIT Press.

Krugman, P. 1994. *Peddling Prosperity: Economic Sense and Nonsense in the Age of Diminished Expectations*. New York: W. W. Norton.

Krugman, P. and Obstfeld, M. 1991. *International Economics: Theory and Policy*. New York: HarperCollins Publishers.

Lazear, E. and Moore, R. 1984. "Incentives, Productivity and Labor Contracts." *Quarterly Journal of Economics* (June): 275-296.

Leamer, E. E. 1984. *Sources of International Comparative Advantage: Theory and Evidence*. Cambridge, Mass.: MIT Press.

Letourneau, R. 1992. "Canada's Trade Performance: World Market Shares and Comparative Advantage." *Working Paper*, Economic Council of Canada.

Lewis, S. R. 1989. "Primary Exporting Countries." In H. Chenery and T. N. Srinivasan (eds.), *Handbook of Development Economics, Volume 2*. Amsterdam: North Holland Elsevier Science Publishers.

Lewis, W. A. 1980. "The Slowing Down of the Engine of Growth." *American Economic Review*, 70 (4): 555-564.

Lipsey, R. G. 1988. "Global Imbalances and American Trade Policy." *Atlantic Economic Journal*, 41 (June): 1-11.

Lodh, B. 1990. "Global Market Shares in Traded Goods and Canada's Comparative Advantage 1971-87." *Mimeo*, Economic Council of Canada (February).

Loxley, J. 1986. *Debt and Disorder: External Financing for Development*. Boulder, Colo.: Westview Press.

Luciani, P. 1996. *Economic Myths: Making Sense of Canadian Policy Issues*. Toronto: Addison-Wesley Publishers.

Magun, S. and Rao, S. 1989. "The Competitive Position of Canada in High-Technology Trade." *Mimeo*, Economic Council of Canada.

Mahmood, A. 1996. "Pakistan's Edible Oil Crisis and the Comparative Advantage of Edible Oil Production under Alternative Oilseed Processing Technologies." *Indian Economic Journal*, 43 (3): 64-73.

Mahmood, A. and Ezeala-Harrison, F. 1997. "Comparative Advantage, Competitive Advantage, and Competitiveness in Developing Countries." *Working paper*, University of New Brunswick.

Markusen, J. R. 1987. *U.S. Canada Free Trade: Effects on Welfare and Sectoral Output and Employment Levels in the Short and Long Run*. Washington. D.C.: U.S. Department of Labor.

Markusen, J. R. 1992. *Productivity, Competitiveness, Trade Performance, and Real Income*. Ottawa: Economic Council of Canada for Minister of Supply and Services Canada.

McCallum, J. 1995. "National Borders Matter: Canada-U.S. Regional Trade Patterns." *American Economic Review*, 85 (3): 615-623.

McCulloch, R. 1988. "International Competition in Services." In M. Feldstein (ed.), *The United States in the World Economy*. Chicago: University of Chicago Press for National Bureau for Economic Research.

McRae, J. J. 1992. "An Exploratory Analysis of Canada's International Transactions in Service Commodities." *Working Paper*, Economic Council of Canada.

Medoff, J. L. and Abraham, K. G. 1981. "Are Those Paid More Really More Productive? The Case Experience." *Journal of Human Resources*, 16: 186-216.

Meier, G. M. 1976. *Leading Issues in Economic Development*. New York: Oxford University Press.

Moon, H. Chang and Peery, N. S. 1995. "Competitiveness of Product, Firm, Industry, and Nation in a Global Business." *Competitiveness Review*, 5 (1): 37-43.

Nafziger, E. W. 1990. *The Economics of Developing Countries* (2nd ed.). Englewood Cliffs, N.J.: Prentice Hall.

O'Brien, P. K. 1982. "European Economic Development: The Contribution of the Periphery." *Economic History Review*, 35: 1-18.

O'Brien, P. K. and Engerman, S. L. 1991. "Exports and the Growth of the British Economy from the Glorious Revolution to the Peace of Amiens." In B. L. Solow (ed.), *Slavery and the Rise of the Atlantic System*. Cambridge: Cambridge University Press.

OECD. 1988. *The Newly Industrializing Countries: Challenge and Opportunity for OECD Industries*. Paris: 18.

Oshikoya, T. W. and Hussain, M. N. 1998. "Information Technology and the Challenge of Economic Development in Africa." *Economic Research Papers, African Develop ment Bank*, 36: 1-29.

Porter, M. E. 1987. "From Competitive Advantage to Corporate Strategy." *Harvard Business Review* (May-June): 43-59.

Porter, M. E. 1990a. "The Competitive Advantage of Nations." *Harvard Business Review* (March-April): 73-93.

Porter, M. E. 1990b. *The Competitive Advantage of Nations*. New York: The Free Press.

Powelson, J. P. 1977. "The Strange Persistence of the Terms of Trade." *Inter-American Economic Affairs*, 30 (4).

Prebisch, R. 1959. "Commercial Policy in the Underdeveloped Countries." *American Economic Review Papers and Proceedings*, 49 (2).

Prebisch, R. 1964. *Toward a New Trade Policy for Development*. Report of the Secretary-Gerneral of UNCTAD. New York: United Nations.

Prebisch, R. 1984. "Five Stages in My Thinking on Development." In G. M. Meier and D. Seers (eds.), *Pioneers of Development*. New York: Oxford University Press for the World Bank.

Rao, P. S. 1992. "The Asia Pacific Rim: Opportunities and Challenges to Canada." *Working Paper*, Economic Council of Canada.

Rao, P. S. and T. L. Lempriere. 1992a. "Canada's Manufacturing Cost Performance and Trade Flows." *Working Paper*, Economic Council of Canada.

Rao, P. S. and T. L. Lempriere. 1992b. "A Comparison of the Total Factor Productivity and Total Cost Performance of Canadian and U.S. Industries." *Working Paper*, Economic Council of Canada.

Rao, P. S. and T. L. Lempriere. 1992c. *Canada's Productivity Performance*. Ottawa: Canada Communication Group.

Rao, P. S. and Preston, R. S. 1984. "Inter-factor Substitution, Economies of Scale, and Technical Change: Evidence from Canadian Industries." *Empirical Economics*, 9.

Reidel, J. 1984. "Trade as the Engine of Economic Growth in Developing Countries Revisited." *The Economic Journal*, 94 (March): 56-63.

Riddell, R. C. 1992. "The Contribution of Foreign Aid to Development and the Role of the Private Sector." *Development:* 7-15.

Rodney, W. 1972. *How Europe Underdeveloped Africa.* London: Bogle-L'Ouverture Publications.

Romer, P. M. 1986. "Increasing Returns and Long-Run Growth." *Journal of Political Economy*, 94: 1002-1037.

Romer, P. 1989. "Capital Accumulation in the Theory of Long Run Growth." In R. Barro (ed.), *Modern Business Cycle Theory.* Cambridge, Mass.: Harvard University Press.

Romer, P. M. 1994. "The Origins of Endogenous Growth." *Journal of Economic Perspectives*, 8: 3-23.

Rugman, A. and D'Cruz, J. 1989. *Fast Forward: Improving Canada's International Competitiveness.* Toronto: Faculty of Management, University of Toronto.

Sachs, J. 1997a. "Nature, Nurture, and Growth: The Limits of Convergence." *The Economist* (June 14): 19-22.

Sachs, J. 1997b. "Asia's Miracle Is Alive and Well." *Time* (September 29): 36.

Salvatore, D. and Hatcher, T. 1991. "Inward Oriented and Outward Oriented Trade Strategies." *Journal of Development Studies*, 27 (3): 7-25.

Sapir, A. 1985. "North-South Issues in Trade-in Services." *The World Economy*, 8 (1): 27-41.

Sapir, A. 1986. "Trade in Investment-Related Technological Services." *World Development*, 14 (5): 605-622.

Schumacher, D. 1988. "Determinants of the Major Industrialized Countries Exports to Developing Countries." *World Development*, 10: 1317-1328.

Shiells, C. 1995. "Regional Trade Blocs: Trade Creating or Diverting?" *Finance and Development*, 32 (1): 30-32.

Singer, H. 1950. "The Distribution of Trade between Borrowing and Investing Nations." *American Economic Review*, 40: 473-485.

Steer, A. 1997. "Ten Principles of the New Environmentalism." *Finance and Development*, 33 (4): 4-7.

Streeten, P. 1981. "World Trade in Agricultural Commodities and the Terms of Trade with Industrial Goods." In P. Streeten (ed.), *Development Perspectives.* London: Macmillan.

Sunkel, O. 1973. "Transnational Capitalism and National Disintegration in Latin America." *Social and Economic Studies*, 22 (1): 135-140. (Reprinted in Meier, 1976).

Tapscott, D. 1996. *The Digital Economy: Promise and Peril in the Age of Networked Intelligence.* New York: McGraw-Hill.

Thomas, V. and Belt, T. 1997. "Growth and the Environment: Allies or Foes?" *Finance and Development*, 34 (2): 22-24.

Viner, J. 1953. *International Trade and Economic Development.* Oxford: Clarendon Press.

Warda, J. 1990. *International Competitiveness of Canadian R&D Tax Incentives: An Update*, Ottawa: Conference Board of Canada.

Warr, P. G. 1992. "Comparative Advantage and Protection in Indonesia." *Bulletin of Indonesian Economic Studies*, 28 (3): 41-70.

Warr, P. G. 1994. "Comparative and Competitive Advantage." *Asian-Pacific Economic Literature*, 8 (2): 1-14.

Weiss, A. 1990. *Efficiency Wages: Models of Unemployment, Layoffs and Wage Dispersion*. Princeton, N.J.: Princeton University Press.

Williams, G. 1994. *Not for Export: The International Competitiveness of Canadian Manufacturing*, 3rd. ed. Toronto: McClelland and Stewart.

Wimpffen, J. L. and Capelle, R. B. 1990. "Assessing the Early Effects of Emerging Trade Blocs." *Canadian Journal of Regional Science*, 13 (2&3): 367-373.

World Bank. 1985-1993. *World Development Report* (Various Issues). New York: Oxford University Press.

World Bank. 1994a. *Adjustment in Africa: Lessons from Country Case Studies*, Washington, D.C.

World Bank. 1994b. *Adjustment in Africa: Reforms, Results, and the Road Ahead*, Washington, D.C.

World Economic Forum. 1989-1997. *World Competitiveness Report*. Geneva: IMEDE.

Index

About the Author

FIDELIS EZEALA-HARRISON is Professor of Economics at the University of New Brunswick. He is the author of *Economic Development: Theory and Policy Applications* (Praeger, 1996) and coeditor of *Perspectives on Economic Development in Africa* (Praeger, 1994).

ISBN 0-275-96414-0

90000>

EAN

9 780275 964146

HARDCOVER BAR CODE